Coronado's Journey
to
The Seven Cities of Gold

*

Discovering His 16th Century Route to Cibola

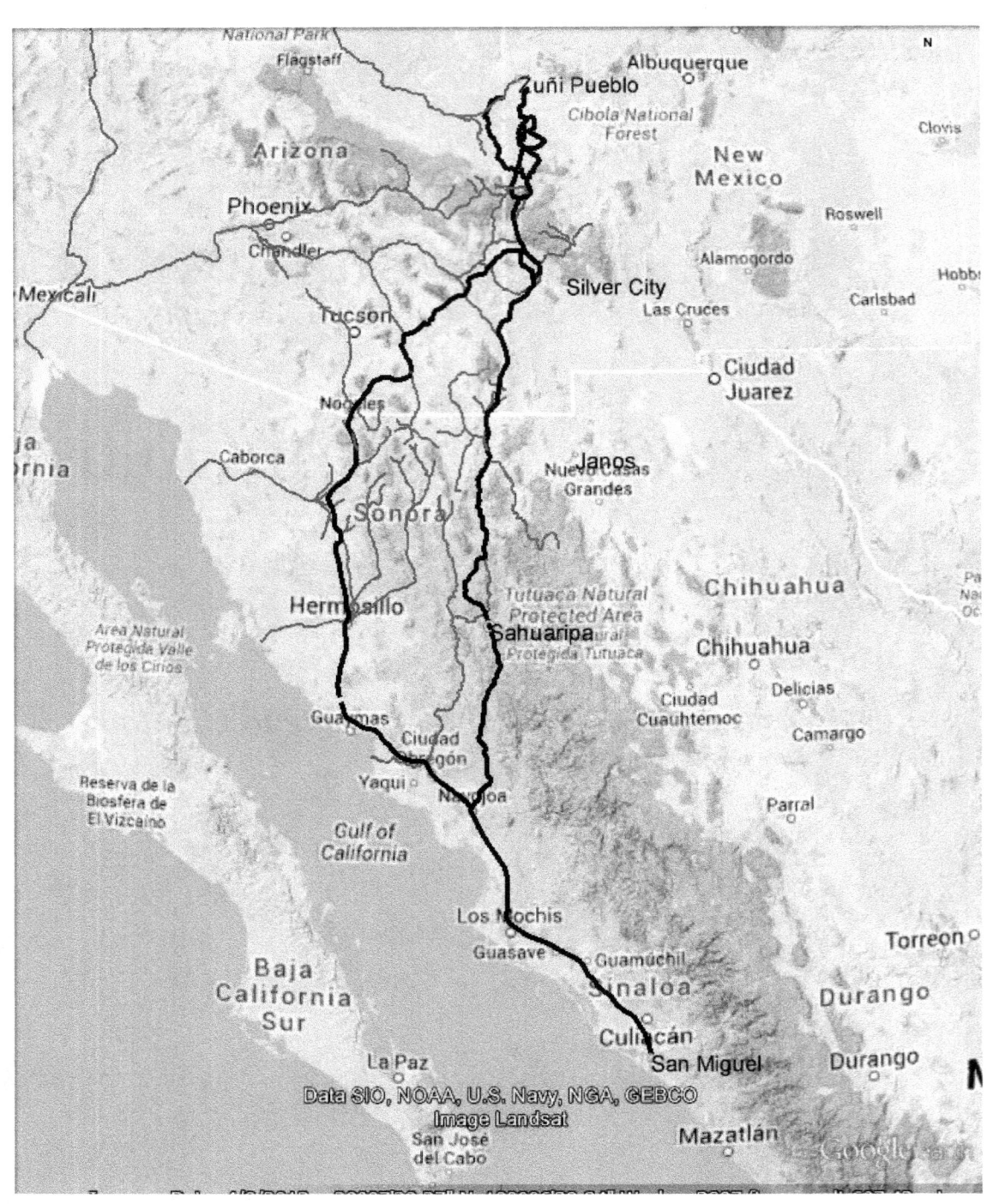

Map of Coronado's Route to Cibola

Coronado's Journey
to
The Seven Cities of Gold

*

Discovering His 16th Century Route to Cibola

JAMES J. (PETE) DREXLER

papaya press
Montrose, Colorado USA

Coronado's Journey to The Seven Cities of Gold. © Copyright 2015 by James J. Drexler. All rights reserved. No part of this book may be reproduced in any form or by electronic or mechanical means, including information storage and retrieval systems, without permission, in writing, from the author, except by a reviewer who may quote short passages in a review. James J. Drexler.

Library of Congress Control Number: 2015903800

ISBN 978-0-9779831-1-7

website: www.petedrexler.wordpress.com

Cover Design: Kateri Drexler
Cover art:
   Coronado Sets Out for the North
   by Frederic Remington
   via Wikimedia Commons

Table of Contents

Preface……………………………………………………………………………ix
List of Graphics…………………………………………………………………vii
Acknowledgments………………………………………………………………xii

Part 1: The Coronado Expedition to Tierra Nueva and Places Visited along the Route to Cíbola
    Chapter 1. Background of the Coronado Expedition…………………3
    Chapter 2. Composition of the Expedition………………………………17
    Chapter 3. Organization and Travel……………………………………41
    Chapter 4. Places Along the Route……………………………………55
    Chapter 5. San Gerónimo and the Traffic………………………………77
    Chapter 6. The Expedition's Return to Culiacán………………………87
    Chapter 7. Close to Cíbola……………………………………………93

Part 2: Possible Routes Taken by the Colorado Expedition to Tierra Nueva in 1540
    Chapter 8. Cíbola in 1540………………………………………………103
    Chapter 9. Search for the Bad Pass……………………………………115
    Chapter 10. The Small Stream…………………………………………137
    Chapter 11. Search for the Rio Frio……………………………………147
    Chapter 12. Arroyo de la Barranca……………………………………155
    Chapter 13. Rio de las Balsas…………………………………………165
    Chapter 14. To the Rio San Juan………………………………………177

v

Chapter 15. The Deep Canyon..185
Chapter 16. Chichilticale..195
Chapter 17. Dogleg on the Rio Nexpa..207
Chapter 18. The Three Sites of San Gerónimo...213
Chapter 19. To the Arroyo de los Cedros...225
Chapter 20. Into Culiacán...239
Chapter 21. The Routes in Summary...251
Chapter 22. Epilogue..259

Appendix A. Method of Travel...267
Appendix B. Distances Between Named Places..269
Appendix C. Searching for Locations near Cíbola....................................283
Appendix D. Tracing the Trail...293
Appendix E. Climate History of the Cíbola Region..................................297
Appendix F. Pack Animals...301

Bibliography and Reference Key..305
Index..309

List of Graphics

Illustrations and Maps

	Map of Coronado's Route to Cibola	ii
Fig 4.1	Magnetic North Pole Wanderings	59
Fig 8.1	Locations of Cíbola Pueblos	107
Fig 8.2	Relative Sizes of Cíbola Pueblos	111
Fig 9.1	Map of Bad Pass and Last Camp	123
Fig 9.2	Map of Possible Rio Bermejo Crossing Locations	129
Fig 10.1	Map of Rio Bermejo and Small Stream Sites	141
Fig 11.1	Map of Western Cíbola Region and Rio Frio Sites	149
Fig 11.2	Map of Eastern Cíbola Region and Rio Frio Sites	151
Fig 12.1	Map of Arroyo de la Barranca Region	157
Fig 13.1	Map of Rio de las Balsas Candidates	167
Fig 14.1	Map of Rio San Juan Candidate Sites	179
Fig 15.1	Map of Deep Canyon Candidate Sites	187
Fig 16.1	Map of Deep Canyon to Chichilticale Region	197
Fig 17.1	Map of Candidate Locations of Dogleg on Rio Nexpa	209
Fig 18.1	Map of Three Candidate Sites of San Gerónimo	215
Fig 18.2	Image of Small Pass on The Rio Bavispe	219
Fig 19.1	Map of Los Corazones to Arroyo de los Cedros	227
Fig 20.1	Map of Region North of Culiacán	241
Fig 21.1	Map of Possible Routes	253
Fig C-1	Detail of Distances Near Cíbola	291

Fig E-1   Reconstructed Temperature History..298
Fig E-2   Reconstructed Precipitation History..298

Tables

Table 2.1   Probable Composition of the Two Groups............................39
Table 11.1   Summary of Candidate Sites to Rio Frio.............................153
Table 19.1   Candidate Site Associations...237
Table 21.1   Western Route...254
Table 21.2   Eastern Route Branch A..254
Table 21.3   Eastern Route Branch B..255
Table 21.4   Eastern Route Branch C..255
Table 21.5   Modern Names and Locations along Western Route...........256
Table 21.6   Modern Names and Locations along Eastern Route............257
Table 21.7   Modern Names and Locations along Northern Route.........257
Table B-1a   Distance Chart Based on 5 Leagues per Day.......................272
Table B-1b   Distance Chart Based on Estimated Rate of Travel.............273
Table B-2a   Distance Chart with Lifted Restrictions...............................276
Table B-2b   Distance Chart with Modified Input....................................277
Table B-3   Distance Chart for Actual Mileage on Western Route.........278
Table B-4   Distance Chart for Actual Mileage on Eastern Route..........279

Preface

There are a surprisingly large number of documents relating to the Coronado *entrada* into the Cíbola region and even beyond to Gran Quivira in present-day Kansas. These include reports made at the time of the Expedition, official documents of later court proceedings and narratives by two men who were with the expedition but who wrote about it some 20 years later. In all this material there is, however, very little detail to directly and specifically identify geographical features or the locations of the sites visited.

Apparently, the Expedition followed existing Indian trade routes and trails and were guided by local Indians along the way. Perhaps for that reason the chroniclers did not feel the need to supply details about the route sufficient to allow un-guided people to retrace their path. Another possible reason for the sparse knowledge about the route is the lack of any known report by the Expedition's official chronicler. This man apparently died shortly before or soon after Coronado's return from Cíbola and very likely never finished writing an official report.

Coronado's northward route in the USA has been speculated to lie anywhere from central Arizona to western New Mexico, but definitive evidence of the route has not yet surfaced. Several authors have attempted to discern the specific route (or routes) traveled by Coronado's forces but no two authors seem to agree on the specifics of the route. In Part II of this volume, I, too, have attempted to discern some most likely portions of the route, but the reader is cautioned that all such "likely" routes remain in the realm of speculation and will probably remain so until hard archaeological evidence is discovered.

In the meantime, it is fun to search and to speculate!

A note of appreciation.

A large portion of the information presented in this book is derived from the work of Richard and Shirley Cushing Flint. Cooperatively and independantly, they have been responsible for making much information about the Coronado Expedition and the people involved with it available to modern scholars. Everyone interested in that period of history is deeply indebted to them for their translations of original Spanish documents and for their involvement in various conferences and publications relating to this subject. I, especially, am deeply grateful to them for their efforts.

A more technical note about references.

Because sections of this book are so heavily based on knowledge gained from others, I have had difficulty in properly and thoroughly citing sources for every piece of information included here. I have, however, attempted to present a sufficient number of references throughout the text to provide the reader with a reasonable guide for verifying the information from the source material. The method chosen to present these references is to mark the appropriate text with a superscript numeral and to expand that reference in the left-hand column on each page. This expansion has the form: "N. Ref, pxx" where

"N" represents a sequential numeric indicator, "Ref" is a shorthand indicator for the author and/or chapter within the referenced document and "pxx" gives the page number within the reference document. In some cases the "pxx" is replaced with "nxx" when it refers to the number of a chapter endnote in the referenced document. A full reference for each document is also presented in the bibliography at the end of the book. This bibliography is keyed to the shorthand indicator, "Ref".

At first glance this may seem to be somewhat cumbersome. It does, however, provide an efficient mechanism to present the detail that is required to allow the reader to effectively find the referenced information, if desired.

Acknowledgments

First and foremost, I would like to acknowledge the people who originally told this story and to the scribes who re-copied the words throughout the intervening years. Acknowledgment is also gladly given to those have translated the original, old Spanish language into modern English -- especially to Richard and Shirley Cushing Flint.

Thanks are also due to my sister Joan, my brother Mark and my daughter Kateri. They not only offered necessary encouragement but also proofread the several iterations of the book.

Part 1

The Coronado Expedition to Tierra Nueva

and

Places Visited along the Route to Cíbola

Chapter 1

Background of the Coronado Entrada

In the early part of July 1540, a group of Spaniards and Native Americans from central Mexico, under the leadership of Francisco Vazquez de Coronado, found themselves approaching the region of Cíbola in the west central part of the present State of New Mexico in the vicinity of the present Pueblo of Zuñi. They had been sent by the Spanish Viceroy of Mexico, Antonio de Mendoza, to seek out the fabled "Seven Cities of Gold" for the Spanish Crown. Coronado's expedition was the first armed *entrada* by the Spanish into the territory far to the north of their existing colonized regions in the New World. The story of that entrada begins several years earlier when Panfilo de Narváez landed about 300 men on the west coast of Florida on April 15, 1528 to "conquer and govern" the unsettled lands lying adjacent to the Gulf of Mexico between the Cape of Florida and the mouth of the Rio Grande far to the west[1]. Of this entire force of 300 men only four would survive after an arduous trip spanning eight years and covering nearly the entire expanse of land from Florida to the Sea of Cortes on the western coast of present-day Mexico.

1. Covey, p27ff

Those four survivors, Alvar Nunez Cabeza de Vaca, Andres Dorantes, Alonso del Castillo, and Esteban de Dorantes (Andres Dorantes' black slave), once again made contact with some Spaniards in the Spring of 1536 when they came across a group of slave hunters. This slaving party was headed by Diego de Alcaraz[2] and was based in the northern Spanish outpost of Culiacán. By

2. A&P, p160

Background 3

late July they were in Mexico City reporting to Viceroy Mendoza. The stories and official reports by these four men about the existence of gold, silver and jewels and of large populations of intelligent peoples with skills and industry ignited a great interest in this northern *Tierra Nueva* (New Land) among the Spaniards of Mexico. With the great wealth extracted from Mexico and Peru by Cortes and the Pizarro brothers still fresh in their minds, the Spaniards anticipated yet another source of fame and fortune in these regions far to the north. In addition to the possibility of extracting portable wealth such as gold, silver, gemstones and manufactured products, the Spaniards were also eager to acquire souls for God and Church by converting the Native Americans to Christianity. They were equally eager to establish *encomiendas* for themselves– a system very similar to the feudal system in Europe. Under this system, a few individuals favored by the Spanish Crown acquired vast tracts of land in new territories along with the rights to use the native people's labor for their own benefit.

By the time Coronado returned from Cíbola in 1542, there had been at least five major exploratory groups sent out to obtain information about the pueblos and people of Cíbola. They were also to obtain knowledge of the lands and routes between the established Spanish city of Culiacán in the northern province of Nueva Galicia and the region of Cíbola in this unexplored Tierra Nueva. The first such group (that of Marcos de Niza) and the second group (that of Melchior Diaz and Juan de Zaldivar) were commissioned directly by Viceroy Antonio Mendoza and the remaining three were various components of Coronado's expedition. All of these groups have contributed documentary evidence about the new territory and the reader deserves some background about each of them. Much of the information known about these groups and their endeavors is due to two men. The first is Pedro de Castañeda de Nájera[3,4] who was attached to the main body of the Coronado expedition. It appears that he served as an unofficial chronicler by obtaining information from others who participated in the various campaigns. The second such man is Juan Jaramillo[5] who served in the Advance Party with Coronado and whose accounts are probably actual first hand information. His interest was centered on the Quivira portion of the expedition from the Rio Grande near present-day Bernalillo, New Mexico through the Texas panhandle and into present-day Kansas. However, much of the knowledge of the geography the Expedition encountered between Culiacán and Cíbola comes only from his narrative.

Both of these men wrote their accounts about 20 years after the expedition ended. Translations of both of their accounts, as well as several others, are readily available in Richard and Shirley Cushing Flint's monumental book "Documents of the Coronado Expedition, 1539-1542"[6].

The official chronicler of the Coronado entrada was a man named[7] Pedro Méndez de Sotomayor, but no report of his is known to exist. Since his wife is known to have been widowed[7] by 1546, he probably died soon after the expedition ended if not before. It is likely that he may not have ever compiled or completed a report.

Marcos de Niza

Within a few months of hearing the reports of Cabeza de Vaca – and certainly before the year 1536 ended – Viceroy Mendoza had decided to send an expedition of discovery under the command of Andres Dorantes to Tierra Nueva in order to verify and locate the places and things of which he and the other three Narváez survivors had heard and reported. However, by the end

3. F&Fdocs28, p378
4. Winship, Cas

5. F&Fdocs30, p512

6. F&Fdocs

7. F&Fdocs28, n201

of the following year, arrangements for that expedition had not been finalized and Dorantes decided to withdraw from the endeavor[8]. Mendoza then placed the command of that expedition in the hands of a Franciscan friar, Marcos de Niza, who was to take the black man, Esteban de Dorantes, along as guide. The de Niza party left Mexico City in the Fall of 1538 accompanying Francisco Vázquez de Coronado to Culiacán where Coronado was to assume his duties as the newly-appointed Governor of the province of Nueva Galicia. It is not clear if Viceroy Mendoza had already decided that Coronado would be in charge of the planned future entrada to Cíbola, but it is known that Marcos de Niza reported his progress and findings back to Coronado in Culiacán during this first expedition to Cíbola.

In anticipation of supporting that planned future entrada from the sea coast, Viceroy Mendoza charged de Niza with obtaining information about the coast along the route to Cíbola. At point in time, very little was known about the location of Cíbola or about the distance it lay from the coast. Some reports even had it laying on the coast[9]. Marcos de Niza was later able to report that the coast continued in a northwesterly direction and that Cíbola lay in a northeasterly direction so that Cíbola could be expected to be far from the coast.

Marcos de Niza left Culiacán in early March of 1539, taking with him another priest, fray Onorato, Esteban de Dorantes and an unknown number of Indians. Esteban and some of these Indians had been purchased by Viceroy Mendoza and freed for the purpose of joining the de Niza entrada and a "great multitude" of additional Indians came from Petatlan and the pueblo of Cuchillo[10]. Sometime around the end of March 1539, de Niza sent Esteban and a few others ahead along the "northern route"

8. F&Fdocs6, p59

9. F&Fdocs15, p189

10. F&Fdocs6, p67

while the main part of the group rested for almost two weeks waiting for the return of two parties de Niza had sent westward to the coast. Esteban had been instructed to limit his excursion to fifty or sixty leagues and then to report his findings in person to de Niza.

However, once Esteban got started, he simply kept going until he reached Cíbola. According to Frank Cushing's telling[11,12] of an old Zuñi story, Esteban arrived at the pueblo of Kiakima at the base of Corn Mountain (also known as Thunder Mountain or Dowa Yalanne) where he was killed within a matter of days. Some of the Indians who had accompanied Esteban to Cíbola escaped and found de Niza on the trail several days distance from Cíbola. In his report to the Viceroy[13] probably written in late August 1539 in Culiacán and presented to Viceroy Mendoza in Mexico City on Sept 2, 1539, de Niza states that he personally continued on to Cíbola and saw one of the pueblos before beating a hasty retreat back to Culiacán. In spite of the death of Esteban and his own fear of the Cíbolans, de Niza was able to report the existence of the cities in the north and their wealth (as perceived from a distance). This was sufficient to keep the fires of hope and expectation burning strongly after his return to Viceroy Mendoza in Mexico City.

There seems to be a widely held opinion among historians that the report of Marcos de Niza to Viceroy Mendoza contains many errors, inaccuracies and rather blatant falsehoods. This was certainly the opinion expressed directly to the Viceroy by Coronado himself when he wrote

I can say truthfully that he has not spoken the truth in anything he said

in his letter of August 3, 1540[14] just after capturing the first

11. Ladd TN, pg 187

12. Rodack TN, pg 91

13. F&Fdocs6, p74

14. F&Fdocs19, p258

pueblo of Cíbola. However, some of the harsh opinions toward Marcos de Niza may be tempered by considering a few factors.

In defense of de Niza, there is little or no indication that the Coronado entrada followed the same trails as the de Niza group and, therefore, the differences of conditions along the route cannot be solely attributed to a shortcoming on de Niza's part. A statement by Castañeda holds an intriguing clue that the routes may have been different. Referring to Coronado and the Advance Party, Castañeda says[15]

15. F&Fdocs28, p393

> *...he did not fail to feel some distress. [This was] because although the news of what lay ahead was marvelous, there was no one who had seen it, except the Indians who had gone with the Black, [Esteban], who already had been caught in several lies.*

Could it be that these "lies" were simply true descriptions of a different route? Was everyone who had been along the route (de Niza and the Indians) actually lying about their experiences? It may be more likely that the two groups, each being guided by different local Indians, used different trails, perhaps each suited to the composition of the group. De Niza's group supposedly was composed only of people on foot while Coronado's Advance Party consisted of men, horses, pack animals and herds of stock. There are, even today, many trails in that country which are suitable for a man on foot but not at all suited to horses or herds of cattle.

Also, the discrepancy between the description of the "first pueblo" of Cíbola encountered by Coronado (presumably – but by no means certain – the pueblo of Hawikuh) and the pueblo "seen" by de Niza is fully understandable if de Niza actually saw the pueblo Kiakima where Esteban was killed. Marcos de Niza's description fairly well describes Kiakima as it would have appeared from a distance – perhaps with some details supplied by a keen imagination.

Marcos de Niza writes down much of what he learns in the first person, even though it is very probable that his information was obtained from the reports of trusted informers and could easily have been second- or third-hand information. To modern sensibilities, this seems to be a matter of his appropriating undeserved personal credit but perhaps the kindest thing is to consider it simply as an expedient literary device.

Even with these considerations, many problems still remain embedded in Marcos de Niza's report, so the reader is cautioned to be wary of the "information" therein. (However, the same caution should be exercised on any documentation concerning the Coronado entrada into present-day New Mexico and Arizona.) It would seem to be a mistake to summarily dismiss everything de Niza has to say – as some authors tend to do – simply because it came from him.

Melchior Diaz and Juan de Zaldívar

Well before the Coronado entrada began, Viceroy Mendoza must not have been satisfied with the report of Marcos de Niza. Immediately after hearing that report in September of 1539, he dispatched another reconnaissance group to verify de Niza's findings. On November 17, 1539 he sent a group of 16 armed horsemen under the command of Melchior Diaz and Juan de Zaldívar from Culiacán but that group was stopped by winter snows in the mountainous regions before reaching Cíbola and was forced to winter in the region of Chichilticale. They gathered a wealth of information from the natives of the region concerning Cíbola, but not much of it compared favorably with the de Niza reports. Without continuing on to Cíbola, the Diaz group returned south and met up with the full advancing Coronado Expedition at Chiametla which was about half way between its departure point at Coronado's Nueva Galicia capital, Compostela, and its immediate destination at Culiacán. This meeting of the groups would likely have occurred about two weeks after Coronado's departure from Compostela on February 23, 1540[16,17]. The lackluster news brought by the Diaz group about the expectations concerning Cíbola disheartened some in the Coronado group, but they continued on to Culiacán, regardless.

16. F&F460, p58

17. Winship, Preface

Coronado and the Advance Group

Coronado left Compostela with the entire body of the expedition on Feb 23, 1540 and reached Culiacán one month later on the day before Easter. On modern maps the straight line distance between Compostela and Culiacán is about 250 miles. The ground-path distance can be estimated to be about 10% greater than that – or about 275 miles. The expedition rested "several days" at Chiametla where the Diaz group had found them, so there is an opportunity to calculate an estimated rate of travel for the full body of the expedition. Assuming a rest period of about five days would result in a travel rate of about 11 miles per day. According to George Parker Winship in the preface[17] to his translation of Castañeda's "The Journey of Coronado," the expedition leaving Compostela consisted of

> *some two hundred and fifty horsemen and seventy Spanish foot soldiers armed with crossbows and harquebuses. Besides these there were three hundred or more native allies and upward of a thousand negro and Indian servants and followers, to lead the*

spare horses, drive the pack mules, carry the extra luggage and herd the droves of oxen and cows, sheep and swine.

Before leaving Culiacán, Coronado divided the expedition into two groups. He selected perhaps two hundred men including about 60 to 75 horsemen, perhaps 30 footmen, many Indian allies and an unknown number of livestock to constitute an Advance Party to be led by himself. He directed the remainder of the expedition to remain in Culiacán until the end of May under the command of don Tristán de Arellano[18,19]. This delay was likely ordered to allow time for the corn crops along the planned route to ripen. Coronado provisioned his Advance Party for an 80-day march and led it toward Cíbola which they expected to be as much as 350 leagues away based on the reports of Marcos de Niza and Melchior Diaz. They departed Culiacán on April 22, 1540 and arrived at the first pueblo of Cíbola on July 7, 1540[19].

18. F&Fdocs28, p392
19. F&Fdocs22, p291

The average rate of travel that Coronado apparently expected for this Advance Party was 350 leagues per 80 days, or about 4.4 leagues/day (11.5 miles/day). A more common estimate of the distance between Culiacán and Cíbola is 300 leagues and Coronado actually took about 75 days to cover that distance. This results in an estimated average rate of travel of 4 leagues/day (10.5 miles/day).

20. F&Fdocs19, p255

From Coronado's letter[20] to Viceroy Mendoza dated August 3, 1540 and written at Cíbola, it appears that the Advance Party had started from Culiacán with some number of livestock which they had to leave behind at the Rio Yaquimí because the trail was too rough for them. In the same letter, Coronado says that they had expected to find that

the route was excellent and flat and that there was

Background 11

> *only one insignificant grade half a league long*

as de Niza had reported, but what they actually found was

> *... that there are mountains... a very difficult trail that could not be traversed without either ourselves preparing one or restraightening the track that was there. And even if the trail is well repaired, it cannot be traversed without great danger of the horses rolling there.*

These factors certainly would contribute to an average pace that was slower than anticipated. The loss of the livestock to feed the group and the loss of much of their other foodstuff while crossing rivers as well as the fact that they were traveling before the Indians' crops had ripened, caused severe hardships. As a result, the entire Advance Party was near starvation when the Cíbolans saw them approaching the first pueblo early in July.

The lack of correlation between de Niza's report and Coronado's actual experiences may be an indication that the two groups did not follow the same route. However, de Niza was traveling with the Advance Party so it is a wonder that there is no record of his defending his reputation against all the negative statements made by Coronado and others. Of course, by the time Coronado wrote his letter to the Viceroy in early August 1540, he may have been so completely disgusted with de Niza that he was not talking to him anymore.

Arellano and Main Body of Coronado's Expedition

After waiting in Culiacán until about the end of May 1540 as ordered by Coronado, Tristán de Arellano took the main body of the expedition with all the supplies they could transport to the the Indian village called Los Corazones. Upon reaching Los Corazones, Arellano immediately started to build a villa which they called San Gerónimo de Corazones and which was to serve as a supply depot for the Expedition. A short time later he moved the settlement and the entire main body of the Expedition northward 10 leagues (about 26 miles) to the valley the Indians called Senora but which the Spaniards called Señora[15]. Again they established a villa and stayed in the Señora valley until the rainy season ended. Around the middle of September 1540[21] Arellano left perhaps 80 men (probably meaning 80 Spaniards and an unknown number of servants and slaves) at San Gerónimo and took the rest of the main body of the Expedition to Cíbola. They arrived at Cíbola during a surprise snow storm probably in in early November.

21. F&Fdocs28, p394

Arellano's group may have been the largest group to reach Cíbola during the Coronado entrada, but it was certainly not the last. Several other groups of varying sizes continued to travel between Cíbola and San Gerónimo and on to Culiacán or even to Mexico City during the entire period of the entrada. Most of these travelers were probably couriers exchanging messages and carrying orders, but some were also men returning to Mexico City for various reasons. San Gerónimo was established as a mid-way re-supply base and was instrumental in the operation of the Coronado Expedition. It is a good place from which to view the character of the Expedition, as will be discussed in more detail in later chapters.

Alarcón's Expedition by Sea

In keeping with a recently developed sensitivity to the humanity of the native peoples, Viceroy Antonio Mendoza charged[22] the Coronado Expedition to

22. F&Fdocs15, p185

> *not inflict injury on or [exercise] force against the Indians.... They are not to take anything they may*

> *possess from them against their will.*

To this end, the viceroy supplied the Expedition's ground force with many head of livestock and other foodstuffs and supplies. In addition, he commissioned Captain Hernando (or, perhaps, Fernando) de Alarcón to outfit two ships with supplies and arms in order to re-supply the ground forces from the coast. According to Bernal Diaz del Castillo[22], one of Alarcón's ship captains, the ships carried

> *hardware, some artillery pieces, gunpowder, crossbows, and arms and armor of all sorts, as well as olive oil and hardtack.*

as well as

> *the clothing the men-at-arms could not take [with them].*

On May 9, 1540 while Coronado was on his way from Culiacán to Cíbola and while Arellano was waiting with the main component of the Expedition at Culiacán, Hernando de Alarcón left the port of Colima in Nueva Espana on the Pacific coast west of Mexico City with his two *navios*, the San Pedro and the Santa Catarina and proceeded up the coast to the port of Aguayaval where he added another ship, the San Gabriel, to his fleet[23]. Flint and Flint identify this port as the modern-day port of Bahia Santa Maria which is just north of Culiacán at the mouth of the Rio Guayabal[24].

According to Alarcón's report[23], the navio San Gabriel was also carrying foodstuffs for Coronado's ground forces. When Alarcón reached Aguayaval, he learned that the entire Expedition had already left Culiacán, so he must have reached that port sometime after the end of May, 1540 when Arellano had been instructed

23. F&Fdocs15, p188

24. F&Fdocs15, n23

to leave. This would imply that the San Gabriel must have been laden with any supplies that Arellano could not take with him on his march to Los Corazones. None of the supplies on Alarcón's three ships ever reached the Coronado Exedition.

Alarcón continued sailing up the west coast of Mexico to its head where the present-day Colorado River empties into the Gulf of California. He then proceeded upriver for a distance he states to be 30 leagues (approximately 80 miles) but apparently did not get as far as the confluence with the Gila River since he made no mention of it. Alarcón questioned the Indians along the river, seeking news of Coronado and information about the location of Cíbola. From the Indians he learned that Coronado had already reached Cíbola which lies more than ten days travel (for the Indians) from his location.

Supply Effort of Hernando Arias

Viceroy Mendoza sent livestock and other food supplies overland along with the Expedition to Culiacán. He also sent supplies by sea with Alarcón's two ships in a fruitless attempt to support the land expedition. Almost lost in the footnotes of history is one more supply effort organized and probably funded by Mendoza. It is recorded[25] that Mendoza had sent Hernando Arias de Saabedra to Culiacán prior to the Expedition's arrival to ensure it had adequate supplies.

25.F&FdocsAp3 p614

It is unknown when Arias de Saabedra went to Culiacán, what he took with him or how he got there, but it is known that the Expedition found a plentiful supply of food when it arrived at Culiacán. It is also known that the ship *San Gabriel* was anchored there during the Expedition's stay. Although it is unknown to be a fact, it might be conjectured that Arias de Saabedra transported supplies to Culiacán with that vessel.

Geographical Legacy

The geography of the territory involved with the Coronado Expedition was almost completely unknown to those explorers. Several major excursions by detachments of the Coronado expedition were sent out from various points along the route to explore a significant part of the area comprising what is now northwestern Mexico and the southwestern United States. This includes portions of California, Arizona, New Mexico, Texas, Oklahoma, Kansas, Colorado and Utah. Although the Seven Cities of Gold turned out to be little more than a myth and although Coronado failed to find the wealth and fame he was seeking, his expedition added immensely to the body of geographical knowledge of an unexplored part of the Spanish world.

Chapter 2

Composition of the Expedition

In the middle of the sixteenth century, by the time Álvar Nuño Cabeza de Vaca had reached the west coastal regions of present-day Mexico in 1536, the town of Culiacán was the northernmost Spanish settlement along the west coast of Mexico. This town was in the most recently organized province, Nueva Galicia, and is now in the present Mexican state of Sinaloa. By 1540, Francisco Vasquez de Coronado had been appointed governor of Nueva Galicia and also had been assigned to lead a group of Spaniards and their Indian allies into the unexplored territory of Tierra Nueva, a vast region to the north of Culiacán. There were multiple purposes of this *entrada,* including the expectation of wealth and fame for the participants, the opportunity to lay claim to a vast amount of land for the Spanish Crown and the hope of converting many native souls to Christianity and the Church.

Coronado's Expedition to Cíbola and Quivira was the first large Spanish penetration into the Tierra Nueva (New Lands) far to the north of the settled regions, but it was not the last. Over the following 300 years there were many Spanish and Mexican excursions into the region for conquest, trade, mining and/or settlement. These later entradas would certainly have traveled different routes for part of their journeys since their purposes and destinations were different. As a consequence, the many period artifacts which certainly would have been lost, traded, stolen or abandoned by all of the groups cannot be taken as defining the route of any particular entrada. To have any reasonable expectation of finding the route of Coronado's journey, one must first have a good understanding of the composition of the Expedition. He must know the size of the various groups within the expedition and what each group was carrying with them. It is also necesary to develop some understanding of the reasonableness of the various possible routes with respect to the composition of the individual groups. To that end, this investigation will begin with the initial recruitment of Expedition members in Mexico City.

Mexico City Contingent

After returning from Tierra Nueva, Marcos de Niza presented a report of his journey to Viceroy Mendoza at Mexico City in the province of Nueva España on September 2, 1539. Within a matter of days, news of his account was circulating throughout the province and firing people's imaginations. Recruitment of men for the Coronado Expedition began immediately. Very soon thereafter, according to Castañeda[1],

1. F&Fdocs28, p389

> *more than three hundred Spaniards were assembled, and about eight hundred Indians native to Nueva España*

and he was probably counting only men-at-arms. Castañeda apparently was greatly impressed by the large number of men of high status who were among these 300. This group of Spaniards (including Portuguese and perhaps other Europeans) and Indian allies whom the Spaniards called "*indios amigos*" comprised the core of the expedition forces, but additional Indians and Europeans joined the group as the expedition mustered at Compostela and marched north to Culiacán.

Muster Roll at Compostela

Coronado assembled the members of his expedition for inspection by Viceroy don Antonio Mendoza in Compostela, the capital of Nueva Galicia, on February 10, 1540[2]. At that time, Compostela was located at the site of present-day Tepic[3]. Most members had proceeded from Mexico City individually or in small groups after being organized there by Mendoza. According to Pedro de Castañeda's account[2], when Mendoza finished making preparations in Mexico City

2. F&Fdocs28, p390

3. F&FdocsGeo, p600

> *he [himself] departed for Compostela, accompanied by many caballeros and noblemen. He spent New Year's Day of [one thousand five hundred and forty] at Pátzcuaro, which is the Episcopal seat of Michoacán. From there he crossed the entire land of Nueva España, met by great pleasure and happiness and splendid receptions, all the way to Compostela (which is, as I have said, [a distance of] a hundred and ten leagues). There he found the whole company assembled, well cared for and given lodging by Cristóbal de Oñate, who at that time was the person who had sole charge of that jurisdiction. He had supported and was captain of all that land, even though Francisco Vázquez [de Coronado] was governor.*

At that time in the Spanish world, the new year began on Christmas day, December 25. Mendoza and his entourage left Pátzcuaro the next day (December 26, 1539) and most likely were accompanied by an unknown number of Pátzcuaro natives[4]. Thus the number of indios amigos in the Coronado Expedition must have been well in excess of 800 men at the time of the muster at Compostela.

4. F&Fdocs28, n113

Composition of the Expedition 19

The Spaniards of the Expedition passed in review before Mendoza on Feb 22, 1540, presumably. As they did so, the scribe Juan de Cuevas recorded the individual men by name along with the number of horses each man was taking as well as giving an indication of the type of arms and armor each had. Cuevas' report[5] tallies 266 horsemen and 62 footmen present at the review. The horsemen had 552 horses and one mule amongst them and the footmen had an additional six horses belonging to five of the men. Coronado is the only man identified as having any armor for his horses and he took four sets for his 23 horses.

5. F&Fdocs12, p139

It should be noted that the count of people attached to the Coronado ground expedition as of February 22, 1540 is incomplete in the muster at Compostela. It includes only "Spanish" fighting men (two of whom are actually noted to be Portuguese) and does not include the indios amigos or servants or slaves. It also does not include any of the religious men, who evidently preceded the expedition to Culiacán, nor other Spaniards who were still expected from the Mexico City region or those who preceded the Expedition north. Among these latter individuals would be the group of 16 armed horsemen and an unknown number of indios amigos under the command of Melchior Diaz and Juan de Zaldívar who had gone to corroborate the report of Marcos de Niza.

Including the Diaz-Zaldívar group, the total number of "Spaniards" attached to the Expedition at the time of the Compostela muster would have been 306 known and an additional unknown number still expected from Mexico City and those who were waiting in Culiacán.

The number of pieces of arms and armor is not possible to determine with a high degree of certainty except for items that Juan de Cuevas singled out for counting. He tallied 55 swords (3 among the horsemen and 52 among the footmen), 20 crossbows (5 among the horsemen and 15 among the footmen), 26 arquebuses (4 among the horsemen and 22 among the footmen) and 12 daggers (1 among horsemen and 11 among footmen). There were 80 pieces of chain mail (77 among horsemen and 3 among footmen) of various types including vests, sleeves, breeches, corselets and one gauntlet. Also listed were 50 sets of headgear (only one among the footmen), some including face guards, throat guards or neck guards. From the manner in which they are listed it would appear that some of the headgear may have been non-metallic, native items. Cuevas also listed 67 protective "elk hide" jackets (62 of which belonged to the horsemen). The majority of both horsemen and footmen also took unspecified "native arms and armor" (262 sets were tallied). This tally of weapons at the Compostela review was certainly not complete as Juan de Cuevas, himself, noted[6]

6. F&Fdocs12, p150

> *These horsemen were carrying their lances, swords, and other arms, in addition to the arms and armor declared [above].*

It seems reasonable to expect that each of the 226 horsemen would have had at least one lance and one sword not tallied by Cuevas. In that case, it can estimated that the group at Compostela had a total of about 280 swords and 230 lances in addition to an unknown number of native obsidian-edged swords.

The Expedition Assembled at Culiacán

The present-day city of Culiacán sits on the site of the original settlement of that name founded in March 1531, but the settlement of *San Miguel de Culiacán* had been established approximately 30 miles south at a

Composition of the Expedition

location about 10 miles up the Rio San Lorenzo in late October of that same year due to a measles pandemic among the native populations at Culiacán[7].

On February 23, 1540, the day after mustering a large part of his Expedition in Compostela[8], Francisco Vásquez de Coronado began the 100 league (260 mile) journey to the northern Spanish outpost of San Miguel de Culiacán. The Viceroy, don Antonio Mendoza, accompanied the Expedition northward from Compostela for two days before he dropped off and returned to Mexico City while the Expedition continued toward its intermediate destination of Chiametla. Chiametla lay about 45 leagues (117 miles) north of Compostela (Tepic) and about 50 leagues (133 miles) south of San Miguel de Culiacán. Chiametla was almost certainly at the site of present-day Chametla in the southern part of the Mexican State of Sinaloa.

The chroniclers fail to record the number of days it took for the Expedition to reach Chiametla, but by the time it arrived there the foodstuffs were running low. The Expedition stayed at Chiametla for "several days" while raiding parties were sent out to acquire food from the local Indian pueblos. It was on one of these raids that the Expedition lost its first member. The second-in-command, *maestre de campo* Lope de Samaniego, died from an arrow shot through his eye and into his brain. Several other men in his group also were wounded by arrows. It was here at Chiametla that the group under Melchior Diaz and Juan de Zaldívar, returning from their attempt to reach Cíbola, met with the advancing Coronado group[9]. The entire group, except for Juan de Zaldívar, then continued the northern journey and reached Culiacán (the chroniclers often use this short form to refer to San

7. Reff DDCC

8. F&F460, p58

9. F&Fdocs28, p391

Miguel de Culiacán) on March 27, 1540.

10. F&F460, p62

Richard Flint has estimated[10] that 360 or more Spaniards, along with an unknown number of indios amigos, were with the Expedition by the time Coronado was ready to leave Culiacán late in April 1540.

rate of travel

The journey of about 95 leagues from Compostela to Culiacán, then, took about 40 days marching (allowing 5 days for the unspecified "several days" stop at Chiametla). The average rate of travel for the combined Expedition on this leg of the trip is then estimated as 2.5 leagues (about 6.5 miles) per day. This very slow pace might have been due to the Compostela-to-Chiametla leg of the trip serving as the "shake-down" learning experience for many novice members. Month's later during the journey when the entire Expedition was once again traveling together, Castañeda says[11] that in marching 37 days on the route from Tiquex to Quivira the Expedition covered 250 leagues and that

11. F&Fdocs28, p410

> *[This is known] because one person was given the responsibility of making an estimate, and one was counting the paces.*

This yields an average rate of about 6.75 leagues per day (almost 18 miles per day). Much of this route was flat and smooth and at that later point the members of the Expedition would have been well seasoned travelers. This rate of six or seven leagues per day could be considered a "normal" pace to be expected over any part of the journey. Castañeda's statement is a very rare insight into the Expedition's method of determining distances traveled.

men

There is no detailed description of the Coronado

Expedition and no count of its membership or a listing of its belongings while it was in Culiacán. However, in late 1546 or early 1547, Viceroy Mendoza stated that two hundred and fifty horsemen left Culiacán with Coronado on his expedition and Coronado testified to the validity of that number[12]. This number agrees well with the 226 counted at the muster at Compostela plus the 18 horsemen in the Diaz and Zaldívar group. Richard and Shirley Flint have been able to compile a list of 358 European members[13] of the Expedition known by name. The Compostela muster roll accounts for a total of only 306 "men" (presumably including only fighting men) including Diaz and Zaldívar and their 16 horsemen who were all absent at the time of the muster. Almost all of the Flints' 358 members probably would have been present at Culiacán.

12. A&R, p314

13. F&FdocsA3, p605

In addition to these 358 men, most, if not all, of them would have had wives, *criados* (servants) and/or slaves to perform the cooking, cleaning and other housekeeping chores. Coronado, alone, had several criados (among whom he distributed 12 or 15 of his 23 horses) and "four black men and three black women"[14]. It must be surmised, then, that the actual number of non-Indian people on the Expedition easily could have been 700 or even considerably more. An estimate in excess of 1000 is not inconceivable – and that doesn't include the Indians.

14. F&Fdocs11, p118

The Flints have also tabulated[10] eleven indios amigos whose names are known, while Arthur S. Aiton and Agapito Rey write[12] that on Jan 18, 1547, in response to question 200 of a legal inquiry into Viceroy Mendoza'a affairs, it was recorded that

Mendoza claimed that thirteen hundred Indians

voluntarily accompanied Coronado from Culiacán and that every care was exercised to care for them and to support their families in New Spain

and that Franscisco Vasquez de Coronado agreed with that number to within "a few more or less". Since the count of European men appears to have included only fighting men, it is highly probable that the count of indios amigos also included only fighting men. In that case the total number of Indians from the central regions of Mexico who were traveling with the Expedition could have easily exceeded 2600. In other testimony at the same Mendoza inquiry, Coronado supports Mendoza's claim of benevolent treatment of the indios amigos by saying

That this witness has seen soldiers of high rank march on foot because they carried their food and other belongings on their horses, as they were not allowed to use any Indians to carry burdens

in answering question 203 and that

he knows and is sure that according to the reckoning of this witness thirty Indians did not die in the said expedition, including the stops and trip back and forth

in responding to question 204. It is easily conceivable that estimates of the number of people attached to the Coronado Expedition at Culiacán could exceed 3600 individuals.

weapons

The number and types of weapons and armor listed in the muster also needs to be recognized as incomplete. Not only would there have been more weapons as well as more horses and mules for the additional 56 fighting men, but it is known that one entire class of weapon is not mentioned . In testimony supporting Juan Troyano's contribution[15] to the Expedition, it is revealed that he was in charge of six versillos at Cíbola and at Tiquex. A versillo was a type of light swivel gun apparently designed to be mounted with a pin on the gunnel of a ship[16]. There is no mention of additional versillos but that possibility cannot be dismissed.

15. F&Fdocs31, p527

16. F&Fdocs28, n589

One additional shortcoming of the known listings of war-fighting items is the absence of any mention of war dogs, although they prominently appear in a number of incidents throughout several of the chroniclers' narratives.

livestock

During the muster, the scribe Juan de Cuevas tallied 558 horses and one mule among the men assembled there. The horsemen accounted for 552 horses and the one mule while the footmen had a total of six horses. From testimony of Juan Bermejo[14] in 1545, it is known that Francisco Vásquez de Coronado, himself, had an additional 15 head of mules not counted in the muster at Compostela. It is highly probable that many other mules also were accompanying the group since mules appear to have been the favored beasts of burden. In testimony[17] at a trial in 1552, Juan Bermejo stated that the expedition had "much livestock (cattle, sheep and pigs)" while Coronado testified[12] in 1547 in response to question 199

17. F&Fdocs11, p124

> *That this witness ordered the horses, mules, and stock that were carried in the said expedition counted at a certain narrow pass where they could be easily counted and there were found to be by count fifteen hundred animals.*

Sheep are mentioned repeatedly throughout the

narratives of the Coronado Expedition, but Bermejo is the only Expedition member to have indicated that "cattle" were taken along and it is unknown how they were acquired. The indication of pigs is also somewhat unique but is consistent with Melchoir Pérez's testimony[18] that he took along "more than a thousand head of livestock (pigs, sheep, and rams)". The presence of cattle and sheep is verified somewhat independently by Captain Fernando Alarcón's report[19] of his passage up the lower Colorado River. There he met some local Indians who had recently returned from Cíbola where they had met Christians (presumably the Advance Party).

18. F&Fdocs32, p537

19. F&Fdocs15, p201

> *[The locals said] that many of them had cattle like those of Cíbola and other small black animals with wool and horns.*

Bermejo and Pérez both list pigs among the livestock of the Expedition, but some historians have questioned this, suggesting instead that pigs may have gone along as salted pork. Coronado's count of 1500 "animals" does not appear to be consistent with Pérez's statement that he, himself, took "more than a thousand" head of livestock and with the known 558 horses listed at the Compostela muster. In addition, many head of livestock probably were taken along by the other high-ranking members of the Expedition, since each person was expected to support himself and his servants.

The Expedition is Split

The Expedition to Cíbola stayed in Culiacán for an extended period of time until leaving in two separate groups. During this stay in Culiacán the Captain General Francisco Vásquez de Coronado apparently finished the organization of the Expedition and completed the assignments of men to the various companies. Coronado split off an Advance Party around the middle of April 1540 and led it toward Cíbola. Apparently, this Advance Party was not composed of complete companies for, according to testimony from Rodrigo Maldonado[15] taken on February 20, 1560,

> *In the [course of] appointment[s] which General Francisco Vazquez made at Culiacán, from some captains he took with himself some of the men-at-arms they had [in their companies].*

He goes on to say that the Advance Party was formed by Coronado such that

> *in choosing, he left other persons among the caballeros, captains, and men-at-arms who remained, both captains and men-at-arms, with as much competence and courage for whatever might be presented as those he took with him.*

These statements lead one to surmise that Coronado divided his forces with the intent of achieving comparable capabilities in each part. The Advance Party was to have fewer European men-at-arms than the remaining group, so it stands to reason that Coronado probably took with himself a biased share of the European-style weapons. Since there is no known record of the numbers of weapons carried by the Advance Party or by the following main body, this statement remains solidly in the realm of supposition regardless of its seeming reasonableness.

Coronado's Advance Party

The Advance Party departed from San Miguel de Culiacán on Thursday April 22, 1540 (Julian date) according to Franscisco Vasquez de Coronado in his letter to the Viceroy[20] dated August 3, 1540 and written shortly after the capture of the first pueblo of Cíbola. The author[21]

20. F&Fdocs19, p254

21. F&Fdocs22, p291

of the *Traslado de las Nuevas* (Copy of the News) agrees with this date, but Castañeda de Nájera's Narrative states[22] that they left one week earlier, 15 days after entering Culiacán on March 29. The *Traslado de las Nuevas* was written during the Expedition, while Castañeda wrote his account about 20 years after the event, so he may well have been mistaken.

22. F&Fdocs28, p392

men

The composition of the Advance Party is not certain. Castañeda says it included as many as 50 horsemen, a few footmen and most of the indios amigos[22]. Juan Jaramillo's Narrative[23] says "only we sixty horsemen went with the general". The Traslado de las Nuevas (Copy of the News) says it was 75 horsemen and 30 footmen and implies that each man had additional "followers". The Relación del Suceso[24] (Report of the Outcome) has "80 horsemen, 25 footmen and part of the artillery". Coronado, himself, says in his testimony[25] of September 3, 1544 in Guadalajara that he took 80 horsemen "more or less" and Don Garcia Lopez de Cárdenas as maestre de campo.

23. F&Fdocs30, p512

24. F&Fdocs29, p497

25. H&R, p319

Since there were approximately 1300 indios amigos at Culiacán and "most" of them went with the Advance Party, it seems reasonable to expect that the Advance Party included at least 1000 individuals (100 European men at arms, 800 indios amigos and perhaps 100 servants). This estimate could swell to as many as 2000 individuals if most of the men took along more than one support person (e.g., wife or servant) and if the 800 indios amigos included only warriors and not their support people. A reasonable estimate of the number of individuals attached to the Expedition's Advance Party leaving Culiacán would be 1500 – roughly half of them fighting men and the other half support people.

Composition of the Expedition

weapons

The weapons carried by the Advance Party would have been primarily "native arms and armor" since almost all of the Europeans at the Compostela muster had them and all of the indios amigos would have had them. In addition, all of the 75 or 80 horsemen probably had lances and swords while all of the 25 or 30 footmen probably had swords, since 52 of the 62 footmen at the Compostela muster were listed as having them. It is known from Coronado's letter[20] to the viceroy that the Advance Party carried both crossbows and arquebuses, but the numbers of each are unknown. It is known from the muster that there were 15 crossbows and 22 arquebuses among the 62 footmen and that no man had both. That implies that there were 25 footmen with neither weapon at Compostela. If the premise that the fighting capability was divided nearly evenly before leaving Culiacán is accepted, then it would be expected that the smaller number of Spaniards in the Advance Party would have been better armed than those in the "main body" under Arellano's command. In that case, it might be surmised that all 25 or 30 footmen in the Advance Party had either a crossbow or an arquebus. But the number of each would be a matter of unsupported conjecture.

It is also known that there were six versillos[15] (light-weight swivel guns) in the Advance Party which were undoubtedly transported by pack horse or mule as were the arquebuses[20]. In addition to these artillery pieces, Castañeda says that there were seven "bronze pieces" held by the residents of Culiacán when the Expedition arrived there[9]. However, there is no indication that either Coronado or Arellano took any of these with them upon leaving Culiacán. The probability of any of these bronze pieces being taken seems very low due to their size and weight and the difficulty of transporting them.

livestock

A significant number of the fifteen hundred or more animals[12] (horses, mules, cattle, sheep and possibly pigs) belonging to the Coronado Expedition seems to have accompanied the Advance Party. Not only were there riding horses for the "horsemen" and pack horses and mules for carrying foodstuffs and weapons, there was also the[26]

26. F&Fdocs19, p255

> *great number of the livestock Your Lordship sent as provisions for the armed force remained behind at this [point of the] journey, because of the roughness of the rock. The lambs and wethers lost their hooves because of the roughness of the ground. And I left the greater part of those I had brought from Culiacán at the Yaquimí River because they could not travel*

as Coronado informed Viceroy Mendoza. The place where the "greater part" of the sheep was left was the Rio Yaquimí valley. This was two day's travel short of the Indian settlement at Los Corazones, the nominal half-way point on the route to Cíbola.

rate of travel

There are several instances when the chroniclers supply enough information to provide an estimate of the rate of travel of the Advance Group. The first comes from Coronado's letter to the Viceroy[20]

> *Thirty Leagues before [the company] reached the place the father provincial describes so thoroughly in his report, I sent Melchior Diaz with fifteen horsemen on ahead. I directed him to make [each] two-day journey in one... He traveled four days*

Composition of the Expedition

> *through some very rugged mountains and found nothing to subsist on....*

to reach the (unspecified) place that Marcos de Niza described. From the context of this statement, it is not clear that Diaz took four days to travel the 30 leagues or if he spent those four days exploring beyond that point. If the former is correct, then Diaz would have traveled at the rate of 7.5 leagues per day (or about 20 miles/day). Since this was double speed, the "normal" rate would have been about 3.8 leagues per day (or 10 miles/day). A somewhat faster rate would be expected through country that was not so rugged. If, on the other hand, the four days were spent exploring, then there is no information about how long it took him to travel the 30 leagues and therefore no information on the rate of travel.

Coronado's letter also states that the Advance Party reached Los Corazones, 150 leagues from Culiacán, on May 26 about 34 days after leaving Culiacán on April 22, 1540. This yields an average rate of travel of 4.4 leagues per elapsed day (11.6 miles/day) for that half of the journey to Cíbola. This period of 34 days includes an unknown number of "rest days" so the actual rate of travel on marching days remains unknown, but must be greater than 4.4 leagues per day. Castañeda provides an opportunity to calculate a travel rate for a marching day when he reports that the Advance Party took one day to go the six leagues[27] from the Rio Bermejo to a point two leagues short of the first pueblo of Cíbola. This is a rate of 6 leagues per day (or almost 16 miles/day).

27. F&Fdocs28, p393

In addition to these estimates of the rate of travel over portions of the trip, there are two sources that yield an average rate for the entire 300 leagues from Culiacán to the first pueblo of Cíbola. Coronado told the Viceroy that the trip took 80 days[20] while the unknown author of the Relación del Suceso[24] says that they arrived at Cíbola on "the seventy-third" day. However, Coronado also says that the Advance Party rested four days at Corazones and another two days at Chichiticale, so the 73 days may be the more correct number of days of travel. On that basis, the average rate of travel from Culiacán to Cíbola is estimated as 4.1 leagues per day (or almost 11 miles/day) including an unknown number of additional "rest days".

In summary, from the above information it appears that the Advance Party of Coronado's Expedition to Cíbola probably traveled at an average rate between 10 miles/day over rough ground and 16 miles/day over smoother ground. It is also expected that the Advance Party spent some days of slower travel when searching out food and when they were travelling weak from severe lack of food. This weakened condition seems to have been prevalent during the latter stages of their approach to Cíbola where they arrived near the point of starvation. The expectation of acquiring food may have been a major contributor to the rapid rate of travel over the final six or eight leagues before Cíbola.

The Main Body of the Expedition

When Coronado left Culiacán with the Advance Party, he named Velasco de Barrionuevo as maestre de campo of the remaining forces in place of Cárdenas who was going with the Advance Party. Coronado placed the entire "main body" of the Expedition in Culiacán under the leadership of don Tristán de Luna y Arellano. This second part of the Expedition left Culiacán sometime during the latter part of May, 1540 with orders to advance to the site of Los Corazones and establish a supply depot there[21]. They probably departed from the valley of Culiacán, near the present-day city of Culiacán, Sinaloa. Arellano's command was organized into several individual companies, each under command of its own captain.

men

Since the Advance Party took about 100 European men at arms, Arellano would have left Culiacán with about 258 European men at arms – if the Flints' count of 358 "Spaniards" is accurate. Castañeda says the "servants and native allies amounted to more than a thousand persons" before the Advance Party left Culiacán[22]. He would also have had about 500 of the estimated 1300 indios amigos warriors for a total of about 760 fighting men. If it is again conjectured that each fighting man was supported by only one non-fighter, then one is led to an estimated number of approximately 1500 to 1800 individuals in Arellano's contingent. The two groups seem to have been split with a comparable number of people in each, although Arellano's group was probably somewhat larger than this estimate because each fighting man likely would have been supported by more than one other individual. A reasonable estimate of the number of individuals attached to the Expedition's main body leaving Culiacán would be 1500 to 2000. Again, roughly half of his people would have been fighting men and the other half support people.

weapons

There is no known tally of the numbers or types of weapons carried by Arellano's force, but it is known that almost all of the men had native arms and armor. Most, if not all, of the European men probably had swords, as well, and the horsemen, of which there were about 145, probably all had lances. It is highly likely that

Coronado left Arellano with a few crossbows and a few arquebuses. It is unknown if Arellano carried any swivel guns (versillos) since the total number of them belonging to the Expedition is never mentioned. The Advance Party carried six versillos and it is possible there were more.

livestock

The Compostela muster shows that each of the 226 horsemen had 2.5 riding horses on average and if this can be used as a guide, it would be expected that the 145 horsemen in Arellano's group had a total of about 360 riding horses. Castañeda says[22] that Arellano left Culiacán with "more than six hundred loaded pack animals". However, from the context of his statement, it cannot be certain that all of these 600 pack animals went with Arellano or if that number included the pack animals that accompanied the Advance Party. Castañeda later relates[27] that all of Arellano's horsemen left Culiacán

> *on foot with their lances over their shoulders. This was so that they could take the horses loaded, down.*

Arellano, then, probably had the 360 riding horses and perhaps as many as 240 additional pack horses and/or mules loaded with foodstuffs and supposedly had several more loaded with weapons and other supplies.

rate of travel

The chroniclers are strangely silent about the distances and travel times between locations visited by Arellano's main force. Arellano and the "main force" of the Coronado Expedition departed Culiacán on an unknown date and there is some apparent confusion among the chroniclers about that date. Castañeda says that Arellano was to delay 15 days[22] after Coronado left before departing himself with the main force. The author of Relación del Suceso says the delay was to be 20 days[24] while the author of Traslado de las Nuevas says that they were supposed to delay leaving until the end of May 1540[21]. It is known, however, that Arellano left Culiacán with orders to proceed to the region of Los Corazones[27] (half way between Culiacán and Cíbola) and to build a settlement there to serve as a way station and supply depot.

Further Comments on the Numbers

Table 2.1 summarizes the estimated numbers of men, weapons, livestock and support people in the various components of the Coronado Expedition. These numbers are imprecise but are based on the known statements of individuals involved with the Expedition. Before leaving the subject of the composition of the Coronado Expedition to Tierra Nueva, several additional considerations should be addressed.

men

Part of the estimate of the number of people in the Coronado Expedition to Cíbola was based on the arbitrary assumption that each named Spaniard was supported by just one other support person (wife, servant or slave). This is likely to be a gross underestimate. For example, it is known that Coronado, himself, had several criados (probably 12 or 15) and "four black men and three black women"[14] and that Melchoir Pérez took "many other attendants (both men-at-arms and servants)"[18]. It is highly probable that most of the other caballeros (many of those listed in the Compostela muster) also took multiple numbers of support men and women.

28. F&Fdocs28, p432

Castañeda estimates[28] that there were "more than one thousand five hundred persons among the allies and servants" when the Expedition was on the march from Tiquex to Quivira around the end of May, 1541. This would have been in addition to the men-at-arms and may not have counted the many "allies and servants" attached to the company of Melchoir Diaz which was returning from its entrada to the Mar del Sur (lower Colorado River region). It certainly did not include those "allies and servants" attached to the contingent manning the supply depot at San Gerónimo.

There might have been approximately 300 "Spaniards" in the Expedition in May, 1541 on the way to Quivira. As noted previously, Flint and Flint[13] have named 358 Spaniards known to have been attached to the Expedition, but that may not be an accurate total. Several Spaniards had died and several others were stationed elsewhere, so the estimate of 300 men-at-arms present when Castañeda made his estimates in May, 1541 seems reasonable. This would make the total number of people at that place and time more than 1800.

livestock

At that same point on the journey to Quivira, Castañeda says there were "a thousand" horses (possibly including mules). The total number of horses counted at the Compostela muster was 558 which belonged to about 230 men but which included only riding horses. If pack horses and mules are included then Castañeda's estimate of a "thousand horses" does not seem unreasonable. He also says that there were "more than five thousand rams and ewes" but does not mention any cattle. By Castañeda's count, then, there was a total of about 6000 animals when the Expedition left Tiquex for Quivira. Earlier, when the Expedition was just beginning, Coronado had counted only 1500 "horses, mules and stock" and, by implication, these were supposedly supplied by Mendoza. The "stock" (apparently including cattle, sheep and pigs) was intended to feed the Expedition. However, after a year that included a long, cold winter in Tiquex, Castañeda says there are at least 4000 stock animals. He could have exaggerated the numbers of animals to emphasize the point he was trying to make, but if his estimates are accepted, one must wonder about the source of the larger number of animals or the earlier under-reporting of their numbers.

An insight into this discrepancy comes from "Melchior Perez's Petition for Preferment, 1551" in which he claims[18] that he took

> *more than a thousand head of livestock (pigs, sheep, and rams)*

and that

> *maestre de campo Garcia Lopez took the livestock from me in order to feed the expeditionary force at Culiacán (because it lacked [food]).*

In the same document this claim is verified by witness Juan Galeasso

> *this [individual] who is testifying ([who was] alguacil mayor and billeting officer for the expedition) seized the aforesaid livestock by order of don Garcia Lopez.*

29. F&Fdocs33, p558

Another petitioner, Cristóbal Escobar[29], establishes by statement and by the testimony of two witnesses, that he took "a certain number of livestock" from Nueva España on the expedition.

It appears to have been common for men of means to take livestock in order to feed themselves and their criados. If so, then it would be very likely that many more than Mendoza's 1500 head would be accompanying

Table 2.1 Probable Composition of the Two Groups
Estimated Numbers of Items

	At Muster	At Culiacan	Advance Party	Main Body
war men				
horsemen	266	250+	75	175
footmen	62	unk	25	37+
natives	800	1300	800	500
total war men	*1128*	*1550+*	*900*	*758+*
support				
non-indios	no count	700	100	600
indios	no count	1300	800	500
total support	*unk*	*2000*	*900*	*1100*
weapons				
swords	280	300	100	200
lances	230	250	75	145
crossbows	20	15	7	8
arquebuses	26	22	11	11
versillos	no count	6	6	unk
native arms	*262*	*1900*	*900*	*1900*
livestock				
horses	558	600+	250	360
mules	1	unk	unk	240
sheep	no count	unk	unk	unk
total animals	*no count*	*1500*	*unk*	*unk*

the Expedition. Although Castañeda's seemingly large count of livestock in May 1541 cannot be verified, it also cannot be presumed to be incorrect.

Composition of the Expedition

Trade Goods

In addition to all the people, animals, equipment and supplies that the Expedition took along to sustain itself, they also took a significant quantity of "trade goods". The primary purpose of the trade goods apparently was to bargain with the native peoples along the way for additional food and supplies. However, a second, but unstated, purpose may have been to create the illusion that the Expedition was a trading party interesting in establishing commerce between the Spaniards in the south and the native communities in the north. Since trade between the natives of the south and the natives of the north was a common occurance, this new "trading partner" would probably have seemed a natural development to any peoples the Expedition encountered.

Chapter 3

Organization and Travel

As discussed in Chapter 2, the Coronado Expedition to Cíbola in the northern territory of Tierra Nueva consisted of approximately 2000 people (perhaps 2/3 of whom were the indios amigos), about 1000 horses and 4000 or more other livestock including cows, mules, sheep and possibly pigs, as well as several dogs. Five or six hundred of the horses apparently were riding horses but the other horses and probably almost all of the mules were used as pack animals for carrying supplies and arms. The method used to move this great assemblage is not specifically stated or explained by any of the chroniclers of the Expedition. However, the information they supply in bits and pieces, taken together with information gleaned from some of the testimony at later legal proceedings, yields a great deal of insight into this matter.

Richard Flint has pointed out that the muster roll at Compostela contains a wealth of information[1,2] relating to the organization of the Expedition. Even though the Expedition was not fully formed at that point, it is clear that Coronado was organizing it into several companies, each with its own captain. Perhaps not all companies had been formed and perhaps not all captains had been appointed nor were all of the men assigned to companies at the time of the muster, but the intent is apparent. At the Compostela muster there were eight (or, perhaps ten) companies and their captains and some of the other officers were identified. These were as follows:

1. F&F460, p58
2. F&Fdocs12, p135

1. Francisco Vásquez de Coronado, Captain General

> Lope de Samaniego, maestre de campo
> Pedro de Tovar, alférez mayor (chief lieutenant)
> Lope de Gurrea
> Hernando de Alvarado, captain of artillery
> 34 additional horsemen

2. García López de Cárdenas, Captain

> Juan Navarro
> Alonzo del Moral, alférez (lieutenant)
> 6 additional horsemen

3. Diego Gutiérrez de la Caballería

> Juan de Villareal, alférez (lieutenant)
> 9 additional horsemen

4. Diego López, Captain

> 9 additional horsemen

5. don Rodrigo Maldonado, Captain

> Juan Torquemada, alférez (lieutenant)
> 9 additional horsemen

6. don Tristán Arellano, Captain

> 7 additional horsemen

7. Diego de Guevara, Captain

> Diego Hernández, alférez (lieutenant)
> 7 additional horsemen

8. Pablo de Melgosa, Captain of the footmen (absent but appointed)

> 62 footmen

The format of the muster document suggests to Richard Flint[1] that the scribe, Juan de Cuevas, might have been identifying two additional companies:

9. [Probable but unnamed], Captain

> Alonso González, alférez (lieutenant)
> 22 additional horsemen

10. [Francisco de Ovando], Captain

> 104 additional horsemen

although neither is explicitly specified in muster.

Another captain and his company were absent because they were returning from an entrada to Tierra Nueva trying to verify the report of Marcos de Niza. They will be included here to recognize that they were part of the Expedition even though they may not have officially joined the Expedition until it reached Chiametla or Culiacán.

11. Melchoir Diaz, Captian

> Juan de Zaldívar
> 14 or 16 additional horsemen.

After the returning Diaz-Zaldívar entrada met the outgoing Coronado Expedition at Chiametla, Diaz apparently accompanied it to Culiacán and beyond while Zaldívar continued south to deliver their report to Viceroy Mendoza. When Zaldívar returned to Culiacán, he received his commission[3] as captain of a company, also.

12. Juan de Zaldívar, Captain

> unspecified number of men assigned from other companies at Culiacán

A note about groups 9 and 10 is in order. It is not certain these two companies had been formed yet nor if the two captains had been appointed at this time nor if the men had yet been assigned to the companies. It

3. FCruel, p254

seems likely that the indicated division is correct, but it is probable that some, if not all, of the 104 horsemen listed under Ovando's command were eventually assigned to other companies. Also, it is not clear when or where Ovando received his commission as a captain.

4. F&Fdocs28, p389

Twenty years later, Castañeda de Nájera listed[4] the same captains through Diego de Guevara (seventh in the above list) and he listed them in the same order – perhaps suggesting that he had a copy of the muster roll. He goes on to say

> *All the rest of the caballeros went under the standard of the general, because they were distinguished persons. Some of them later were captains ... I will name some of those whom I remember; they were Francisco de Barrionuevo (a caballero from Granada). Juan de Zaldívar, Francisco de Ovando, Juan Gallego, Melchior Diaz ...The captain of footmen was Pablo del Melgosa (a native of Burgos) and the captain of artillery was Hernando de Alvarado (a caballero from Santander).*

Castañeda's inclusion of Francisco de Ovando in this list suggests that his captaincy was not official at Compostela.

5. FCruel, p277

When Francisco Vázquez de Coronado testified[5] on September 3, 1544 at the *pesquisa* (special investigation) conducted by Lorenzo de Tejada, he gave a slightly different list of companies leaving Compostela. This list affords some insight into the reorganization that took place at Culiacán which is not well documented by the Expedition's chroniclers. Combining the information from Coronado's list with Castañeda's information above, it can be deduced that the companies and captains that left Culiacán would have been

1. don Garcia López Cárdenas, maestre de campo
    assigned a company
2. Pedro de Tovar, alférez mayor (chief lieutenant)
    assigned a company
3. don Rodrigo Maldonado
    captain of horsemen
4. don Diego de Guevara
    captain of horsemen
5. don Tristán de Arellano
    captain of horsemen
6. Melchoir Diaz
    captain of horsemen
7. the councilman of Sevilla Diego López
    captain of horsemen
8. don Juan de Zaldívar
    captain of horsemen
9. Hernando de Alvarado
    captain of artillery
10. Pablo de Melgosa
    captain of the footmen

Note that Diego Gutiérrez de la Caballería is missing from Coronado's list. This is a fairly clear indication that he did not leave Compostela with the Expedition. Lope de Samaniego did leave Compostela but was killed at Chiametla before reaching Culiacán. He was replaced as maestre de campo by don Garcia López Cárdenas. Zaldívar received his commission and company at Culiacán. By this accounting, the Expedition consisted of ten companies (eleven, if Captain General Francisco Vázquez de Coronado also had a distinct company) as it left Culiacán. Some of these captains were assigned to

Organization and Travel 45

the Advance Party and their companies were commanded by someone else when Arellano left Culiacán.

The Main Group Departing from Culiacán

When Francisco Vázquez de Coronado left Culiacán with the Advance Party, he named don Tristán de Arellano as general of the troops remaining behind. If the surmise is correct that Coronado did not take complete companies with himself in the Advance Party, then General Arellano would have had the ten companies listed above in his command. Each of these companies would have been commanded by their respective captains or the captains' lieutenants (*alférez*) for those captains who accompanied Coronado to Cíbola in the Advance Party.

It is common practice to call Arellano's command the "main body" of the Expedition, but apparently it was comparable in size and strength to the Advance Party when the indios amigos and servants are considered. This group can be considered "main" primarily in the sense that most (probably over eighty percent) of the "Spaniards" were attached to it.

Eventually, Arellano went to Cíbola with this entire force except for about 80 men-at-arms and an unknown number of indios amigos, other local Indians and servants. These he left in the Señora valley to maintain the second site of the supply station, San Gerónimo. About half of those 80 men later also went on to Cíbola and Tiquex with don Pedro de Tovar[6].

6. F&Fdocs29, p501

Known Individuals in the Advance Party

As was pointed out previously, Captain General Francisco Vázquez probably did not include complete companies in the Advance Party. He did, however, include some of the captains and some of the men-at-arms selected from the ten companies at Culiacán. Even though the precise organization of this Advance Party is unknown, some of the individuals can be named with a reasonable degree of certainty. An analysis of five documents (numbers 11, 19, 30, 31 and 33) in Flint and Flint's "Documents of the Coronado Expedition 1539 – 1542"[7] and the testimony of several individuals in Richard Flint's "Great Cruelties Have Been Reported"[8] has identified at least 28 Spaniards who almost certainly left Culiacán in the Advance Party on April 22, 1540 on their way to Cíbola:

7. F&Fdocs
8. FCruel

Francisco Vázquez de Coronado, Captain General

Hernando de Alvarado	Captain of Artillery
Alonzo Álvarez del Valle	guidon bearer
Hernando Martín Bermejo	Secretary to Coronado
Juan Bermejo	crossbow man, cousin of Hernando
Garcia López Cárdenas	Captain and maestre de campo of army
Juan de Contreras	head groomsman

Melchoir Diaz, Captain

Luis de Figueredo	courier
Rodrígo de Frias	
Juan Gallego	
Juan Jaramillo	
Pedro de Ledesma	
Alonzo Manrique	
Domingo Martín	

Pablo de Melgosa, Captain of footmen

Melchoir Pérez de la Torre

Organization and Travel

Caspar de Saldana	
Gomez Suarez	
Francisco Torres	
Juan Troyano	artillery man
Juan de Villegas	
Rodrígo Ximon	
Juan de Zagala	
Marcos de Niza	cleric
Daniel	cleric
Juan de Padilla	cleric
Luis de Úbeda de Escalona	cleric
Antonio de Castilblanco	cleric

This is certainly not an exhaustive compilation and could easily contain mistakes. Much of the information was recorded from the memories of several different people some years after the events took place.

Formation and Marching

There is good reason to believe that each company traveled independently of the others when the Expedition was on the move and that they traveled with a considerable distance between the companies. The one woman, Francisca de Hozes, who testified at the pesquisa (special investigation) conducted by Lorenzo de Tejada in 1544, told of a pertinent incident[9] that occurred on don López Garcia de Cárdenas' return march from Tierra Nueva. Cárdenas had left Tiguex, according to Castañeda[10], with a few other people soon after Coronado's return from Quivira late in 1541. It is improbable that Francisca de Hozes and her husband, Alonso Sánchez, were traveling with Cárdenas, but she says that when he got to Corazones (this would most likely have been the Suya site of San Gerónimo) he

9. FCruel, p61

10. F&Fdocs28, p425

> *found the town and valley at war. ... She knows that the Indians... would have killed don Garcia López de Cárdenas and those who went with him, if they had not turned back and gotten reinforcements from another captain who was coming close behind.*

11. FCruel, p81

Another witness, Juan Gomez[11], told a very similar story, except that he named don Tristan de Arellano as the one who would have been killed if it had not been for the reinforcements. Who the second captain was is unknown, but this statement implies that Castañeda's "a few other people" was actually a much larger number than one might think.

Since Cárdenas had been the maestre de campo prior to leaving Tiquex, it is reasonable that he would take the lead on the trail. Francisca de Hozes makes it clear that another company (or group) was following Cárdenas' group at some distance. It seems reasonable to think that this was a typical mode of travel and that all the companies of the Expedition traveled the same way, one behind the other and each separated from the one ahead and the one behind.

12. F&Fdocs15, p201

There is also the report by Captain Hernando de Alarcón[12] of information he obtained from some Indians residing along the present lower Colorado River, perhaps near its confluence with the Gila River. These Indians had recently returned from a trading trip to Cíbola which, for them, was a journey of between 8 and 30 days. While there, they had apparently witnessed the arrival of a group of Spaniards. The Advance Party arrived at Cíbola in early July and the main body of the Expedition did not arrive there until sometime in September. Alarcón obtained his information before the middle of September, so it is almost certain that the Indian informants were referring to the arrival at Cíbola of Coronado and the Advance Party. The possibility that the Indians had witnessed the arrival of the main body cannot be totally discounted, but it does seem unlikely.

In addition to identifying the new arrivals as Christians, Alarcón's Indian traders described their cattle and sheep and also said[13]

13. F&Fdocs 15, n91

> *one day, before we departed, from sunrise to sunset these Christians did nothing but get themselves there.*

This statement would seem to support the idea that the Expedition extended over a long distance and did not travel as one large group. The length of the Expedition along its route would have been about one day's march, or about 4.5 to 6 leagues (12 to 16 miles). If the estimate in the previous chapter of 1500 people in the Advance Party is close to reality, then there would have been an average of about 42 feet between persons on the trail. This seems very excessive even for single-file marching and there is no other indication that the entire Advance Party moved in single-file formation. One straight forward way to reconcile this problem is to conjecture that the Advance Party moved in tighter formations within groups which were more widely separated (as Francisca de Hozes may have been describing in her story about Cárdenas' return march from Cíbola to Suya).

If that conjecture is valid, then it would appear that the Advance Party was also organized into companies (or company-like groups) – at least for the purpose of marching. This is a rare glimpse into the possible daily mechanics of Coronado's Advance Party. It is interesting that this insight came from Indians living several hundred miles distant rather than from the Expedition's own chroniclers.

There is another straight forward – and, arguably, more likely – way to reconcile the large average distance between men along the trail. In the previous chapter the number of fighting men in the Advance Party was estimated to be about 100. It is known that the Expedition had pack horses and mules which had to be led along the trail. The estimated number of such pack animals in the Advance Party is estimated to be 160 in Appendix F. Conjecturing that each Spanish fighting man (or his servants) led one or two mules, the average separation of 42 feet between those men no longer seems excessive.

Of course, the Spanish fighting men account for only about a third of the people in the Advance Party. The separation between the rest of the people would be expected to be considerably less than 42 feet unless Alarcón's informants included the herds of livestock in the one day it took the Spaniards to "get themselves there." In that case, it is highly conceivable that the average separtation could be 42 feet or even greater.

The Expedition's usual method of advancement appears to have consisted of a march of one league followed by a rest period which was followed by another one-league march and another rest period. This sequence would have been repeated several times until they reached the desired destination for that day or until daylight faded. The number of marches in one day seems to have varied from about four to eight, as will be seen in later chapters. The pace of marching seems to have varied also and was likely determined by the distance to the next desired camping site. Although not stated directly, it is presumed that a normal overnight camp was followed by another day of marching.

This repeated sequence of daily travels was periodically interrupted by a longer rest period consisting of several days. Four days of rest seems to have been normal, but Coronado mentions one such rest period[14] at Chichilticale as being only two days which he said was too short a period for the horses to recover. The number of these extended rest periods is unknown for either the Advance Party or the main body of the Expedition.

14. F&Fdocs19, p256

The chroniclers of the Expedition also have very little to say about the means or methods of camping. It is known that the Expedition formed *reales* (campgrounds with tents arranged in a compact local area) for that purpose. The tents comprising a *real* probably belonged to each man, or each family group, and would have been of various shapes and sizes. The captain of a company may have had a larger tent which could have also served as the company headquarters. If all of the tents were used for the overnight camps or only for the extended rests periods is unknown.

There are only two known specific places in the narratives where a *real* is mentioned and both are associated with presumed extended rest periods. One of these involves Pedro de Tovar at Tusayán (the Hopi villages of today) where Castañeda says[15]

15. F&Fdocs28, p396

> *The captain and those who were with him looked for a place to establish their* real *near the pueblo.*

The second mention of a possible *real* comes from the narrative[12] of Captain Hernando de Alarcón who

52   Coronado's Journey

reported that some local Indians along the Rio Tizon (the lower reaches of the present Colorado River) had recently been to Cíbola and had seen strangers similar to himself.

> *[The local Indians] said, moreover, that these people called themselves Christians and customarily lived in a single very large residence.*

These Christians were undoubtedly the members of the Advance Party since Arellano's group had not arrived in Cíbola at the time the "local Indians" had been there.

Both of these instances are clear indications that the Advance Party carried tents, but neither the number nor the types they had is known. It is probably safe to presume that the main body of the Expedition under Arellano also formed *reales* for camping. If the surmise is correct that the individual companies marched independently of each other, then it is probable that each company formed its own *real*, as well. There is also no information in the documentation about the configuration in which the *reales* were deployed. It could well be that the *reales* of the Expedition were nothing more than a closely grouped deployment of the many tents belonging to the individual members of the companies. In any case, the arrangement of tents within a real would have been such as to provide a defensive configuration while still providing space for normal camping activities. While cooking, eating, equipment maintenance and resting were the primary functions of any camp, it was also necessary to defend against possible hostile natives.

Chapter 4

Places Along the Route

Along the entire route that the Coronado Expedition traveled between Culiacán and Cíbola, there are only two locations that are known with any reasonable degree of certainty. These are the starting point at Culiacán, Sinaloa and the ending point at the Zuñi Indian Reservation in western New Mexico. But even those two locations are known only to within fifteen or thirty miles, and the route between them has been postulated by various historians to pass anywhere from central Arizona to western New Mexico – a separation distance of well over 150 miles.

Information about the places mentioned by the chroniclers of the Coronado Expedition on the route between Culiacán and Cíbola will be collected in this chapter. Of particular interest are the distances from one place to the next and the description of the routes between them, as well as the descriptions of the places themselves. Some insight into probable locations of those places will be developed. The majority of the information contained in this chapter comes from two sources. The first is the narrative of Pedro de Castañeda de Nájera with translations by Richard and Shirley Flint[1] and by George Parker Winship[2]. The second is the narrative of Juan Jaramillo, also translated[3] by the Flints.

Castañeda travelled with the main body of the Coronado Expedition throughout the entrada, apparently not going on any of the exploration journeys to Hopi, Grand Canyon, Colorado River, Pecos Pueblo, Socorro,

1. F&Fdocs28
2. Winship, Cas
3. F&Fdocs30

Palo Duro Canyon or Quivira. He appears to have obtained his information about those excursions from men who did participate in each of them. He probably collected much of his information from these sources while at Cíbola and Tiguex. However, he could have also interviewed Expedition members during the 20 years he spent at Culiacán after the entrada ended but before writing his account in the 1560s.

Jaramillo, on the other hand, was in the Advance Party leaving Culiacán and spent the entire Expedition in the groups traveling with Coronado himself[4]. He would have gone to Socorro, Pecos, Palo Duro Canyon and Quivira. He seems to write about only his own personal experiences and his account of the route to Cíbola emphasizes the distance and direction of travel. A major difficulty with his narrative is that he seems to be unsure of both distances and directions at the time he wrote his narrative some twenty years after the Expedition.

4. F&Fdocs30, p508

Problems with Locating Places

The locations of places mentioned in the documents are uncertain due to a multitude of factors. For one thing, the names that the Coronado Expedition's chroniclers used for many places and features are not in use today. In some cases where those same names are still in use, they apply to different places on modern maps. The names, themselves, cannot be considered reliable guides for identification. Also, the descriptions given by the chroniclers are most often subjective enough and vague enough that today we could fit those descriptions to many different places.

In many instances we are given distances between places by multiple writers and those different sources are usually remarkably consistent for the distance measurement between the same two features. The reason for this consistency is that, apparently, it was customary to have one or two men assigned to either counting steps or estimating the distance as the group was marching. Many times, however, the distance is not specified in units of length, but rather in units of time. A typical "day's march" (one "*jornada*") seems to have been comprised of a series of six "marches" of one league each, separated by a period of rest, so that a "day's march" typically covered six leagues (about 16 miles) over good terrain. The reported distances, therefore, should represent fairly accurate and reliable information. The primary difficulties with this is that

1. Several different types of "league" were in use at the time. The two most common were the "*legua legal*" equivalent to about 2.63 miles and the "*legua comun*" of 3.46 miles. (Cabeza de Vaca in his famous journey across the land probably reported distance in legua comun[5] with a day's march being 4 leagues (about 14 miles).) There are several places in the Expedition's documentation where the chroniclers' distances in "leagues" can be compared with high certainty to modern maps and these consistently indicate their use of the "legua legal".

2. The chroniclers' existing accounts are usually transcribed copies and translations of copies of the originals. Sometimes this copying process involved several generations of transcriptions, perhaps involving several languages. It may well be that some of the scribes converted one type of league to another during the transcription process. Compounding this problem is that the type of league used by the original chronicler is almost always unknown.

Places Along the Route

3. As we have estimated previously, one day's march was sometimes as little as 4 leagues but may have been as great as 8 leagues at other times. The type of terrain probably influenced the pace and must be taken into consideration when estimating the distance traveled in one day.

The result of these uncertainties is that the measurements of distance as stated in the documentation must be used with caution and must be corroborated for consistency with other information before placing a full measure of faith in it. Even with that caveat, the available distance information still remains one of the best starting points for a study of Coronado's route from Culiacán to Cíbola. It would seem prudent, however, to treat distances derived from travel time simply as guides to locating places that meet feature descriptions, wherever possible.

Latitudes

There are several instances in the documents where the chroniclers report latitudes for various places, but these are always in error with respect to modern maps by about one and a half degrees. Latitude was almost certainly determined by use of an astrolabe for measuring the sun's angle when it crossed the local meridian plane. The astrolabe technique requires sighting on the sun to determine the angle between sun and the local horizontal plane, but the sun has an angular diameter of approximately one-half degree as seen from the Earth. The error in a calculated latitude caused by sighting on the lower limn of the sun rather than the upper limn would then also be about one-half a degree.

This technique also requires that the astrolabe be aligned in the "true" meridian plane when sighting on the sun. This true meridian plane is established by the the

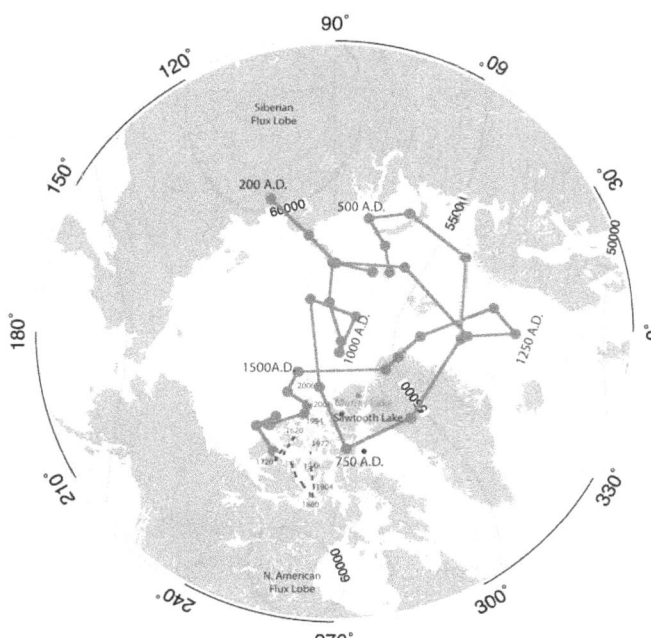

Fig. 4.1 Magnetic North Pole Wanderings. This graphic shows the approximate locations of the magnetic north pole from 200 A.D. to 1700 A.D. At an observer's position, the angle between the "true" meridian plane (passing through the rotational polar axis at the center of the graphic) and the "apparent" meridian plane (passing through the magnetic pole) is the "magnetic declination." Graphic used by premission of Oregon State University. (See reference OSU in Bibliography).

observer's position and "polar north" which is determined by the Earth's axis of rotation. However, the Expedition probably used a magnetic compass to determine North and therefore would have observed the sun angle in an "apparent" meridian plane instead of the "true" meridian. Since the magnetic north pole drifts about (see Figure 4.1) with respect to the polar axis (a phenomenon known as the "magnetic declination"), the North direction determined by the compass will also drift about with respect to polar north. The magnetic declination, of course, varies with the observer's position on the Earth. Since the Spaniard's navigation charts (giving the sun's height for any day at any meridian) were undoubtedly produced in Spain, they almost certainly would not have been corrected for the magnetic declination at the places traversed by the Coronado Expedition. This would have led to a significant error in the apparent meridian plane and a corresponding error in Latitude determination.

Places Along the Route

It is probably reasonable to assume that the Spaniards were skilled in the latitude measurement technique so that the errors in latitude should not be laid to faulty measurements. At this point, it is unknown whether the sun sighting or the meridian determination (if either) was the actual cause of the latitude errors reported, but it is a very plausible explanation. In that case, it also seems reasonable that the measurements relative to one another would be fairly correct.

Indian Guides

There is something else that should be kept in mind also while studying the route of the Coronado Expedition and the places along the way. Each component of the Expedition was guided by native Indians along existing trade and/or migration routes. There is little reason to expect that all parts of the Expedition traveled identical paths. In fact – given the different characteristics of the various components – it is highly likely that the guides would have selected from the available paths the ones most suitable for each component, more or less independently of the pathways selected by other Indian guides for another component. This is one more reason to be somewhat wary of applying distances and descriptions indiscriminately to a place or feature simply because it may have been called by the same name by different chroniclers. That being said, it is important to note that several places seem to have been common to all (or most) groups making the journey. The base of San Gerónimo (in one or another of its three locations), Chichilticale (at least the region) and the routes between and near them are included in such places. The route from Culiacán to Corazones also seems to have been a common segment.

It is by no means certain that the various components of the Expedition traveled different segments of pathways north of Chichilticale, but the possibility remains open.

Climate Change

The descriptions of weather-related and/or climate-related features must also be considered. During the period of the Coronado entrada to Cíbola and Quivira in Tierra Nueva, the region appears to have been midway through the "little ice age" according to the information in Appendix E. The temperatures, rainfall, seasonal changes and vegetation patterns were probably considerably different from what they are today. This could have had major effects on the numbers and locations of fresh water springs and their flow rates and on the availability of grass for grazing livestock. This, in turn, could have had a major impact on the choices of routes to be traveled. These considerations are especially important in the arid desert regions through which the Expedition traveled. Today, many of the streams and rivers in that region flow toward inland basins but they normally dry up long before reaching the collection basins. It is possible that some of these streams would have had much greater flows of water and may have been viable water sources and grazing areas in 1540. In that case, it seems reasonable to suppose that those streams, and the entire region, could have supported a much larger population of native peoples and game animals than would be possible today.

Places between Culiacán and Cíbola

The places known to have been visited by the Coronado entrada between Culiacán and Cíbola will now be listed in sequence. The distances along the route reported by the chroniclers are given in "leagues" with a conversion to "miles" assuming the 2.63 miles per legua legal. As noted previously, this type of league appears to have been used consistently in the two narratives referenced, but caution is advised before accepting the "miles" as absolute truth.

1. Culiacán: This name seems to be applied to three different places: the *villa* of San Miguel de Culiacán, the *valley* of Culiacán and the *original location* of the villa along the Culiacán River.

6. F&Fgeo, p601

The original site of Culiacán had been established by Nuño Beltran de Guzman[6] in 1532 and apparently used as a slave hunting center. By 1540 he had moved the villa south to a new site[6] located on the Rio San Lorenzo and renamed it San Miguel de Culiacán. The chroniclers of the Coronado Expedition often refer to this second site as "Culiacán", " villa of Culiacán" or "San Miguel". The original villa was at the site of present-day Culiacán.

7. F&Fdocs28, p429

According to Castañeda's account of the retreating Expedition[7], the "villa of Culiacán" was 10 leagues (26 miles) to the south of the "valley of Culiacán". Coronado and the entire out-going Expedition rested for several days at the villa of Culiacán. Although Castañeda is somewhat ambiguous on this point, it appears that Coronado and the Advance Party may have left for Cíbola directly from the villa. Since the remainder of the Expedition did not depart for another 20 days or more, it is not unreasonable to suspect that they moved to the valley of Culiacán for that period of waiting, perhaps to relieve the citizens of the villa. This is simple speculation, but it would explain why Castañeda listed the distance to Petlatlán as 20 leagues on the outward trip and as 30 leagues on the return trip (see the entry below for Petatlán).

2. Petatlán (or Petlatlán): This name could apply to either an Indian village or to the Rio Petatlán.

Juan Jaramillo left Culiacán with Coronado's Advance Group in April 1540 and reported a 4-days' travel "at a fairly rapid pace" to the Rio Petatlán. Assuming this implies a rate of seven marches per day (as reported for later marches across the Llano Estacado in the Texas panhandle) this would result in a distance from the villa of Culiacán to Petatlán of about 80 miles. Castañeda followed with the main body of the Expedition about 20 days later and reported both 20 leagues[8] [53 miles] and 30 leagues[7] [79 miles].

8. F&Fdocs28, p416

Castañeda describes this region[8] as:

> *Petatlán is a settlement of houses covered with a sort of matting made from reeds. [The houses are] congregated into pueblos. [They] extend all along a river from the mountains to the sea. They are a people of the same social level and habits as the Tahues of Culiacán. ... The provincia was called Petatlán because the houses were made of mats [petates]. Use of this type of house is continuous throughout that region for two hundred and forty leagues and more, as far as the beginning of the unsettled area [before] Cíbola. At Petatlán that land clearly forms a boundary; that is because from there onward there are no trees without spines, and there are no fruits except prickly pears, mesquite [beans], and pitahayas.*

This "Rio Petatlán" is probably the modern Rio Sinaloa. As Dan Riff[9] has pointed out, in 1533 the entrada led by Diego de Guzman visited the town called Petatlán on that river, some 32 leagues north of the modern Rio

9. Reff

Culiacán which, in turn, is 10 leagues north of the site of San Miguel de Culiacán. At the present, Rio Petatlán is the name of a tributary of the Rio Sinaloa, but names could have changed over time.

3. Rio Sinaloa:

Castañeda states[8]

> *From Culiacán to there [Petlatlán] it is twenty leagues and from Petlatlán to the valley of Señora it is a hundred and thirty. In between there are many rivers settled by the same sort of people. [These rivers] are [ones] such as Sinaloa, Boyomo, Teocomo, Yaquimí, and other, much smaller ones.*

From this it is understood that the Expedition's "Rio Sinaloa" is not the same as their "Rio Petatlán". Supporting this is Jaramillo's statement[10] that it was 3 days' journey from Rio Petatlán to Rio Sinaloa. Some confusion might arise as a result of both names still being used today but applied to different rivers. This will be clarified in a later chapter where the route of the Coronado Expedition in this region is discussed. The distance between these rivers, according to Jaramillo, would then be 47 miles to 54 miles based on the supposition that a "normal" day's travel was 6 leagues (leguas legales) and that the "fairly rapid" day's travel was 7 leagues.

10. F&Fdocs30, p512

4. Arroyo de los Cedros:

Jaramillo says it was 5 days' travel[10] (78 to 91 miles) from the Rio Sinaloa to this arroyo. He and nine other horsemen were sent ahead[11] from the Rio Sinaloa, probably under the command of Melchior Diaz, making double time until they reached the stream called Arroyo de los Cedros. From there they went eastward

11. F&Fdocs19, p255

> *through an opening which the mountains formed to*

the right of [our] route and see what was in those [mountains] and behind them.

This group of 10 horsemen re-joined Coronado back at the Arroyo de los Cedros after a few days (at least the 5 days required for Coronado to reach there from the Rio Sinaloa) and the entire Advanced Party continued its northward trek toward the Rio Yaquimí.

5. Rio Yaquimí:

Jaramillo gives 3 days' travel from Arroyo de los Cedros to the Rio Yaquimí (47 to 55 miles). Coronado left many injured cattle and sheep with 4 horsemen at the Rio Yaquimí to rest and heal before following the Advance Party to Cíbola. It appears that these men and livestock remained here until Arellano and the main body of the Expedition arrived at that location. One of Arellano's men, Cristóbal de Escobar[12], probably took these four men, the livestock and other supplies to Cíbola immediately. They arrived at Cíbola[11] about August 3, 1540.

12. F&Fdocs33, p558

6. Indian Settlement:

Although Jaramillo is not absolutely clear about this segment of the route, it appears that the entire Advance Party went from the Rio Yaquimí to another stream where they found an Indian settlement with thatched huts and fields of corn, beans and squash. This segment took another 3 days (47 to 55 miles) and included a passage through a one-league long (2.6 miles) "dry arroyo". Jaramillo's account[10] does not indicate where in this 3-day journey they came upon the dry arroyo. It could even be read to mean the dry arroyo was the exit to the Arroyo de los Cedros.

7. Settlement of Los Corazones:

This is supposedly the place visited by Cabeza

Places Along the Route

de Vaca on his way south in 1535 and was the first of three locations for the Expedition's base station, San Gerónimo. Jaramillo says that it was "probably about two day's" travel (32 miles) from the previous, un-named Indian settlement to Los Corazones. The unknown author of "Relacion del Suceso[13]", who appears to have been with main body of the Expedition, gives 150 leagues (391 miles) from Culiacán to Los Corazones. He also says it is in "hot lowlands" with a poison herb growing in "slate and barren ground" and has a stream used for irrigation.

13. F&Fdocs29

8. Señora:

The second site of San Gerónimo was located in this valley. The name applies to both the valley and the settlement (sometimes also called the "Villa Señora" and "San Gerónimo" in the documents). The author of "Relacion del Suceso[13]" says that Señora ("a [Spanish] villa was later settled there") was 10 leagues[14] (26 miles) north of Los Corazones. Castañeda[8] and Jaramillo[15] both give a distance of 130 leagues (340 miles) from Petatlán to Señora. This agreement implies that both chroniclers used the same type of league or that someone converted the information. Jaramillo could be referring to any place in the valley since the settlement of San Gerónimo had not yet occurred at the time he passed through. Jaramillo also says that Señora is upstream from Los Corazones and that the Advance Party reached it from Los Corazones by[15]

14. F&Fdocs29, p497
15. F&Fdocs30, p513

> *going through a sort of small pass and, very near this stream, to another valley formed by the same stream, which is called [Arroyo] de Señora. It is also irrigated and [is inhabited] by more Indians than the others. There are the same sorts of settlements and food [here]. This valley probably extends about six or seven leagues, a little more or less. ... There*

are mountain ranges that are little vegetated on both sides [of the valley].

9. Ispa:

This apparently was an Indian settlement in a river valley. Jaramillo says that upon leaving the Arroyo de Señora (presumably from their camp in that valley), the Advance Party[15]

traveled beside this same stream, crossing it at the bends it makes, to another Indian settlement called Ispa. There is probably one day's journey from the last [valley] to this one. [The people there] have the same mode of life as those before.

This would locate Ispa about 6 leagues (16 miles) north of the Señora valley but in another valley of the same river and north of the multiple "bends it makes" in that 16 mile stretch between valleys.

10. Suya:

This name also applies to two entities: it applies to a *valley* at that location and it also applies to the third site of San Gerónimo in that valley. (This place might also be the "Vacapan" of Castañeda's narrative[16] where "there were vast amounts of cactus fruits".) Castaneda gives a distance of 200 leagues (526 miles) from Culiacán to Suya as well as 40 leagues (105 miles) from the Señora valley to Suya. He relates also that there were many pueblos near Suya, peopled by the same kind of natives that they found all along the way (as far as Chichilticale). The Indians here[8] make a wine out of saguaro cactus fruits (pitahayas), make preserves of prickly pear cactus, make a long-lasting bread from mesquite beans and grow large, edible melons.

16. F&Fdocs28, p395

11. Rio Nexpa:

Jaramillo gives "about 4 days" travel (64 miles) "through unsettled land" from Ispa to the Rio Nexpa which he implies to be a north-flowing "rivulet".

Just a few Indians came out to see the general with gift[s] of little value, some roasted maguey stalks and pitahayas.[15]

12. Dogleg:

This is a location on the Rio Nexpa from which the route took an abrupt turn from generally north to generally northeast. Jaramillo gives 2 day's travel (32 miles) from the Rio Nexpa (possibly from their campsite on the river) northward, down river[15] to the dogleg. The author of "Relacion del Suceso" gives 240 leagues (which could be a scribal error for 210 leagues) from Culiacán to the dogleg[17] (552 or perhaps 727 miles). He also gives the latitude as 34.5 degrees North, but latitude measurements at that time were notoriously in error, as mentioned earlier. Castañeda, in telling of Juan Gallego's return[18] toward Cíbola in 1542, says that Gallego and his 22 reinforcements met with Coronado and the retreating Expedition on its second day of march south of Chichilticale. He also says that Gallego had traveled 200 leagues (522 miles) from Culiacán[19]. It would appear that the two groups met at, or very near, the dogleg in the route between the Rio Nexpa and Chichilticale.

17. F&Fdocs29, p498

18. F&Fdocs28, p428

19. F&Fdocs28, p431

13. Chichilticale:

This is another name that seems to be applied sometimes to a local site (or perhaps different sites) and sometimes to a general region. Jaramillo gives 2 days' travel (32 miles) toward the northeast from the dogleg to the foot of the mountains[15] they called Chichilticale.

Castañeda gives no distances derived from the Coronado entrada, but does give a distance of 220 leagues (578 miles) from Culiacán to Chichilticale for the Marcos de Niza journey. It is not certain that Marcos de Niza took the same route to Chichilticale as that taken by Coronado, but Castañeda may have been implying that when he wrote[20] that Esteban had "walked through" Chichilticale before. Castañeda says that Chichilticale was so named because the friars[21] (probably Marcos de Niza's group)

20. F&Fdocs28, p388

21. F&Fdocs28, p417

> *found in this vicinity a building that in former times was inhabited by people who split off from Cíbola. It was made of reddish or bright red earth. The building was large and clearly seemed to have been strong. It must have been abandoned because of the [Indians] of that land, who are the most uncivilized people of those that had been seen until then. They live in rancherías without permanent habitations. They live by hunting.*

He also says that Chichilticale lies at the northern boundary of the plant life region that began at Petatlán and is where [22]

22. F&Fdocs28, n413

> *the Mountain country is broken to permit passage to the land's region of plains.*

This boundary is between the Lower Sonoran life zone, characterized by the large cacti, creosote bush, mesquite, paloverde, and other spiny plants generaly located below 4,500 feet in elevation, and the Upper Sonoran life zone, where piñon, juniper, and oak are typical[23].

23. Epple, Arizona, 5

14. Deep Canyon:

Jaramillo gives no distance to the "deep canyon", but states that they reached it after they "crossed the mountains". Presumably, he is referring here to the

Chichilticale mountains. They found water and pasture in the deep canyon[15]. Castañeda gives a 3-day travel (48 miles) from Chichilticale to the "very deep" canyon in the *despoblado* (unsettled region) where they found a big horn[16] on the banks of a river. On the way from Chichilticale to the deep canyon they saw a large herd of rams which[16]

> *were large bodied; their coats [were] exceedingly long, their horns [were] very large and heavy. In order to run, they lift their faces and throw their horns over their backs. They run much [of the time] over rough land, so that we were unable to lance them and had to let them go.*

Castañeda summarizes the land of the despoblado between Chichilticale and Cíbola as[21]:

> *All the rest [of the region] is uninhabited, covered by great pine forests. There are huge quantities of pinon nuts. The pines there are spreading [and] from two to three estados tall. There are oak forests with sweet acorns and juniper trees that yield a fruit [that looks] like dry coriander candy. It is very sweet, like sugar. At several springs there are watercress, rosebushes, pennyroyal, and oregano. In the rivers of this unsettled region there are whiskered and freshwater carp like [those] in Spain. There are leopards [jaguars] which were seen from the beginning of the unsettled region.*

It is not certain that Jaramillo and Castañeda were discussing the same "deep canyon" but it does seem probable that they were. That premise will be accepted unless later evidence indicates otherwise.

15. Rio San Juan:

Jaramillo gives an uncertain three day travel (48 miles) toward the northeast from the deep canyon to the Rio San Juan which the Advance Party reached[15] on St. John's day, June 24, 1540.

24. F&Fdocs19, p 256   From Cíbola on August 3, 1540 Coronado writes[24] to Viceroy Mendoza:

> *I crossed the boundary of the unsettled region on the eve of San Juan's [feast] day. With no relief from the previous difficulties, during the first days we found no grass, but rather a worse mountain route and more dangerous passes than any we had negotiated behind us.*

16. Rio de las Balsas:

Jaramillo gives an uncertain two day travel (32 miles) toward the north from the Rio San Juan to the Rio de las Balsas. Leaving the Rio San Juan[15]

> *we went more toward the north through land [that is] somewhat broken to another river we called [Rio] de las Balsas, for we crossed it on [rafts, or balsas] because it was swollen. It seems to me we took two full days [going] from the one river to the other.*

If Jaramillo was emphasizing the "two full days", he may be implying two long, 7-league days (or about 36 miles), but he seems so uncertain about the distance that it probably should not considered be very precise, in any event.

17. Arroyo de la Barranca:

Jaramillo gives an uncertain two "short" days (less than 32 miles) traveling "nearly" northeast from the Rio de las Balsas and crossing to another stream they named

Places Along the Route   71

Arroyo de la Barranca[15]. He does not indicate if they left the valley of the Rio de las Balsas after the crossing or if that river turned toward the northeast and they continued following it.

18. Rio Frio:

Jaramillo gives a one day's travel (16 miles) from the Arroyo de la Barranca to the Rio Frio, so named because its waters were cold[15], probably in July 1540. On the return trip he gives the distance from Cíbola to the Rio Frio as 5 days[25] (80 miles) toward Chichilticale.

25. F&Fdocs27, p 329

19. Small Stream:

Jaramillo gives an uncertain one day travel[15] (16 miles) from the Rio Frio going through a pine forest at almost of which they found a small stream. A Spaniard named Espinosa and two others died at the small stream from eating a poisonous plant.

20. Rio Bermejo (possibly the Rio del Lino):

Castañeda gives a 15-day travel (235 miles) from Chichilticale to the Rio Bermejo and says that the river was so named because its waters[26]

26. F&Fdocs28, p 393

> *flowed muddy and bright red. In this river there were whiskered carp like [those] in Spain. It was here that the first Indians of that land were seen.*

In his letter[24] to the Viceroy dated August 3, 1540, Coronado says of some river:

> *I saw that there was flax in very large quantities on the bank of one river, and therefore it is called Rio del Lino.*

The identification of the "Rio del Lino" and the "Rio Bermejo" as the same river is by means of the descriptions of the river by the various chroniclers. The further possible association of that river with the modern Little Colorado River is suggested by the names "bermejo" and "colorado" (both meaning "red" in Spanish). This association is further enhanced by a map in General Carleton's 1864 report[27] which labels the river presently known as the "Little Colorado" as "Rio del Lino or Colorado". No single chronicler mentions both the Rio del Lino and the Rio Bermejo in his writings, so it seems unlikely that these are two different rivers. It is also interesting to note that Coronado is the only one who mentions a "Rio de Lino" and he does not mention any "Rio Bermejo". If the two names actually refer to the same river, it would be an extremely rare occurrence where the various chroniclers disagree on the names of any feature.

27. Carleton

Jaramillo gives a two day travel (32 miles) from the small stream to the Rio Bermejo[15] traveling in "same general direction but more to the northeast [or perhaps northwest[28]]". This distance and description would indicate that the Rio Bermejo is at the end of the most northern despoblado.

28. F&Fdocs30, n67

21. First Pueblo of Cíbola:

Castañeda says that Cíbola was 8 leagues (21 miles) from their position on the Rio Bermejo[26]. Jaramillo recalled a two day journey – but not two full days – so Castañeda's distance is probably close to the actual distance. In his letter to Viceroy Mendoza, Coronado states that Cíbola is four day's travel from the small stream where Espinosa and "two Moors" died. From Chichilticale, Castañeda records that it is a distance of 80 leagues [209 miles] toward the north[26] to Ciboa. From Corazones, the author of "Relacion del Suceso, 1540s" gives 150 leagues[14] (391 miles) to Cíbola.

Places Along the Route   73

Two additional sites are mentioned between the Rio Bermejo and the first pueblo of Cíbola. These are a "last camp" and a "bad pass" and those sites will be discussed in detail in a later chapter.

Overview of the trail from Culiacán to Cíbola

Coronado tells Viceroy Mendoza that he reached Cíbola[11] from Culiacán in 80 days. This would have been the number of elapsed days, including an unknown number of rest days. He had left Culiacán on April 22, 1540 and arrived at Cíbola on July 7, 1540 for an actual elapsed period of 77 days.

The author of "Relacion del Suceso, 1540s" gives 300 leagues (783 miles) to Cíbola and says[14] it took 73 days. At the usual conversion rate of 6 leagues per day, this would yield 438 leagues (1143 miles) in strong disagreement with the 300 leagues (780 miles) given by multiple chroniclers. If both the 300 leagues and the 73 days are correct, then the travel rate was about 4.1 leagues (10.7 miles) per day. Here, again, it is unknown if the author meant 73 elapsed days or 73 travel days. Of the actual 77 elapsed days, the Advance Party rested at least 6 days (four days at Los Corazones and two days at Chichilticale), so this "73 days" was probably meant as elapsed time.

29. F&Fdocs22, p 291

The author of "Traslado de las Nuevas" states[29] that it is "more than" 350 leagues (913 miles) and took 77 days "enroute". This seems to imply an elapsed time and not a "days traveled" time. This yields an average rate of 4.5 leagues (12 miles) per day.

Castañeda gives a distance of 300 +/- 10 leagues (783 +/- 26 miles), but this was in reference to the Marcos de Niza entrada which may not have taken the exact route of the Coronado Expedition.

Perhaps the best estimate of the average rate of travel is made by taking the most-agreed upon distance of 300 leagues and the actual 77 days of elapsed time to arrive at a rate of 3.9 leagues (10.2 miles) per elapsed day. Without knowing the number of rest days, it is not possible to estimate an average travel rate per marching-day from this information.

Another note on distance and rate of travel

It appears that each component of the Coronado Expedition marched for some variable number of days and then took "several" days off to rest the men, horses other animals being herded along. It seems reasonable that those men assigned to counting paces and estimating distances would tally their information and record it during the rest days, or perhaps at every night's camps. It is reasonable that the distances reported in leagues between camps can be taken as fairly reliable, regardless of the type of terrain being traversed. The distances reported for longer segments of the route were probably simply summations of the shorter segments and would be equally reliable. Caution needs to be exercised when applying the "days traveled" and/or "days elapsed" reports. For instance, it is rarely clear which an author means when he reports the number of days required to go from one place to another. It should be reasonably safe to interpret "one day's journey" or one "jornada" as the distance traveled during one day between overnight camps. However, converting that information into equivalent distances traveled in that day presents a problem. Over smooth terrain, the "6 or 7" leagues per day might be reasonable. But over rough terrain, where the Expedition members might even be forced to stop to build or widen the paths, the daily rate of travel was probably much less. The chroniclers offer very little insight into this.

In the above listing of places identified by the chroniclers, when only the time duration of route segments is given, the distance in leagues has been converted at the nominal rate of 6 *legues legales* (16 miles) per day. The reader is advised that some of those distances may well be drastically inflated, especially considering that the average rate for the entire Culiacán to Cíbola journey was much closer to 4 leagues per day.

Chapter 5

San Gerónimo and the Traffic

At the time of the Coronado Expedition to Tierra Nueva, the town of Culiacán in the northern part of the Spanish province of Nueva Galicia was the last Spanish settlement on the Expedition's route northward. But it was still another 300 leagues (about 800 miles) to the expected location of their destination, Cíbola. The leader of the expedition, Francisco Vásquez de Coronado, decided to establish a supply base at a position approximately halfway between Culiacán and Cíbola. This chapter will be concerned with the three different locations of that base and the Expedition's activities associated with each of those locations.

Fortunately, the region around the Indian settlement of Los Corazones (where Cabeza de Vaca had found the natives to be friendly and helpful) lay at the proper distance from Culiacán (150 leagues). Coronado and his Advance Party arrived at this settlement on their way to Cíbola on May 26, 1540 and rested there for four days[1] before continuing their march to Cíbola. Tristán de Luna y Arellano and the main body of the Expedition arrived at this location about the middle of July 1540 and began to build a Spanish settlement, calling it San Gerónimo de Corazones. The precise location of this villa is unknown today but the consensus of modern historians favors the proximity of the modern village of Ures in the Sonora river valley in the state of Sonora, Mexico. The location will be discussed in more detail in a later chapter.

1. F&Fdocs19, p255

It was probably from this first location of San Gerónimo de Corazones that Cristóbal Escobar departed from the main body of the Expedition with the livestock Coronado had left behind[2] at the Yaquimí River. He also took with him other relief supplies for the Advance Party at Cíbola. Although Escobar, himself, gives no dates for his re-supply effort, Coronado does mention in his August 3, 1540 letter to the Viceroy that the remnants of his stock and some supplies that had been with Arellano had just recently arrived at Cíbola. It is not certain that Coronado was referring to Escobar's effort, but it seems highly probable. If so, Escobar must have left San Gerónimo immediately upon Arellano's arrival there and he would have made the trip to Cíbola in a relatively short time. Escobar does say that he was "travelling quickly" because he knew the Advance Party was in dire straits. This might imply that Coronado had sent a message to Arellano prior to his arrival at Corazones, but Arellano probably also got news about the Advance Party from the four men Coronado had left with the stock at the Rio Yaquimí.

2. F&Fdocs33 p556

Before this first villa was fully established, Arellano concluded that the location was not sustainable and moved the base "10 leagues farther on" (about 26 miles) upriver to the place they called "Señora". The author of the "Relacion de Suceco[3]" called Señora "the best of all the settled places". This move to the second location of San Gerónimo was probably made early in August 1540. It was from this location that Arellano sent don Rodrigo Maldonado "down river" to the coast in search for any news of the supply ships[4] of Hernando de Alarcón. Meanwhile, in Cíbola around the first of August 1540, Coronado was sending don Pedro de Tovar westward to explore Tusayan (the Hopi villages). At

3. F&Fdocs29, p497

4. FFdocs28, p393

the same time he was sending Melchior Diaz and Juan Gallego southward to San Gerónimo. Diaz and Gallego arrived at this second location of San Gerónimo at Señora around the "middle of August" according to Castañeda[5]. Gallego was on his way to Mexico City in Nueva España carrying Coronado's letter dated August 3, 1540 (Julian calendar) to Viceroy Mendoza and taking the disgraced Marcos de Niza back with him[6]. Melchior Diaz carried orders for General Arellano to advance to Cíbola with the bulk of the main body of the Expedition. Diaz also had orders for himself to take charge of a force of eighty horsemen and perhaps an unknown number of other Spaniards and their native allies who were to be left at Señora by Arellano. Diaz was also ordered to search for Alarcón's supply ships along the coast. About the middle of September, Arellano set out for Cíbola where his group arrived during a surprise snow storm[5], probably in late October or early November 1540.

5. F&Fdocs28, p394

6. F&Fdocs29, p498

Apparently sometime in October 1540, Melchior Diaz took perhaps 25 to 40 horsemen and others of the men left at San Gerónimo to search for the Rio Tizon (the present-day Colorado River) and the ships of Hernando de Alarcón. He left Diego de Alcaraz in command of the remaining forces at the Señora location of San Gerónimo[5]. (Alcaraz is the same man who had been in charge of the slaving party who were the first Spaniards contacted by Cabeza de Vaca five years earlier).

While Maldonado had searched "downriver" and had restricted his search to the vicinity of the mouth of the river, Diaz left Señora in a north-northwest direction and reached the region of the Rio Tizon after a journey of about 150 leagues[5] (400 miles). He then searched down the Colorado River for three days (perhaps 48 miles) to a point about 15 leagues (40 miles) north of the river's mouth. There he found messages from Alarcón saying that Alarcón had returned to Nueva España with his ships and the supplies they were carrying for Coronado and the Expedition[5]. This total distance of about 88 miles from the mouth of the Colorado River to the place Diaz reached the Rio Tizon is remarkably close to the confluence of the Gila and Colorado rivers at Yuma, Arizona. Diaz was killed in an accident with his own lance on this exploration and the rest of that group returned to San Gerónimo where they arrived[7] perhaps in early February 1541. Soon after their arrival, Alcaraz sent messengers to Coronado with the news of Diaz's death and the news that there was no hope of being re-supplied by Alarcon's ships.

7. F&Fbio, p593

Tristán de Arellano arrived at Cíbola from San Gerónimo around November 10, 1540 and Coronado immediately left Cíbola to explore the Indian province of Tutahaco near present-day Socorro, New Mexico. From Tutahaco, Coronado traveled north to the province of Tiguex on the banks of the Rio Grande near present-day Bernalillo, New Mexico. This is where don Garcia López de Cárdenas had set up winter quarters[8] for the entire expedition. Alcaraz's messengers from Señora arrived at these winter quarters at Tiguex at the "end of March" 1541[8] and on April 23, 1541, the same day he left Tiguex for Quivira[9], Coronado sent don Pedro Tovar to San Gerónimo to bring back half the men there to Tiguex. Tovar arrived at San Gerónimo at Señora about the first of June 1541 and shortly thereafter (perhaps about the first of July) he moved the settlement to its third location. This new site was located at the Indian village of Suya, another 40 leagues (105 miles) closer to Cíbola. This move was necessitated by some trouble the Spaniards

8. F&Fdocs28, p405

9. ExpTN, p5

had with the Indians around the Señora valley and by the more plentiful supply of food at Suya[10], but it also put the supply base closer to midway between Culiacán and the new winter quaters at Tiguex.

10. F&Fdocs28, p416

Pedro de Tovar remained at San Gerónimo/Suya until about the first of September 1541 when he departed for Tiguex with half the men. He, presumably, left Diego de Alcaraz once again in charge at San Gerónimo. Tovar and the men from San Gerónimo (probably most of the men who had gone with Diaz to the Rio Tizon) arrived at Tiguex around the middle of October, about the time Coronado returned from his journey to Quivira[11].

11. F&Fdocs28, p424

Shortly after his arrival at Tiguex from Quivira, Coronado sent don Garcia López de Cárdenas and "ten or twelve" other Spaniards to Suya[12] and on to Mexico City perhaps carrying Coronado's letter to the King dated October 20, 1541. When Cárdenas arrived at San Gerónimo at Suya probably in late November or early December 1541, he found it burned and vacated. Apparently the former slave trader Alcaraz had been mistreating the local Indians and had also lost any remaining respect of his men. Half of the 40 men who Tovar had left at San Gerónimo had mutinied[13], led by Pedro de Ávilar, and left the settlement to flee back to Culiacán. In this weakened condition the villa at Suya was attacked and overrun by the Indians, killing two of the defenders. The remaining twenty or so men were forced out by the Indians and also fled back to Culiacán[14]. When they saw the conditions at Suya, Cárdenas and the others in his group turned around and returned to Tiguex where they would have arrived probably around the middle of January 1542.

12. F&Fdocs26, p319

13. F&Fdocs28, n519

14. F&Fdocs29, p502

Since the expedition had failed to find any of the

San Gerónimo and the Traffic   81

wealth or the large populations it was seeking, Coronado decided to end the entrada and the entire force left Tiguex around the first of April 1542 on its way to Cíbola, Chichilticale, San Gerónimo (or, rather, the former site of it at Suya) and Culiacán. Meanwhile, Juan Gallego, one of the earlier couriers from Cíbola to Viceroy Mendoza, had put together an additional group of 22 men in Mexico City and Culiacán. This group included several of the former mutineers and final defenders of Suya[15]. Gallego had been marched toward Coronado's position had been prepared to go as far as Cíbola, Tiguex and Quivira. He probably passing through all three of the former sites of San Gerónimo. He met the southbound, retreating Coronado Expedition around the middle of April 1542 during the Expedition's second day of marching south from Chichilticale. This meeting would then have been approximately halfway between San Gerónimo/Suya and Chichilticale, very near the "dogleg" on the Rio Nexpa. The combined groups then marched back through San Gerónimo/Suya and on to Culiacán where the Expedition was either disbanded or, more likely, simply fell apart.

15. F&Fdocs28, p426

It appears that all but about 40 men who had left Compostela on February 23, 1540 with the original Expedition actually completed the journey to Cíbola via San Gerónimo. Those approximately 40 men (or perhaps about 100 people[13]) stayed behind to man the San Gerónimo villas at Los Corazones, Señora and Suya and were the only ones who did not eventually reach Cíbola. A large number of the other Expedition members went on to explore the Hopi villages, the Grand Canyon, the lower Colorado River, parts of California, Arizona and New Mexico, hundreds of miles of the Rio Grande valley, parts of the Texas panhandle and further north into parts of present-day Oklahoma and Kansas and Colorado.

Courier Traffic through San Gerónimo

In addition to the troop traffic, it is known that messages also travelled along the route between Coronado and San Gerónimo and that some continued beyond there to Culiacán and Mexico City. Two such messages have already been mentioned. The first was the August 3, 1540 letter from Coronado to Viceroy Mendoza carried by Juan Gallego who travelled from Cíbola to San Gerónimo (at Señora) with Melchoir Diaz in early August, 1540. The second message mentioned earlier was the October 20, 1541 letter from Coronado to King Carlos I, carried (probably) by don Garcia López de Cárdenas on his aborted attempt to return to Mexico City. There was only one other known, documented courier run between Coronado and San Gerónimo although the content of that communication is unknown. This run was made by Luis de Figueredo probably sometime in August or September or 1540. It is possible that Figueredo travelled with Gallego, but there is no indication of that in the record.

It is very probable that Luis Figueredo carried messages along the route through San Gerónimo on many more occasions, but that is not documented. Figueredo is a rather unique and interesting member of the Coronado Expedition and deserves some special attention.

Luis de Figueredo: Figueredo does not appear on the Compostela muster of February 22, 1540 and he is known only because of testimony he gave on March 12, 1545 in support of Francisco Vásquez de Coronado. This testimony was given in the legal investigation into Coronado's treatment of the natives encountered by the Expedition to

16. Fcruel, p408

Tierra Nueva during 1540 to 1542[16]. Figueredo apparently was at Compostela during the muster and was on the march between there and Culiacán. He was also at the battle at the first pueblo of Cíbola on July 7, 1540 and witnessed the entradas out of Cíbola by don Pedro de Tovar (to Tusayán/Hopi in July 1540), don López Garcia Cárdenas (to Mar del Sur in July 1540), Hernando Alvarado (to Tiquex, Cicuique and the bison plains in August 1540) and Francisco de Ovando ("in another direction" [date uncertain]). Ovando's entrada would have left Cíbola prior to the date in November 1540 when Coronado left Cíbola upon Arellano's arrival from San Gerónimo/Señora. Figueredo testified that he did not know about the conditions at Tiquex when the Expedition first arrived nor was he present during the Tiquex wars in the Fall and Winter of 1540–1541 because at the time he had gone "with some messages to the valley of Señora".

It is tempting to conjecture that Figueredo left Cíbola at about the same time that Coronado left and was likely carrying the message that the Expedition was moving its quarters from Cíbola to Tiquex. He does not say when he returned to Tiquex, but his testimony indicates that he was there[12] when Coronado left for Quivira on April 23, 1541. It would appear, then, that Figueredo would have arrived at San Gerónimo/Señora in late September or October 1540. This would have been very close to the time that the Diaz/Gallego group arrived there, also, making it uncertain who carried the orders for Arellano to proceed to Cíbola. Figueredo was not asked directly, so did not say, if he returned to Cíbola with Arellano, continued on with Gallego to Culiacán or went with Diaz to locate the Rio Tizon. Whatever he did, he apparently was back in the Tiquex region in the Spring of 1541 (perhaps in time to see Coronado leave for Quivira, as he testified) but did not go on the entrada to Quivira.

One other courier run is known and documented, but this one went from Culiacán to Mexico City with messages from Cíbola. It was made by Juan de Cepeda[17] who fell ill at Culiacán and did not go any farther with the Expedition to Tierra Nueva.

17. ModHist, 1/15/13

Extrapolating from this small amount of information, it seems reasonable to conjecture that regular communications may have travelled along the entire route with exchanges of couriers occurring at San Gerónimo and Culiacán. During the latter stages of the Expedition, another route of communications bypassing San Gerónimo may have developed. Apparently there is no documented evidence to support that supposition[18], but the last men at San Gerónimo/Suya thought that was the case[15].

18. F&Fdocs28, n518

Chapter 6

The Expedition's Return to Culiacan

After returning from Quivira in the late Summer of 1541, Coronado's Expedition wintered for the second time at Tiquex along the Rio Grande near the present city of Bernalillo, New Mexico. The following Spring of 1542 the entire expedition left Tiquex on its way back to Culiacán and Mexico City. Specific dates are extremely rare in the chroniclers' narratives for this return journey. The only firm date known is the camp at the Rio Frio and that is only because a dated legal document was executed there. In this chapter, the places that the Expedition visited between Cíbola and Culiacán on this return journey, as recorded in the documentation, will be considered.

1. F&Fdocs28. p429

Cíbola: Castañeda clearly identifies this location[1] when he says

> ... the seven pueblos of Cíbola, the first to be seen and the last to be left, the expedition set out, traveling across the unsettled region ... For two or three days' journey the natives never stopped, following the expedition, behind the rear guard in order to pick up a little of the baggage or a few servants. ...

They would have left Cíbola around April 4, 1542.

Rio Frio: This location and date are known from a promissory note[2] executed by Rodrigo Trujillo for the purchase of one chestnut horse for 450 *pesos de oro de minas* from the estate of Juan Jiménez

2. F&Fdocs27, p347

> *The document was prepared within this expeditionary force...while it was quartered on the banks of the river which is called Rio Frio, which is between Chichilticale and Cíbola, on the ninth day of the month of April in the one thousand five hundred and forty-second year* [April 9, 1542] *since the birth of Our Savior, Jesus Christ.*

3. F&Fdocs30, p513

The Expedition had stopped at the Rio Frio on the northbound trip, also, and Jaramillo[3] reports that it was a five day journey from the Rio Frio to Cíbola. This is a strong indication that the return trip followed the same route as the outbound trip, at least in leaving Cíbola. This also might imply that the Expedition rested for an extended period of time at the Rio Frio, since they had time to execute proceedings in the Juan Jiménez case.

Chichilticale: Castañeda seems to be the only chronicler who mentions the portion of the return trip from the Rio Frio to the Señora valley and even he covers the entire segment with only[1]

> *The unsettled region was traversed without opposition. They left Chichilticale and Juan Gallego reached the expedition during the second day's travel.*

This is enough to establish that the returning expedition and the northbound Gallego party were on the same trail near Chichilticale. This is another strong indication that the northbound and southbound routes of the Expedition were the same.

Señora Valley (or perhaps Suya): It is known that the returning Expedition passed through the Señora Valley because of the testimony of Juan de Contreras on June 4,

1544, during the investigation of the Expedition's cruelty to the Indians of Tierra Nueva[4].

4. FCruel, p115

> *when don Tristán de Arellano was returning from the reconnaissance with the vanguard, as he came through the valley called Señora, he went in pursuit of two Indians who were fleeing. ... And the Indians there had killed Alcaraz, who had been left as captain, and many other Spaniards.*

It is likely, but not certain, that Contreras was referring to the valley at Suya, the third location of San Geronimo, instead of the valley of Señora, since Suya is where Alcaraz was killed. Since the outgoing Expedition had traversed both the Señora valley and the site of Suya, it is relatively certain that the returning journey was still following the same path as the outgoing journey at this point.

Batuco: It is, again, Castañeda who recorded that the Expedition passed through an Indian village named Batuco on its return journey but there is no information about its location. Castañeda says that the Expedition experienced battles or harassments from the native Indians from the point where it met Gallego south of Chichilticale

> *until [the expedition] reached Batuco. There, Indian allies from the valley of Los Corazones came to the camp in order to see the general, like [the] friends they always were.[1]*

Apparently the Spaniards did not meet with the Los Corazones natives until Batuco. This seems to imply that the Expedition bypassed Los Corazones (the first location of San Geronimo) on the return trip. Since Batuco was not mentioned by the chroniclers on the northward trip, this is a relatively strong indication that the Expedition took a different route back in that segment of the journey.⁵ It is, however, possible that Batuco was the un-named Indian village the northbound Expedition visited just prior to reaching Los Corazones. In that case, this would be an indication that the return route coincided with the outgoing route at this point, also.

5. F&Fdocs28, n406

It seems highly reasonable to conjecture that the returning Expedition bypassed the highly populated river valleys between Suya and Los Corazones. It had been just a matter of a few days since Gallego had cut a bloody path through that territory and the natives were understandably in a hostile mood.

Petatlán (Petlatlán): Castañeda records[1] that

> *The expedition was traveling without taking rest because already at this time there was a lack of food. Because [the people of] those areas were up in arms, there was nowhere to get provisions until [the expedition] reached Petlatlán.*

Petatlán was located in the province of Nueva Galicia (of which Coronado was governor) and the people of that territory were apparently not in armed revolt. The expedition rested there for a few days in order to resupply.

Culiacán: According to Castañeda, the Expedition left Petatlán[1]

> *with greater speed than previously, they sought to cross those thirty leagues which there are to the valley of Culiacán.*

Note that Castañeda is referring to the *valley* of Culiacán. The villa of San Miguel de Culiacán was another 10 leagues farther south. San Miguel was the final destination and the place where the Expedition was disbanded or, perhaps, simply fell apart.

Summary

It is apparent that the route of the returning Expedition coincided with the northbound route for the vast majority of the distance between Cíbola and Culiacán. It also seems likely that the returning Expedition bypassed some of the previous route through the southern part of the Señora valley and Los Corazones (perhaps to avoid additional conflicts with the natives). This conclusion does not preclude the possibility that different components of the Expedition may have taken separate paths over some portions of the trail on the northbound trek. Neither does it preclude the possibility that the couriers may have found a better route to Mexico City bypassing San Geronimo/Suya during the final months of the Expedition's stay in Tierra Nueva. However, there is no direct evidence that either of these possibilities actually occurred.

Chapter 7

Close to Cíbola

In a previous chapter is a discussion of the major places along Coronado's route between Culiacan in the present state of Sinaloa, Mexico and Cíbola which, in all probability, lies in the modern Zuñi Pueblo Reservationn in the state of New Mexico, USA. Interesting sites in the immediate vicinity of Cíbola and some pertinent nearby features mentioned in the documentation of the Coronado entrada will be discussed in the present chapter. These sites will be addressed in the order in which they were visited by the Coronado Expedition on its march northward. The paragraph headings below will identify the site and its distance from the "first pueblo of Cíbola".

In Part 2 of this volume, these sites will be associated with geographic features in an attempt to determine a specific route taken by the Coronado Expedition.

1. Coronado's last camp before Cíbola: {3 to 4 leagues}

1. H&R, p343

The testimony[1] of García López de Cárdenas, recorded on February 20, 1546 gave his eyewitness recollection of the arrival at Cíbola of Coronado and the Advance Party. At this point of the journey, Cárdenas and perhaps twenty other horsemen were serving as advance scouts and had been sent ahead of Coronado and the Advance group[2]:

2. LdeC, 3/9/12

> *The expedition came within three or four leagues (8 to 12 miles) of Cíbola, without having any skirmishes*

with the Indians. When we reached that position, I was ahead with eight or ten horsemen and noticed some Indians on a hilltop. I advanced alone to the place, making signs of peace and offering presents of things I carried to trade. With this, some of them came down and took the articles that I offered. I shook hands with them and remained at peace... and I remained there to await Francisco Vásquez and the others... At this very place, the soldiers camped for their last night before reaching Cíbola.

Pedro de Ledesma also gave testimony for the investigation into Coronado's conduct during the Tierra Neuva entrada to Cíbola and Quivira. There he stated[3] that the Expedition's Advance Party was met by several Cíbolans "when they had gotten within 3 leagues of Cíbola" and that the camp was a bit beyond that meeting point, closer to Cíbola.

3. FCruel, p235

For that same investigation, Domingo Martín's testimony[4] reveals that the two or three Indians who came out to meet with Coronado "within 3 leagues from Cíbola" were from "the province and principal pueblo" of Cíbola.

4. FCruel, p93

The last camp site for Coronado's Advance Party before reaching Cíbola, then, appears to have been near the foot of a hill laying almost 3 leagues (8 miles) from the first pueblo of Cíbola and 5 leagues (13 miles) from the Rio Bermejo. It is probable that the Expedition had camped at the Rio Bermejo the previous night to take advantage of the fresh water and pasture. This, then, is another of the rare instances where a rate of travel can be estimated: the 5 leagues from the Rio Bermejo were covered in one day. However, this rate is probably less than typical since the day's travel was cut short by the encounter with the Indians.

2. Site of heavy early snowfall: {3 leagues}

Probably in the early part of November, 1540, the main body of the Coronado Expedition under the command of Tristán de Luna y Arellano had traveled to within a one-day march (6 leagues or 16 miles) from Cíbola. There, Castañeda[5] records, they experienced cold winds and heavy snows that started falling late in the afternoon. By the time the snowfall began, the group would have traveled most of a one-day march. If one estimates that they had covered 5 leagues, this would put the snowfall site about 3 leagues (8 miles) from Cíbola and about 5 leagues (13 miles) from the Rio Bermejo toward Cíbola. If the main body of the Expedition traveled along the same path as the Advance Party, then the site of the snowfall would have been very close to the site of the "last camp" of Coronado before reaching Cíbola.

5. F&Fdocs28, p395

3. bad pass / first battle: {2 leagues}

From his last camp site, Coronado sent López de Cárdenas ahead with a small group of horsemen to guard a "bad pass" which they thought the Indians could easily block. In rebuttal of charges made against him by judge licenciado Tejada, Coronado stated[2] that Cárdenas camped that night at the bad pass which was "half a league" to the east of the Captain General's camp. Many Indians attacked at midnight and Cárdenas stayed there until morning waiting for Coronado to arrive. Castañeda says[6] that the first battle and, hence the bad pass, was two leagues (5.26 miles) before Cíbola.

6. F&Fdocs28, p393

This information along with the estimated position of the "last camp" would put the bad pass about five and a half to six leagues (16 miles) from the Rio Bermejo or about two to two and a half leagues from the first pueblo of Cíbola.

Domingo Martín's testimony[4] includes the information that at the bad pass, Cárdenas "established a bivouac in a woodland" where the Spaniards were attacked after night had fallen. Pedro de Ledesma[3] further says that "there were some boulders" at the dangerous pass that Cárdenas was sent ahead to guard.

4. Site of Big Boulders: {2 leagues}

Apparently, when the main body under Arellano was caught in the snow storm in the late afternoon, they were in a place with no cover since they continued marching. They reached some "hollows" in big boulders after "it was fully dark". It can be estimated that it was about 3 hours from "late afternoon" to "fully dark" and that the group was traveling through the snow storm at about half the normal rate of speed. It can then be surmised that they traveled about 1 or 2 leagues (2.6 to 5 miles) from where they were when the snowfall began to the place with the big boulders. This would put the site of the big boulders about 1 to 2 leagues (2.6 to 5 miles) from Cíbola and about 6 or 7 leagues (16 to 18 miles) from the Rio Bermejo. This seems to be a reasonable distance, since Castañeda says[5] that the next day they made it to Cíbola fairly early in the day while implying that they traveled slowly and spent a considerable amount of time looking after their Indian allies who had suffered greatly because of the cold and snow.

This "site of big boulders" of the main body of the Expedition would have been very close to the "bad pass" of the Advance Party. Since "there were some boulders" at the "bad pass" also, it seems likely that the two descriptions refer to one and the same place.

5. Site of Confrontation outside Cíbola: {1 league}

López de Cárdenas reports[2] that Coronado and the remainder of the Advance Party met up with Cárdenas and his 10 men at the bad pass the morning after the midnight battle and they all marched on toward Cíbola on July 7, 1540. They saw 4 or 5 Indians about one league (2.63 miles) before Cíbola or about 7 leagues (18.4 miles) from Rio Bermejo, but the Indians left without meeting with the Spaniards.

6. Cíbola:

After confronting the 4 or 5 Indians, Coronado's troops continued their march toward the first pueblo of Cíbola and about a crossbow's shot (about 150 feet) outside the pueblo they

7. F&Fdocs22, p292

found a large number of the Indians in the country outside the pueblo[7]

8. F&Fdocs19, pg257

...they approached the horses' legs to shoot their arrows. ...some of them fled quickly to the pueblo, which was nearby and well fortified[8].

9. F&Fgeo, pg599

According to some testimony[9] at the Coronado inquiry, the Spaniards approached the first pueblo from the west. However, this does not necessarily indicate the direction of travel approaching the pueblo. Since the battle at the pueblo almost certainly occurred in the afternoon, Coronado probably would have chosen to make his final approach and attack from the west simply to have the sun at his back.

The anonymous author of "Traslado de las Nuevas"

Close to Cíbola

says that the pueblo[7]

> *was all surrounded by a stone wall like a city wall. The houses [were] very tall, of four and five [stories] and [some] even of six stories, each one with its flat roof and covered passageways.*

10. Winship, p16

Castañeda describes the first pueblo of Cíbola as "spilling down a cliff"[6] or "looking as if it [had] been crumpled all up together"[10] and says there are other pueblos very much larger and stronger than Cíbola[6]. This latter statement would seem to suggest that the "first pueblo of Cíbola" was not necessarily the "principal" pueblo. Castañeda also says that the Spaniards succeeded in capturing the pueblo with some significant difficulty

> *"because [the Indians] have a narrow entryway [with] twists and turns"*[6] or

> *"since they held the narrow and crooked entrance".*[10]

11. Davis, p155

William Watts Hart Davis in his 1869 book[11] says of the first pueblo of Cíbola

> *Instead of the large city as the friar had represented, they found it to be a village of not more than two hundred warriors, situated upon a rock, and the only means of reaching it was by a narrow and tortuous road difficult to ascent.*

Attempting to Locate the Sites

As noted previously, the main body of the Expedition seems to have followed the same route as the Advance Party up to some point approaching Cíbola. But there is little in the chroniclers' narratives or in the other known accounts to indicate that they followed the same path in the immediate vicinity of "first pueblo of Cíbola". However, the locations and descriptions of the "site of big boulders" (of Arellano's main force) and the "bad pass" (of the Advance Party) are glaring exceptions. It is highly probable that they refer to one and the same place. This "bad pass" with boulders in a wooded area will serve as a starting point in attempting to locate the sites mentioned above in the following chapters.

None of the other sites mentioned near the "first pueblo" is quite so clearly identified as the "bad pass", including the "first pueblo of Cíbola" itself. According to Frank Cushing's telling of an old Zuñi story[12], Esteban the Black of Marcos de Niza's entrada reached the pueblo of Kiakima when he arrived at the province of Cíbola. Since Marcos de Niza traveled with Coronado, presumably as a guide, it is possible that Coronado might have first approached Kiakima as well. However, it is widely held by modern scholars that Coronado first approached the Cíbola pueblo of Hawikuh, instead.

When Fredrick Hodge[13] excavated the ruins of Hawikuh around 1920, he did indeed find several Spanish artifacts, but nothing to positively identify it as the site of the first Spanish conquest of Cíbola. During the half century following Coronado's entrada, there were several other Spanish entradas into that region. In addition, the Spanish established a mission church at Hawikuh in 1629. Many Spanish era artifacts would be expected in the pueblo as well as in the entire region, even if it were not Coronado's "first pueblo". There is no known old Zuñi story similar to Cushing's story about Kiakima that would identify Hawikuh as Coronado's captured pueblo.

Most of the descriptions of the "first Pueblo of

12. Green, p174

13. Hodge

Cíbola" given above could equally well apply to either Hawikuh or Kiakima and perhaps to other pueblos, notably Kechiba:wa as will be discussed in later chapters.

Ostensibly, some other pueblo could have been reached first, but none has been seriously suggested by modern scholars. If Davis' description[11] of the approach to the first pueblo ("the only means of reaching it was by a narrow and tortuous road difficult to ascent") is correct, then the probability of Kiakima being the "first pueblo" would be enhanced. Hawikuh was on a hill with broad slopes leading up to the pueblo in several places and Kechiba:wa has a single broad slope leading up to it. Unfortunately, Davis does not state the source of his information nor does he say who translated it. Davis, himself, may have been the translator but he gives credit to Samuel Ellison of Santa Fe for translating material appearing later in his book. Since this information cannot be verified at present, it is not possible to conclude that Kiakima was the first pueblo visited by Coronado. To date, the archaeological evidence is insufficient to clearly identify any of the Zuñi Reservation ruins as the "first pueblo of Cíbola".

Since the identification of Coronado's "first pueblo of Cíbola" is unknown, any additional insight into the route taken by the Advance Party on its approach to the region will likely come from an attempt at matching the known place descriptions and distances to geographical terrain features. This will be the focus of the remaining chapters.

Part 2

**Possible Routes Taken by the
Coronado Expedition to Tierra Nueva
in 1540**

Chapter 8

Cíbola in 1540

What is known about Cíbola when Coronado first arrived in the mid 16th century? For one thing, it was a center of trade over a vast and active trading network that covered most of northern Mexico and much of the the western United States. Cíbola trading extended eastward to the Great Plains region where they obtained bison hides and westward to at least the lower Colorado River (where Alarcón interviewed local traders from Cíbola). The trade network extended to the west coast of Mexico where the natives of Cíbola obtained seashells and southward into present-day Mexico where they obtained various brightly-feathered birds. The Cíbolans were aware of the Mississippi River, the Gulf coast of Texas and Mexico, the west coast of California, the Grand Canyon of the Colorado River and the rivers and plains of Oklahoma and Kansas. These were civilized people with an ancient culture and tradition.

It appears that the peoples of other provinces encountered by the Coronado Expedition each had their own names for the various pueblos of Cíbola. It is likely that the name applied by the Spaniards to any one of the pueblos would have depended more upon the home province of the interpreters than on the Cíbolans' own name for that pueblo.

Surprisingly little information was recorded by the Coronado Expedition about the geographical positions of the "seven" pueblos of Cíbola or of their size, structure and population. The names of only two, or possibly three, of the pueblos are given in the documents of the Expedition and it is not certain who supplied those names. One of these two pueblos was almost certainly Mats'a:kya, called "Mazaque" by Castañeda[1], and almost certainly was the one he described as[2]

1. F&Fdocs28, p417
2. F&Fdocs28, p393

> *the largest, best, and most beautiful pueblo of that provincia [of Cíbola]. Only this pueblo has seven-story buildings. ... They are special buildings which serve as strongholds in the pueblo. They are taller than the others and rise over [them] like towers. In them there are loopholes and embrasures for defense of the roofs. [This is necessary] because the pueblos do not have streets; the roofs are level, and they come and go among themselves by first climbing up to the roofs. These taller buildings [then] protect them. ... [edges of the roofs] of the pueblo some of which extend out like balconies with wooden pillars beneath.*

Castañeda also says that the first pueblo encountered by Coronado and the Advance Party was called "Cíbola" by the Spaniards and he describes it as[3]

3. F&Fdocs28, p393

> *a small pueblo crowded together and spilling down a cliff. ... It is a pueblo with three and four upper stories and with up to two hundred fighting men. The houses are small and not very roomy: They do not have [individual] patios; a single patio serves a neighborhood.*

4. FFdocs19, p259

Coronado, in his letter[4] to Viceroy Mendoza dated August 3, 1540, says that no individual pueblo was called Cíbola but that name applied to the entire region. However, all of the chroniclers and individuals testifying at later legal hearings do call the "first pueblo of Cíbola" by the name "Cíbola".

None of the chroniclers record the name any of the Indians used for this "first pueblo of Cíbola", but Coronado may have given it the name "Granada". However, no one else seemed to use that name for any of the pueblos of the Cíbola region. Coronado describes Granada by[4]

> *In this one, where I am now lodged, there could be some two hundred houses, all encircled by a wall. It seems to me that together with the other [houses] that are not [encircled] in this way, they could reach a total of five hundred hearths [households]. There is another neighboring town, one of the seven [that] is somewhat larger than this one. [There is] another one the same size as this [one], and the remaining four are somewhat smaller.*

Coronado does not explicitly say that Granada is the same pueblo as "Cíbola" or that Granada was the first pueblo he encountered. It would seem that only the walled portion of Granada (not including the other 300 or so houses outside the wall) was the size ascribed to Cíbola by Cantañeda. It is probable, but not certain, that Castañeda meant to include the entire pueblo in his description. If so, it must be considered possible that Granada and Cíbola were two separate pueblos. The other primary chronicler, Juan Jaramillo, states[5]

5. F&Fdocs30, p514

> *From this first pueblo of Cíbola we went, as I have said, to another one of them, which is about one short day's journey*

but from the context it is not clear if he is referring to

Cíbola in 1540   105

an exploration from Cíbola during the early part of the Expedition's occupation or to the first part of the later journey from Cíbola to Tiguex.

In summary, we have an Indian name of one Cíbolan pueblo, Mazaque, which is called Mats'a:kya by the Zuñi, but for which we do not have any Spanish name. There is also have one (or two) pueblos for which we have no Indian name, but for which we do have the Spaniard's names of "Cíbola" and/or "Granada". Since Mats'a:kya was the largest of the pueblos, it cannot be Coronado's Granada. Mats'a:kya is also highly unlikely to be the "first pueblo of Cíbola" since it was not identified as such in any of the several references to it by multiple chroniclers.

It is recognized that the ruined Zuñi pueblo of Hawikuh is customarily identified as the pueblo "Cíbola" (or the "first pueblo of Cíbola"), but, at this point, making that connection seems unjustified without further investigation.

The Province of Cíbola

The province of Cíbola was described only slightly better than the pueblos by members of the Coronado entrada.

6. FFdocs19, p259

Coronado states that[6]

> *The seven ciudades are seven small towns, all consisting of the [sort of] houses I describe [here]. They are all located within close proximity; within four leagues.*

Castañeda says that[1]

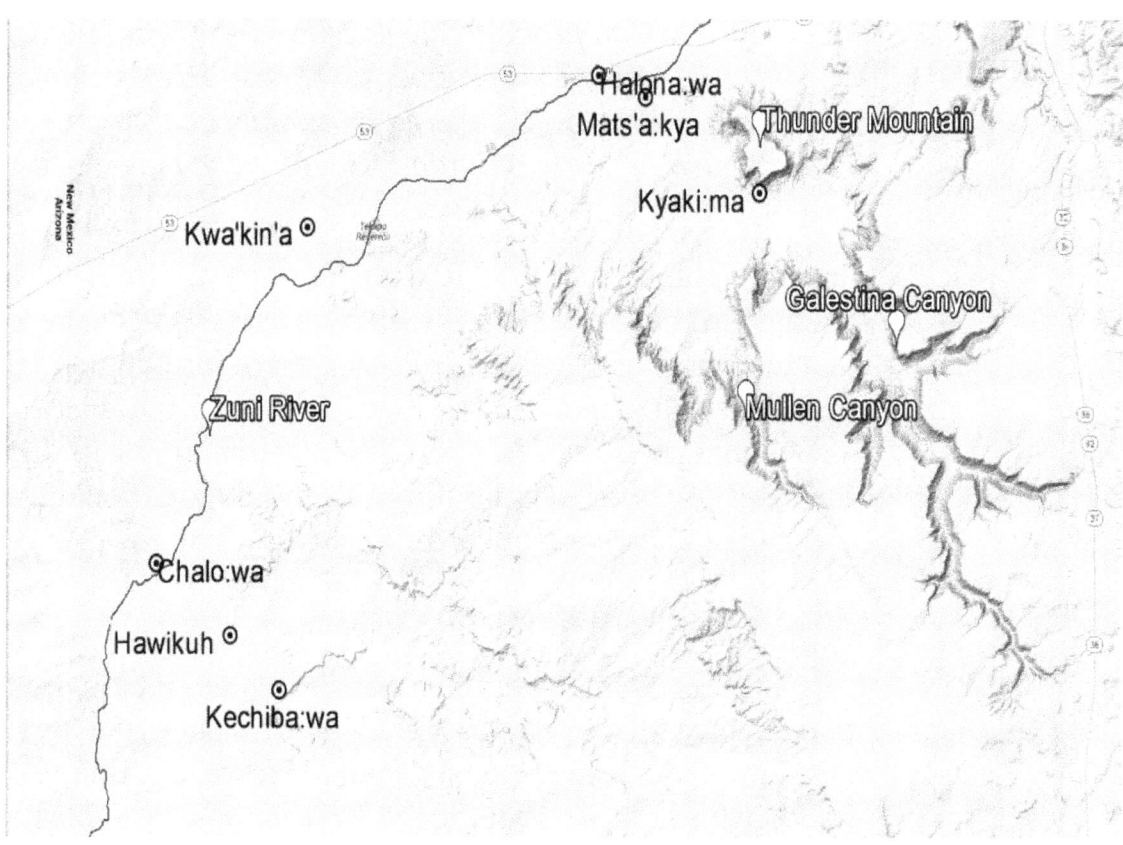

Fig. 8.1. Approximate locations of the pueblos of Cíbola when the Coronado Expedition arrived in the region in July 1540. Geographic features and modern highways are shown for orientation.

> *Cíbola comprises seven pueblos. The largest is called Mazaque. Usually the buildings are three- and four storied. At Mazaque there are buildings of four and [even] seven stories. ... This land is a valley between short ranges of mountains [which are] like bluffs.*

7. F&Fdocs30, p513   In Juan Jaramillo's narrative, he says[7]

> *In this provincia of Cíbola there are five small pueblos including this one. ... . These pueblos are separated from each other by about a league or*

more, which probably turns out to form a circuitous route of about six leagues.... It is somewhat sandy land and not well covered by pasture. ...The forests around here are of juniper trees for the most part.

Castañeda's and Jaramillo's descriptions of the land and topography agree well with the arid hill and mesa country in the present Zuñi region. Jaramillo also states that the province of Cíbola lies just west of the continental divide, which also is true of Zuñi. The Zuñi oral history also contains a tradition of first encounters with the Spaniards. There can be little doubt that Coronado's Cíbola is the present-day Zuñi Reservation region.

The Cities of the Province

There is no definitive count or identification of the pueblos that were occupied at Cíbola at the time the Coronado Expedition arrived. However, Edmund Ladd, who is a member of the Zuñi nation, provides a map[8] showing the names and locations of eight sixteenth century pueblos. These include: Hawikuh, Kwa'kin'a, Kechiba:wa, Binna:wa, Halona:wa, Mats'a:kya, Dowa Yalanne and Kyaki:ma. His map applys the label "Dowa Yalanne" to the entire mesa of Corn Mountain, but it is included here as a pueblo because it was at that time a place of refuge and almost certainly would have had at least one pueblo atop it. Binna:wa may not have been occupied when Coronado arrived since Kintigh[9] lists it with an abandonment date of 1500.

In their Appendix 2 entry for the Geographical Data of Cíbola, Flint and Flint[10] list nine pueblos occupied in 1540 according to modern archaeology. These include Hawikuh, Kechiba:wa, Kwa'ki'na, Kyaki:ma, Mats'a:kya,

8. LaddTN, p191

9. Kintigh, p176

10. F&Fgeo, p599

Halona:wa north, and possibly Chalo:wa, Binna:wa, and Ah:kya:ya.

The pueblos listed by Flint and Flint will now be discussed individually beginning with the westernmost and proceeding eastward in order of location. The information about these pueblos has been taken from Keith Kintigh's 1985 book[11] "Settlement, Subsistence, and Society in Late Zuñi Prehistory" except for the entry for Kyaki:ma where T. J. Ferguson[12] is also referenced. The occupation dates which are given on the heading lines here were taken from the Appendix[13] in Adams and Duff "The Protohistoric Pueblo World, A. D. 1275-1600".

11. Kintigh, 1985

12. Ferguson, 1996

13. Adams&Duff

Chalo:wa (occupied 1425 – 1540)

Chalo:wa lies about 100m (333ft) west of the Zuni River and in the floodplain on a low knoll with steep slopes to the north, east and south. To the west, the slope is more gradual and forms a natural approach. There is a row of hills to the west, but there are no rock outcropping in the vicinity of the site. The ruin mounds are basically rectangular in shape with dimensions of 60m X 64m (200ft X 213ft) and include an unknown number of rooms. Kintigh says that Mindeleff [circa 1885] indicated he was told that the ruins of Chalo:wa had been occupied at the time of Spanish contact.

Ah:kya:ya (occupied 1400 - 1500)

The site lies about 400m (1330 ft) east of the Zuñi River on top of a low ridge extending west into the river valley. There are a total of five rooms at this site. Four rooms are within a 9m X 36m mound and one room occupies a separate 6m X 7m mound.

Hawikuh (occupied 1400 - 1680)

Hawikuh is located on the southern end of a low ridge in the Zuni River valley about 4.3km (2.7miles) east of the confluence of Plumasano Wash and the Zuni River. The ruins lie within a mound measuring 185m X 193m [617 ft X 643 ft]. Kintigh calculated the number of ground floor rooms to be 457 and estimated a total of 800 rooms at the site.

Kwa'kin'a (occupied 1400 - 1680)

Kwa'kin'a is located on a ridge overlooking the Zuni River which runs about 1.3 km (0.8 mile) southeast of the ruin. No sandstone outcrops are apparent in the immediate vicinity of the site, but some do exist on the mesa slopes southeast of the river, about 1.8 km (1.1 mile) to the south of the site. The ruins are evidenced by one large F-shaped mound and two smaller L-shaped mounds. These mounds are located on the tops of natural features and do not appear to be connected. The large mound measures 126m X 45m with an estimated 141 rooms. One of the smaller mounds measures 35m X 25m with an estimated 30 rooms while the other measures 20m X 12m and has an estimated 15 rooms. The total number of rooms at Kwa'kin'a is, then, 186.

Kechiba:wa (occupied 1425 - 1680)

Kechiba:wa is located on a low rise of white gypsum on top of a mesa forming the northern edge of Plumasano Wash. The site sits about 75m (250 feet) from the south rim of the mesa and overlooks the valley to the south. It lies on a grassland plain area but is surrounded by juniper-piñon woodlands. The site of Hawikuh, about 3 km (2 miles) to the west, is visible from Kechiba;wa. The mesa

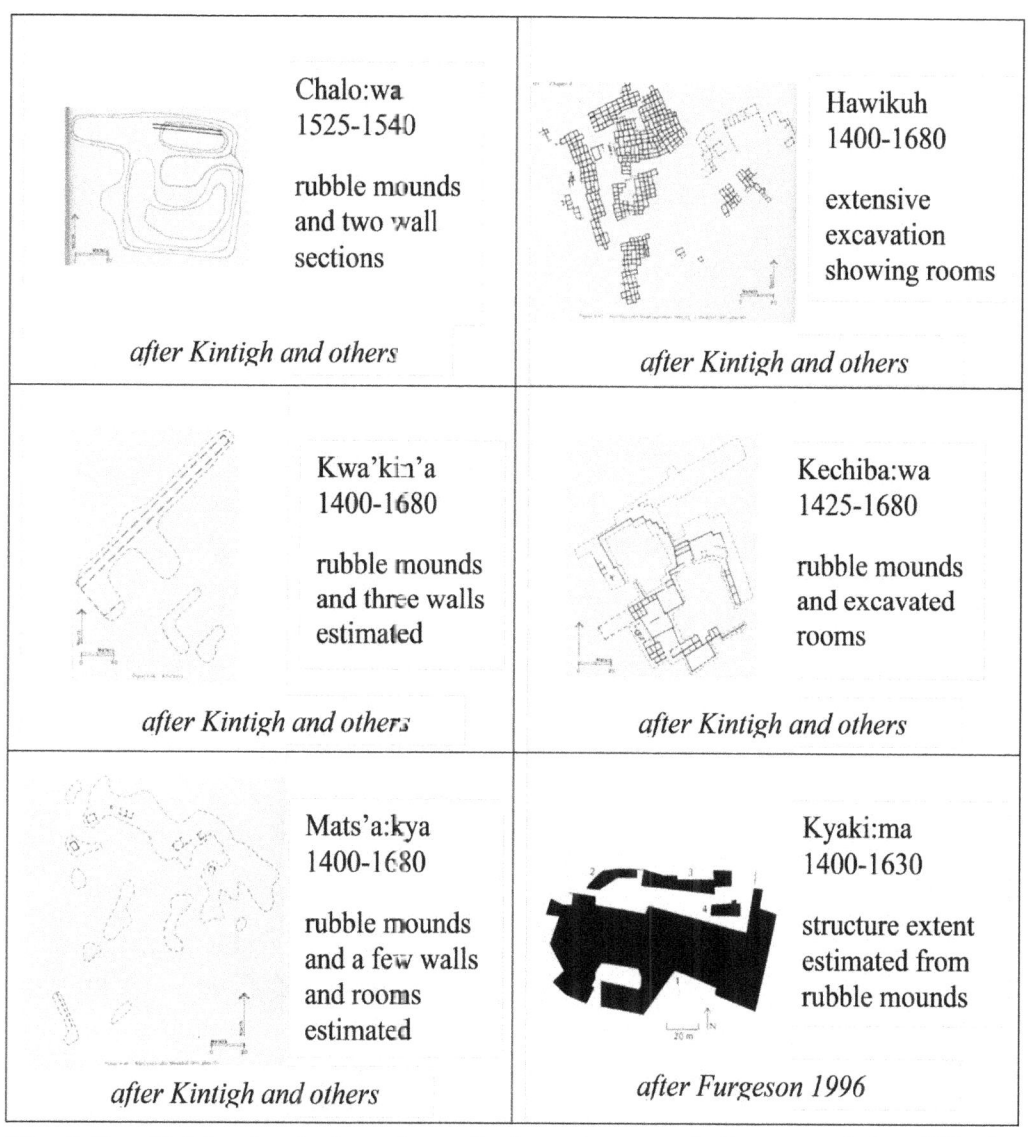

Fig 8.2. Table depicting the relative sizes and shapes of the Cíbola pueblos probably occupied when Coronado arrived. The referenced drawings and sketches were re-sized to the same scale for this table and all are oriented with North up.

has a steep slope to the south, a more gradual downward slope to the west of the site and a gradual uphill slope to the northeast. A spring is located about 750m (about half a mile) south of the site at the bottom of the steep face of the mesa. The ruin mound has dimensions of 128m X 152m (427ft X 507ft) and includes several room blocks similar to Hawikuh. Kintigh estimated that the site includes 471 ground story rooms and a total of 824 rooms.

Binna:wa (occupied 1375 - 1500)

Binna:wa sits on top of a knoll surrounded by Zuni River Valley bottomland. The river runs about 100m (333 ft) to the north of the site. The ruin is in an area of plains grassland, although a deciduous riparian ribbon follows the river about 50m to the north of the ruin. Sandstone outcrops occur on the north slope of the knoll. The ruin mound is irregular in shape and covers a region of approximately 42m X 58m (140ft X 193ft). From the amount of wall rubble, Kintigh estimates that there are 168 rooms at Binna:wa.

Halona:wa (occupied 1375 - present) (presently called Zuñi Pueblo)

The ruins of the 1540 pueblo of Halona:wa lie beneath the modern Zuñi Pueblo and very little extensive archaeological work has been undertaken on those old ruins. Consequently, there are no reliable estimates for the number of rooms at Zuni Pueblo for any specific time. However, Kintigh has estimated a size of about 200 rooms for the 1540s Halona:wa from historical information. The site is situated on the crest and slopes of a small knoll on the north bank of the Zuni River and is surrounded by the Zuñi River floodplain.

Mats'a:kya (occupied 1400 - 1680)

Mats'a:kya is located on the top, sides, and base of a large knoll on the Zuñi River floodplain. The knoll lies about 200m (666ft) south of the river and about 2 km (1.25 miles) northwest of Corn Mountain (Dowa Yalanne). Evidence of the architecture of the ruin is scant and even rough outlines of major room blocks are difficult to discern. Kintigh says the best projection of the site configuration is a major room block completely covering the knoll, with several additional room blocks southwest of the knoll. The ruin mound is contained in an area of 140m X 150m (467ft X 500ft) containing an estimated 515 ground floor rooms. Assuming that one-half of the ground floor rooms supported two-story structures and that one-fourth supported three-story structures, Kintigh estimated the site to have 901 rooms. If Castañeda's observation of this pueblo having up to seven stories is correct, then Kintigh's estimation of 901 rooms would need to be revised to a considerably larger number.

Kyaki:ma (occupied 1400 - 1630)

Kyaki:ma is located in a protected cove on a steep hill that is part of the lowest bench on the southern edge of the base of Dowa Yalanne. Sheer sandstone cliffs stand immediately behind the ruin to the north. The site overlooks the broad area of bottomland where Galestina Wash and Mullen Canyon join. A permanent spring lies about 200m west of the site. Some indication of structure is discernible and according to Kintigh the best assessment is that there was a single linear room block at the top of the ridge that extends from the edge of the mesa. Another square room block (or square composition of linear room blocks) is surrounded a deep depression and several large sandstone slabs are set vertically in the ground east of the upper room block. Noting that an accurate room estimate cannot be made, Kintigh used a mound size of 70m X

140m (233ft X 467ft) to estimate 250 ground floor rooms at the site but did not offer an estimate of the total number of rooms. Ferguson determined a mound size of 101m X 165m (337 ft X 550 ft) and derived an estimate of 834 ground floor rooms and suggested that same number for the total room count, also.

Of the nine pueblos listed above, seven are likely to have been occupied when the Coronado Expedition reached Cíbola in 1540 and those are included on the accompanying map of the area, Figure 8.1. Their locations were determined by matching the above descriptions to geographical features appearing on satellite photographs. Figure 8.2 presents outlines of these pueblos to convey the probable relative sizes of each pueblo at the time of the arrival of the Spaniards. The outlines shown represent current archaeological information and, as such, depict the size at the time of their abandonment.

It is known that the population of the Cíbola region decreased significantly after the arrival of the Europeans, probably due to diseases foreign to the native people of that region. It would seem somewhat reasonable, then, to presume that the pueblos did not increase substantially in size before they were abandoned some 90 to 140 years after Coronado's arrival. The table of pueblos of Figure 8.2 does not include Halona:wa. That site lies beneath the modern pueblo of Zuñi which has been occupied continuously since about 1400, except for perhaps the 12 year period of the Pueblo Revolt from 1680 to 1692. Halona:wa has not experienced any major archaeological excavations that would yield the required information about the ancient pueblo structure in 1540.

Chapter 9

Search for the Bad Pass

The name "Cíbola" was used by the Spaniards in 1540 to refer to a region containing at least six or seven occupied pueblos. "The first pueblo of Cíbola" refers to the first of those pueblos to be visited by Coronado and the Advance Party on July 7, 1540. Precisely which pueblo this was is still not certain. As discussed previously in Chapter 7, for many years there have been two main contenders for this distinction: one being the pueblo of Kiakima (Kyaki:ma) and the other being the pueblo of Hawikuh. Kiakima is almost certainly the place visited by Estevan, the Moor, and the place where he was killed during the Marcos de Niza entrada.

1. Green, p174

The primary support for this assertion is the Zuñi oral history[1] story told to Frank Hamilton Cushing by four old Zuñi men sometime between 1880 and 1884. Cushing relates that the "black Mexicans" and their Indian allies came down "Hemlock" canyon and descended upon Kiakima. The ancient people of that pueblo killed one of the black men (undoubtedly Estevan) where a large stone stood near the arroyo (Galestina Canyon) that runs past the pueblo. Although the name is no longer in use, from the context of the story, "Hemlock" must have been either Galestina Canyon or Mullen Canyon. Another thing supporting Kiakima as the first pueblo is that, when the Spaniards of the Coronado entrada arrived at the first pueblo, they apparently thought they had arrived at the place Estevan was killed.

The other candidate for the "first pueblo of Cíbola," Hawikuh, was one of the three southwestern-most pueblos of the Cíbola group and seems to have acquired its common acceptance as the first pueblo from two factors:

1) the supposition that the Advance Party approached the first pueblo from the west (although the natural final approaches to Hawikuh seem to be from either the northwest or the south), and

2. Hodge, 1966

2) the supposition on the part of Frederick W. Hodge[2] that Hawikuh was the "first pueblo of Cíbola" when he was excavating it from 1917 to 1923. (Opinions of famous and influential people sometimes have a way of being accepted as fact.)

These two pueblos are not, however, the only likely candidates for that distinction. From what was learned in the previous chapters about the seven Cíbola pueblos that were probably occupied when the Spaniards arrived, only one can be ruled out with high certainty. That one is the pueblo of Matsima (Mats'a:kya) which was the pueblo where the defeated people of the "first pueblo" wanted to go to make arrangements for peace. Matsima also does not have a natural final approach from the west since that is a steep slope of the mesa on which it was built. Halona:wa, at the site of present-day Zuñi Pueblo, does not seem to be a likely candidate, either, since Coronado would not have

3. F&Fdocs22, p293

had to travel four leagues[3] to "see" the "rock" (probably Dowa Yalanne) upon which the Indians were fortifying themselves). Also, it would be difficult to imagine that pueblo as "spilling down a cliff" as Castañeda described[4]

4. F&Fdocs28, p393

the "first pueblo".

The ancient pueblo of Kwakina (Kwa'kin'a) cannot be completely ruled out as a candidate. The only reasonable approach to this pueblo is from the west. Coronado could have traveled as far as four leagues to see Dowa Yalanne, but only if he traveled close around the base of it for some distance.

And then there are the two remaining southwestern-most pueblos, Chalo:wa and Kechiba:wa. Both have approaches only from the west. Kechiba:wa lies on top of a fairly high mesa and is the southern-most of the seven pueblos. It could have been the first pueblo encountered if the Advance Party had approached the Cíbola region from the south. Chalo:wa lies on a rise in the flood plain of the Zuñi River and has steep slopes protecting the final approach from the north, east and south. The location of Chalo:wa makes it a possible candidate as the first pueblo if Coronado's entrada approached the region from the west or by traveling up the Zuñi River from the south or southwest. This pueblo was probably abandoned[5] sometime during 1540 but the reason is unknown. Could it have been abandoned in response to the Spaniards' occupation of it?

5. Kintigh, p 68

It seems, then, that there are multiple reasonable candidates for the "first pueblo of Cíbola" based on the known evidence. First is Kiakima, supported by the Zuñi's oral history as having been visited by Estevan; second is Hawikuh, supported by the opinion of a famous archaeologist, who was, perhaps, told that by the Zuñis; the third possibility is Chalo:wa because of its location and description; fourth is Kechiba:wa because of its position and description; and fifth is Kwakima because of its location and description.

Whichever one of these pueblos was encountered first (if any of them) probably would have been on the

Search for the Bad Pass 117

most direct or best trade route determined by the Indian guides leading the Advance Party. The best route for the Coronado Expedition with its horses, pack animals and, possibly, sheep and cattle, may not have been the most direct available alternative nor the route normally taken by Indian traders, who had no beasts of burden. The Expedition's route, then, could well have taken it past other pueblos on its way to the principal trading pueblo – presumably the pueblo of Matsima (Mats'a:kya, Mazaque).

Knowing which pueblo was the "first pueblo" encountered would be a great help in determining Coronado's route in the Cíbola region. However, lacking that knowledge, this investigation of the Expedition's route will be based on feature descriptions and distances presented by the chroniclers.

Beginning the Search

As previously discussed, there are not many points on Coronado's route in the region of Cíbola that can be readily identified and associated with features of the terrain. However, the "bad pass" is one place that should be identifiable on modern maps. This pass where Cárdenas bivouacked was in a wooded area with boulders. Cíbola is a landscape with relatively few such places that could be associated with the path of a trade route. The search for the "bad pass" will begin with a review of the known facts about the local vicinity.

The chroniclers of the Coronado Expedition have supplied distances between several named places on the way to the "first pueblo", but are mostly silent on the direction to one place from another. However, on this part of the entrada approaching the first pueblo there are three occasions where a direction is given. Apparently Coronado approached the "first pueblo" from the west[6], but as pointed out previously, this may have been simply the direction of the final attack and may not be the general direction of march from the "bad pass" to the pueblo. A decision to attack with the sun at his back would have been prudent of Coronado. The second instance of a direction being given is found in the testimony of Francisco Vásquez de Coronado taken probably early in 1545 and recorded in paraphrased and summary form in December 1547[7]. That testimony states that the last camp prior to reaching the "first pueblo" lay to the west of the bad pass. The third instance is Jaramillo's statement[8] that the Rio Bermejo lies somewhat to the "northeast" of the "small stream". (Flint and Flint point out several occasions where "northeast" and "northwest" might have been interchanged in the documents of the Expedition. They offer a quite plausible explanation[9] of the source of this directional confusion.)

In order to gain more insight into the route taken by Coronado and his men on their approach to the "first pueblo of Cíbola", an attempt will be made to match the descriptions and known distances to geographic terrain features. Appendix B presents a table of the given and deduced distances between points on the Coronado Expedition to Cíbola. Only the last few entries in that table – those near the first pueblo encountered – are of present concern. This latter part of the route and the sites encountered are presented in more detail in Appendix C. The task of identifying geographic locations begins by listing the known attributes of the "bad pass" and its vicinity.

The information known about the "bad pass" can

6. F&Fgeo, pg 599

7. FCruel, p468

8. F&Fdocs30, p513

9. F&Fdocs30, n67

be summarized as:

1. It was 2 to 2.5 leagues (5.3 to 6.5 miles) from the first pueblo.
2. It was a place of big boulders with hollows.
3. Cárdenas bivouacked his group in a wooded area at this location.
4. A hill was located one-half league (1.3 miles) along the trail to the west.
5. There was a lake an unknown distance, but more than one-half league (1.3 miles), along the trail south of the hill.
6. The Rio Bermejo was about 5.5 leagues (14.4 miles) south of the bad pass or about 13 miles beyond the last camp.
7. The "small stream" was 13.5 leagues (35 miles) south of the bad pass or about 9 leagues (24 miles) to the south-southwest of the Rio Bermejo crossing.
8. The Rio Frio was about 18 leagues (47 miles) from the bad pass or 4.5 leagues (12 miles) from the "small stream".

For the conversion of "leagues" to "miles" the *legua legal* (equal to 2.63 miles) has been used because that "standard" league appears to have been commonly used[10] by the chroniclers of the Coronado Expedition. Since the documents themselves do not state which type of league was being used to record the distances, it is not absolutely certain that these conversions are accurate. At least one of the members of the Expedition, Juan Jaramillo, may have sometimes used the *legua comun* (or common league, equal to 3.46 miles), but he very seldom states distances in *leagues* – preferring to state travel times in

10. F&Fdocs Intro 11

days instead. The conversion using the *legua legal* seems to be highly reasonable.

A visual search of satellite imagery available in the vicinity of the modern-day Zuñi Reservation revealed several candidate locations for the "bad pass". These are shown on the accompanying Figure 9.1 and are labeled "Pass 1" through "Pass 8" and "Pass 15". The documents do not indicate the type of pass the Expedition encountered. It might be a river crossing, a canyon access trail or simply a restricted, narrow pathway through rough terrain. The "passes" shown in Figure 9.1 include any such features that seemed reasonable to the author from the imagery. The first task will be to determine whether any of these passes fulfill the characteristics listed above for the "bad pass" of the Expedition's chroniclers.

Characteristics of the Passes

Pass 1. This pass is a trail up and over a lava flow that blocks access to the Cíbola region from the south and lies between Jaralosa Draw and Venadito Draw. The pass is about two miles long with two short segments that could be considered "dangerous", but there are no apparent "big boulders with hollows" anywhere along the route. It lies about 7 or 8 miles from the nearest pueblos, Kechiba:wa and Hawikuh. This is too far if the "leagues" given in Appendix C are *leguas legales* but which would be the correct distance if *leguas comun* were adopted. This pass appears unlikely to be the "bad pass" of the Advance Party under Coronado or the place of big boulders of the main force under Arellano.

Passes 2, 3 and 4. These three passes appear to be reasonable access routes from the mesa down into Galestina Canyon and all three are "wooded" and have large boulders. Pass 4 lies about 5.5 miles up the canyon from the nearest pueblo, Kyaki:ma, and the others lie about another 2 miles or more further up the canyon. For any of these to be the desired "bad pass" would require that Coronado have approached the region of Cíbola from the south.

Pass 5. This pass is an access to the western branch of Mullen Canyon from the mesa west of the main portion of Mullen Canyon. This is the same mesa from which Passes 2, 3 and 4 extend into Galestina Canyon, but Pass 5 lies about 5 miles west of Pass 4, across Mullen Canyon. It appears to be a heavily wooded path, even today, with an outcropping of big boulders that extends more than half a mile at the beginning of the pass (i.e., where the path drops off the mesa). This pass lies about 5.5 miles from the nearest pueblo, Kyaki:ma, and appears to well fit the description for the "bad pass".

Pass 6. Pass 6 is a Zuñi River crossing just below the confluence with Venadito Draw but north of the lava flow that is crossed by Pass 1. This pass is about 7 miles from both Hawikuh and Kechiba:wa, which is a bit farther than would be expected for the "bad pass". Also, Pass 6 does not appear to have any big boulders in its vicinity. This is not likely to be the Expdeition's "bad pass."

Pass 7. Pass 7 is another route down off the mesa and lies about 2.2 miles northwest of Pass 5, but instead of leading down into Mullen Canyon, Pass 7 leads down into Trapped Rock Canyon. The pathway through this pass descends along the wooded base of a sheer cliff to the north and through a field of large boulders with an abundance of hollows among the boulders. Of all the possible "bad passes" identified in this imagery search, Pass 7 appears

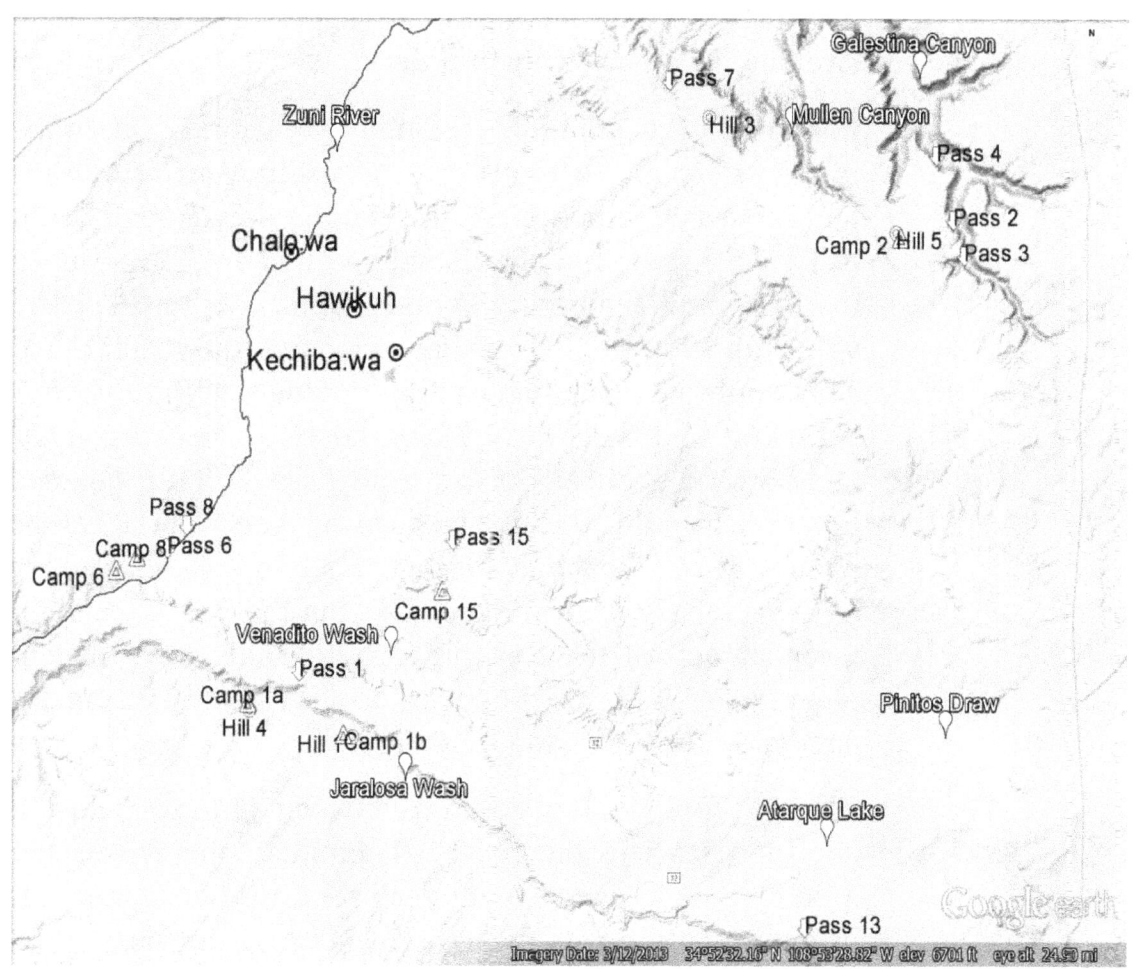

Fig. 9.1. Satellite image showing possible candidate locations of the "bad pass" and the "last camp" of the Coronado Expedition of 1540. Cíbola pueblos and some geographical features are also indicated. Google Earth image.

to be the most likely to have afforded significant shelter from the snow storm that hit Arellano's troops. Pass 7 lies about 5.5 miles along a reasonable path from each of the two nearest pueblos, Halona:wa and Mats'a:kya in close agreement with the two "*leguas legales*" of Appendix C. Of the sites being considered here, Pass 7 seems the best fit to the chroniclers' description of the "bad pass", particularly if one identifies Coronado's "bad pass" with Arellano's "place of big boulders".

Pass 8. This is another crossing of the Zuñi River and is immediately above the confluence with Venadito Draw. Unlike Pass 6 which is about 0.7 mile downstream from it, Pass 8 has both a significant wooded area adjacent to the river and a significant outcropping of big boulders which appear to be somewhat separated from each other. This might be described as "big boulders with hollows". Hawikuh and Kechiba:wa are the two closest pueblos and both lie about 6.5 miles from Pass 8. This distance agrees well with the 2.5 leagues of Appendix B. It is about 25% farther than Castañeda's two leagues (*leguas legales*) tabulated in Appendix C, but that may be within the accuracy of the Expedition's distance measurement techniques. This pass appears to be a reasonably good candidate for Coronado's "bad pass".

Pass 15. The trail here passes between a hill to the north and an arroyo to the south. It could easily have been a "dangerous" pass. A modern road, Indian Route 22, uses this pass on its way to Kechiba:wa and Hawikuh. However, there are no "big boulders" anywhere in the vicinity so that this site is very unlikely to be the "bad pass" of interest.

Candidates for Coronado's "last camp"

Coronado's last camp prior to reaching the "first pueblo" of Cíbola was one-half a league (1.3 miles) to the west of the "bad pass" and was near the base of a hill where Cárdenas had met with several Indians from Cíbola. The possibility of such a campsite associated with each of the various candidate "bad pass" sites will now be investigated.

Pass 1. A study of the satellite imagery reveals two possible candidate camp sites that are both at the correct distance from Pass 1 and are both nearby to a hill. Camp 1a, just north of Hill 4, is to the west of Pass 1 and Camp 1b, west of Hill 1, is to the southeast of Pass 1. Ostensibly, Camp 1a could be an acceptable candidate for Coronado's "last camp" were it not that Pass 1 has the problems of being a bit too far from the nearest pueblos and of not having an abundance of big boulders.

Pass 2. There is a hill, Hill 5, with a possible camp site, Camp 2, the expected distance and to the west from Pass 2. There are also a wooded region in the pass and a large field of big rocks that appear to have "hollows". This pass is, however, about 7.4 miles from the nearest pueblo, Kyaki:ma, along a probable route down Galestina Canyon which is about 15% farther than the expected 2.5 leagues. It should be pointed out that the chart of Appendix C lists the distance from the "first pueblo" to "last camp" as both 2.5 leagues (6.6 miles) and 3 leagues (7.9 miles). The estimate of 7.4 miles from the pueblo to the pass plus the 1.3 miles from the pass to Camp 2 site would result in 8.7 miles from the pueblo to the last camp. This latter figure is only 10% greater than expected and is within the expected uncertainty of Coronado's distance measurements. The combination of Camp 2, Pass 2 and Kyaki:ma seems to well satisfy the known requirements for the final route of Coronado's approach to Cíbola.

Pass 3. There are two hills and a possible camp site southwest of Pass 3. However, Pass 3 is even farther away (another two miles) from the nearest pueblo than is Pass 2. This extra 2 miles would result in a 35% discrepancy in distance. It appears that Pass 3 should not be considered a likely candidate for the "bad pass".

Pass 4. Hill 5 and Camp 2 are both within the expected three-league distance from Kyaki:ma although Camp 2 lies about 1.7 miles from the pass. Hill 5 and Camp 2 lie to the southwest of the Pass 4. There is no possibility of another hill at the expected distance to the west of the pass because another branch of Galestina Canyon lies in that direction. Pass 4 could still be considered a candidate "bad pass" but only if the "west" position requirement for the "last camp" is abandoned.

Pass 5. While pass 5 well fits the description of the "bad pass", there was no hill and camp site pair found within the required distance without going either southward to slight rises in the terrain or northwest to Hill 3. Hill 3 would have been approached from the south and would have been more than a mile out of the way for someone intending to use Pass 5. Pass 5, therefore, appears to be an unlikely candidate for the "bad pass".

Pass 6. Hill 2 and a possible camp site, Camp 6, immediately south of Hill 2 would satisfy the known requirements for the "bad" pass and "last camp". Pass 6, however, does not have big boulders and, in addition, lies just below the confluence of two rivers which would not have been a choice crossing point. Therefore the Pass 6 and Camp 6 combination is considered unlikely to be the sites of interest.

Pass 7. There are no hills or candidate camp sites to the west of this pass which leads down to the west from the mesa top. There appears to be a rather easy route all the way to the nearest pueblos from the west of Pass 7 so that anyone to the west would have had no reason to go through the pass. This pass could be a candidate pass for a route from the south with Hill 3 offering a possible camp site, but Hill 3 is southeast of Pass 7. Pass 7 appears to be a highly unlikely candidate for the "bad pass" unless Coronado's statement that the "last camp" was west of the "bad pass" is ignored.

Pass 8. A possible camp site, Camp 8, immediately to the southeast of Hill 2 lies the required 1.3 miles to the west of Pass 8. As seen earlier, Pass 8 lies about 6.5 miles from both Hawikuh and Kechiba:wa, which is about 25% farther than expected. However, the combined distance from either of those pueblos to Camp 8 is 7.8 miles which is almost exactly the 3 leagues (7.9 miles) given in Appendix C. The combination of Pass 8 and Camp 8 satisfies the stated distance requirements very well.

Pass 15. Another possible camp site, Camp 15, is located the proper distance from Pass 15 but lies almost due south of it instead of to the west as Coronado stated. Since Pass 15 lacks the expected boulders, the Pass 15 and Camp 15 combination are unlikely to be the Expedition's sites.

The sites identified here as possible places for the "bad pass" and the "last camp" visited by the Coronado Expedition are indicated in Figure 9.1. It would seem that the most likely route of Coronado's Advance Party's final approach to the region of Cíbola is one of the following.

1. From Camp 8 through Pass 8 and onto either Hawikuh or Kechiba:wa.
2. From Camp 2 through Pass 2 and onto Kyaki:ma.
3. From Camp 2 through Pass 4 and onto Kyaki:ma.
4. From Camp 1a through Pass 1 and onto Hawikuh or Kechiba:wa.

The first two entries in this list seem to fit expectations

equally well while the third is slightly hampered by the fact that Camp 2 lies southwest of Pass 4 instead of toward the west. The fourth combination in the list is more severely burdened by the fact that Pass 1 lacks the expected boulders and because it lies a bit farther than expected from a possible "first pueblo". All the other identified combinations of campsites, passes and pueblos appear to be much less likely to have been on the route of the Expedition's final approach to Cíbola.

Candidates for the Rio Bermejo Crossing

So far, the current search has resulted in list of three candidate "last camp" sites which are – in order of apparent likelihood – Camp 8, Camp 2 and Camp 1a. It is now necessary to investigate whether any of these campsites lay reasonably close to the required 5 leagues (13.2 miles) (see Appendix C) from possible candidate "Rio Bermejo" river crossing sites. It is required that there must also be a reasonable route between a campsite and a possible river crossing.

Camp 8 (west of Pass 8).

Hardscrabble Wash

There are several possible "river" crossings at about the correct distance of five leagues (13.2 miles) west from Camp 8. These lie along Hardscrabble Wash between the positions marked "Hardscrabble X1" and "Red River X3" in Figure 9.2. At the present time, Hardscrabble Wash is usually a dry channel except just after a rain, but in 1540 there was presumably a much greater average annual rainfall, so the channel could well have been a live river with significant flow. See Appendix E for a history of precipitation in this region. There appear to be several

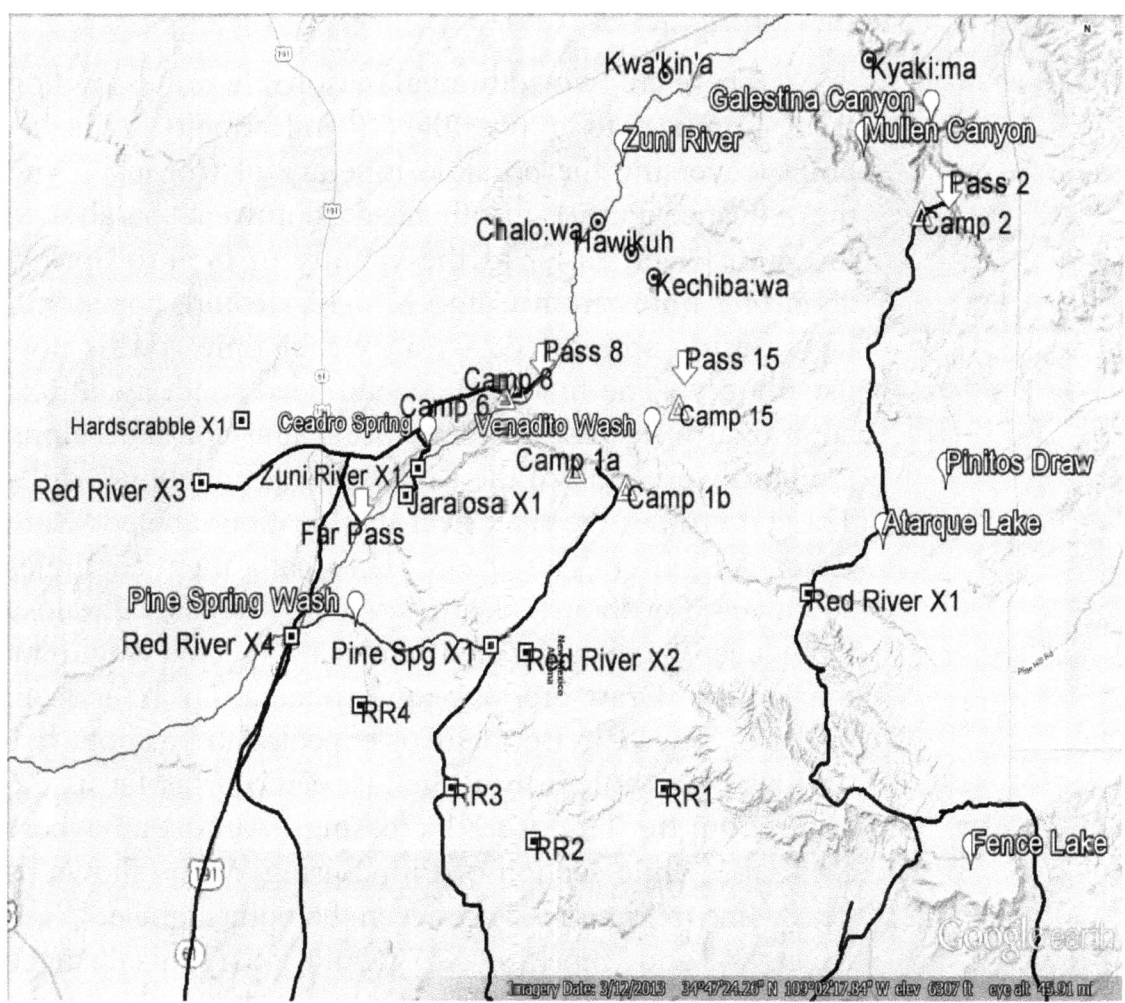

Fig 9.2. Image showing locations of possible "Rio Bermejo" sites. Some of the possible routes in the region are indicated by the lines interconnecting the sites. Major modern roads are also included for orientation and reference. Google Earth image.

places along this section of the draw that would have afforded ready crossings. Hardscrabble Wash drains a sizable area of dark red soil so that the river almost certainly would have been *bermejo* (red) in color. This entire section of Hardscrabble Wash is considered a likely candidate for the Expedition's "Rio Bermejo" crossing.

Pine Spring Wash

There are two additional reasonable routes leading from Camp 8 to a possible "Rio Bermejo" crossing point (reversing the possible itinerary of Coronado and the Advance Party). Both head southwest, parallel to the Zuñi River, as far as the vicinity of Ceadro Spring, about 4.7 miles from Camp 8. This feature appears to have been a spring-fed lake in wetter times but is now usually dry. The first route would head south about one additional mile past Ceadro Spring and continue along the northwest bank of the Zuñi River for about 0.7 mile. There it crosses the river near the location labeled "Zuñi River X1" in Figure 9.2). This path then continues southwest for about 1.2 miles where it crosses Jaralosa Draw near the place labeled Jaralosa X1. This would put the Jaralosa Draw crossing an estimated 7.6 miles from Camp 8. The "Rio Bermejo" is expected to be about five leagues (13.2 miles) from the last camp or as far as 5.6 miles from the Jaralosa X1 crossing. Almost anywhere along a 10-mile section of Pine Spring Wash (shown as heavy line in Figure 9.2) between the points labeled "Red River X4" and "Pine Spg X1" would satisfy this distance estimate. There is no other water course in the region that would satisfy this requirement except for portions of the Zuñi River.

The second of the two routes would continue heading southwest on the high ground northwest of the Zuñi River from the place where the first route headed down to the river, past Ceadro Spring. This route may have crossed the Zuñi River at the location labeled "Far Pass" on Figure 9.2 or it may have continued on the high ground to the present route of Arizona State Highway 61. If it crossed the river at the "Far Pass", then any point along the western half of the previously mentioned stretch of Pine Spring Wash could be a candidate for the "Rio Bermejo" crossing. If the route continued southwest to meet the present Highway 61/191 then it probably would have travelled along the Zuñi River and crossed it below the confluence with the Pine Spring Wash, near the place labeled "Red River X4".

The short section of Hardscrabble Wash and the rather long section of Pine Spring Wash appear to be the only water courses within the expected distance of Camp 8 that also have an apparently reasonable route to them. It is highly likely that the "Rio Bermejo" crossing would have been along one of these sections of the two water courses if the "last camp" actually had been at Camp 8.

Camp 2 (west of Pass 2, southwest of Pass 4)

Pinitos Draw

From Camp 2 on the mesa near Galestina Canyon, the southbound traffic would naturally take one of two routes:

1) a path heading south-southeast for about 3 miles where it intersects a modern unpaved road, Indian Service Route 8, near a present-day ranch headquarters and then turning more southerly, or

2) a path heading south for about ¾ mile to descend the western edge of the mesa and then continuing southward.

Both of these routes would lead to Atarque Lake about 13.5 miles from Camp 2 on either route. Pinitos Draw flows through Atarque Lake and drains a large area of red soil. This stream probably would have well deserved the name Rio Bermejo (Red River). There are two other stream crossings within a reasonable enough distance of Atarque Lake to be considered possible candidates for the "Rio Bermejo". Both cross Jaralosa Draw.

One of these crossings is labeled "Pass 13" on Figure 9.1 and the other is labeled "Red River X1" on Figure 9.2. The crossing at Pass 13 is almost exactly one league (2.63 miles) south of Atarque Lake and would likely have been reached within about an hour before reaching Atarque Lake on the north bound journey. The "Red River X1" crossing is about one and a half leagues from Atarque Lake, but the route through it may have led northward without the eastward diversion required to reach Atarque Lake. Jaralosa Draw also drains an extensive area of "red" soil. However, above its confluence with Pinitos Draw, that soil appears to lack the "bright red" coloration found in Pinitos Draw and implied by the Spanish word "*bermejo*".

If the Camp 2 site is the location of Coronado's "last camp", then it would appear that there are only two reasonable possibilities for the "Rio Bermejo".

1. The most likely possibility would be Pinitos Draw at Atarque Lake or perhaps at about three miles below the lake and about ¾ mile above the confluence of Pinitos Draw and Jaralosa Draw.

2. The second possibility is Jaralosa Draw, itself, at either the "Red River X1" location or the "Pass 13" location.

Camp 1a (west of Pass 1)

Jaralosa Draw

Camp 1a is associated with Pass 1 which was noted to lack any "big boulders" and which was a bit farther away from any possible "first pueblo" than expected. Therefore, the combination of Pass 1 and Camp 1 (or 1a) has a low probability of being the "bad pass" and the "last camp". Nevertheless, it is noted that five candidate "Rio Bermejo" crossings were located on the satellite imagery at about the correct distances from Camp 1. These are labeled RR1, RR2, RR3, RR4 and Red River X4. No reasonable path was identified between RR4 and Camp 1.

The pathway between Camp 1 and both RR2 and RR3 would reasonably go through the vicinity of "Red River X2" but that way to RR2 simply is much too far. RR3 seems to have a good path (the route of a present-day road) to the "Red River X2" location. There also appears to be a good pathway between the "Red River X4" location and Camp 1a. This path lies along Jaralosa Draw to the south of the lava flow crossed by Pass 1. If the difficulty that Pass 1 has no boulders is ignored, then RR1, RR3 and "Red River X4" could be accepted as candidates for the "Rio Bermejo", but at the present time that cannot be justified.

Summary

The search for the "bad pass" of Coronado's Advance Party was based on locating possible passes within "2 leagues" of a possible "first pueblo of Cíbola". These passes had to be within "one half league" of a possible "last camp" site and within five leagues of a possible "Rio Bermejo" crossing. Based on the foregoing analysis, the following "bad pass" candidates and the "last camp" and "Rio Bermejo" candidates associated with them have been identified as having a reasonable chance of being on the Expedition's route as it approached Cíbola.

1. Pass 1. *Low probability: no boulders.*
   a. Camp 1a
      i. RR1, RR3, Red River X4
2. Pass 2. *High probability.*
   a. Camp 2
      i. Pinitos Draw at Atarque Lake
      ii. Jaralosa Draw: Red River X1, Pass 13
3. Pass 4. *Low probability: no camp site to the west.*
   a. Camp 2
      i. Pinitos Draw at Atarque Lake
      ii. Jaralosa Draw: Red River X1, Pass 13
4. Pass 8. *High probability.*
   a. Camp 8
      i. Hardscrabble Wash: Hardscrabble X1, Red River X3
      ii. Pine Spring Wash: Red River X4 to Pine Spg X1
      iii. Red River X4

These results include only those possibilities identified by a visual inspection of satellite imagery and corresponding USGS topography maps. The information for the searches was gleaned from the documents of the Coronado Expedition to Tierra Nueva. Those documents do not specify the locations of any sites in the Cíbola region in sufficient detail for modern readers to readily identify them. However, by careful study of the images and maps it was possible to ascertain some reasonable candidates for those sites relating to the Expedition's "bad pass", "last camp" and "Rio Bermejo". Possible routes between various pairs of these sites have also been found and are presented in Figures 9.1 and 9.2. As might be expected for the major trading center of Cíbola, there are many interconnecting routes leading into the region from all directions and many pathways interconnecting the various pueblos. Only those most pertinent to the present discussion have been indicated on the Figures.

Extending the Search

Of the two likely "bad pass" candidates, Pass 2 would lead to Kyaki:ma while Pass 8 would lead to either Hawikuh, Kechiba:wa or Chalo:wa. The mystery of which pueblo was the "first pueblo of Cíbola" has not been solved. However, the larger mystery of Coronado's route from Culiacan to Cíbola remains to be addressed. The Expedition's chroniclers provide vastly more information about the northern half of the route than about the southern half, so this part of the investigation will begin at the northern end of the route at the "bad pass" candidate sites. The process of discovery-and-refinement utilized to find the "bad pass" candidate sites will be continued to identify and locate other features and places mentioned by the chroniclers of the Coronado Expedition of 1540.

For convenience a point of view of a reverse tracing of the Expedition's journey will be adopted and maintained throughout the next several chapters in an attempt to retrace the route from the "bad pass" all the way southward to Culiacan.

Chapter 10

The Small Stream

While searching for possible locations of the "bad pass" in the previous chapter, several tentative sites for the "Rio Bermejo" crossing were identified. These include

1. about a three-mile section of Hardscrabble Wash between "Hardscrabble X1" and "Red River X3"
2. a nine-mile portion of Pine Spring Wash between "Red River X4" and "Pine Spg X1"
3. three distinct locations along Jaralosa Draw, "Red River X4", "Red River X1" and "Pass 13"
4. the "Atarque Lake" vicinity.

The sites "RR1" and "RR3" were also identified as low-probability candidates because they are dependent on the small chance that "Pass 1" was Coronado's "bad pass".

The viability of these candidates as the "Rio Bermejo" will now be investigated by considering the only evidence provided by the chroniclers of the Coronado Expedition. In addition to the 5 to 5.5-league distance from the Rio Bermejo to the "last camp", Juan Jaramillo says that the Rio Bermejo also lies "2 days" travel[1] from the "small stream" along a north-northeastly route from the south. Along with that information, Juan Jaramillo also admitted that he could easily be mistaken in some of the distances or in the number of days of travel from one place to another. Fortunately, in this case, the author of "Traslado de las Nuevas" also supplies[2] the information that it is "4 days" from the "small stream" to the "first

1. F&Fdoc30, p513

2. F&Fdoc22, p291

pueblo". This latter information is in very good agreement with Jaramillo's "2 days" travel between the Rio Bermejo and the "small stream". However, before any candidate for the "small stream" can be considered viable, it must, in turn, satisfy the chroniclers' descriptions. In this case, Jaramillo's narrative states that the Expedition crossed the "small stream" after a "one day" journey from the "Rio Frio" on its northbound journey. It is required, then, to find a southward access to a "Rio Frio" as well as finding pertinent sites separated by the correct distances.

A note on traveling rates

Since Jaramillo supplies only the number of *days* of travel[1], the *distances* for this portion of the route must be estimated in order to find reasonable candidates for the "small stream". It is already known that the Expedition took two days to travel the 8 leagues from the Rio Bermejo to the first pueblo of Cíbola. However, in all likelihood, neither of these were full days of travel. The first day from the Rio Bermejo seems to have been cut short by Coronado's meeting with the Cíbolan Indians at the spot he subsequently made his "last camp". The second day would also have been a short day of travel because the Advance Party reached the "first pueblo" in the afternoon and took possession of the pueblo before dark.

The four leagues per day average rate of travel for those two days would then be slower than the rate expected for the days prior to reaching the Rio Bermejo. On the other hand, the entire Advance Party was weary and near starvation[3] when it camped at the "small stream". It was here that a Spaniard named Espinosa, two Moors and perhaps some *indios amigos* died from eating poisonous plants. It seems unlikely that the Expedition could have traveled at its normal pace of 6 leagues per day under those conditions but it *could* travel more than four leagues per

3. F&Fdocs19, p256

day since it traveled that distance in "short" days. It then seems reasonable to estimate a nominal rate of travel of between five leagues (13.2 miles) per day and six leagues (16 miles) per day between the "small stream" and the Rio Bermejo. If so, then Jaramillo's recollection of a two day travel would translate into a distance of 26 to 32 miles.

Search for a Possible "small stream"

A search of the satellite imagery and topographic maps for possible water courses that lie about 26 to 32 miles from each of the candidate "Rio Bermejo" crossings found in the previous chapter was conducted. The result of that search is now presented.

Hardscrabble Wash:

Inspection of the satellite imagery revealed four somewhat reasonable stream crossings the correct distance from the Hardscrabble sites within a tolerable uncertainty. The westernmost of these lies along Concho Creek about 12 miles west of St. Johns, Arizona near the location labeled "CC" on Figure 10.1. This "small stream" site would have required that the Coronado Expedition travel downstream, north along Concho Creek for at least 5 miles, staying just to the west of the Black Ridge. The reasonable approaches to this location pose a problem. For the Expedition to have reached this "small stream" location they would have been traveling almost due east. Any southerly, more northerly or northeasterly approaches are blocked by mountains and mesas.

But had they been to the west of this stream, this possible crossing site would have been significantly out of the way and it seems doubtful that any trade route would have taken that course. The only other reasonable route to site "CC" would be northward along the Concho Creek from a position south of the present town of Concho, Arizona. In that case, the Expedition would have come across this stream 12 leagues or more before reaching the "Rio Bermejo", instead of the 8 leagues as stated. It appears that the "CC" location is unlikely to be the Expedition's "small stream".

The other three possible "small stream" crossing points based on the Hardscrabble "Rio Bermejo" crossings all lie nearly due south from Hardscrabble Wash. The one labeled "LC" lies on the Little Colorado River and the two others, "LC trib 1" and "Dry 1", lie on small tributaries of the Little Colorado. In order to have reached the identified crossings on Hardscrabble Wash from any of these three places, the Expedition would have had to cross the Zuñi River and gone several leagues out of their way to their "last camp" (Camp 8). Going this way, the Expedition would have approached Hardscrabble Wash from the south and would not have *crossed* this "Rio Bermejo". It is also probable that the Expedition would have crossed other, more direct routes to Cíbola in its trek to Hardscrabble Wash on this path from any of those three locations. It should be noted that none of the Expedition's chroniclers specifically stated that they *crossed* the Rio Bermejo. It is possible that they simply got to the river and proceeded to the "last camp" without crossing the river. Even so, it seems unlikely that any of the three sites "LC", "LC trib 1" or "Dry 1" would have been the actual "small stream".

There is, however, one more very intriguing possibility. The Zuñi Indians have been making pilgrimages to a sacred lake at the time of the Summer solstice (about June 21 on the current Gregorian calendar or June 11 on the Julian calendar used by Coronado) for as long as their oral history recalls. This lake is near the

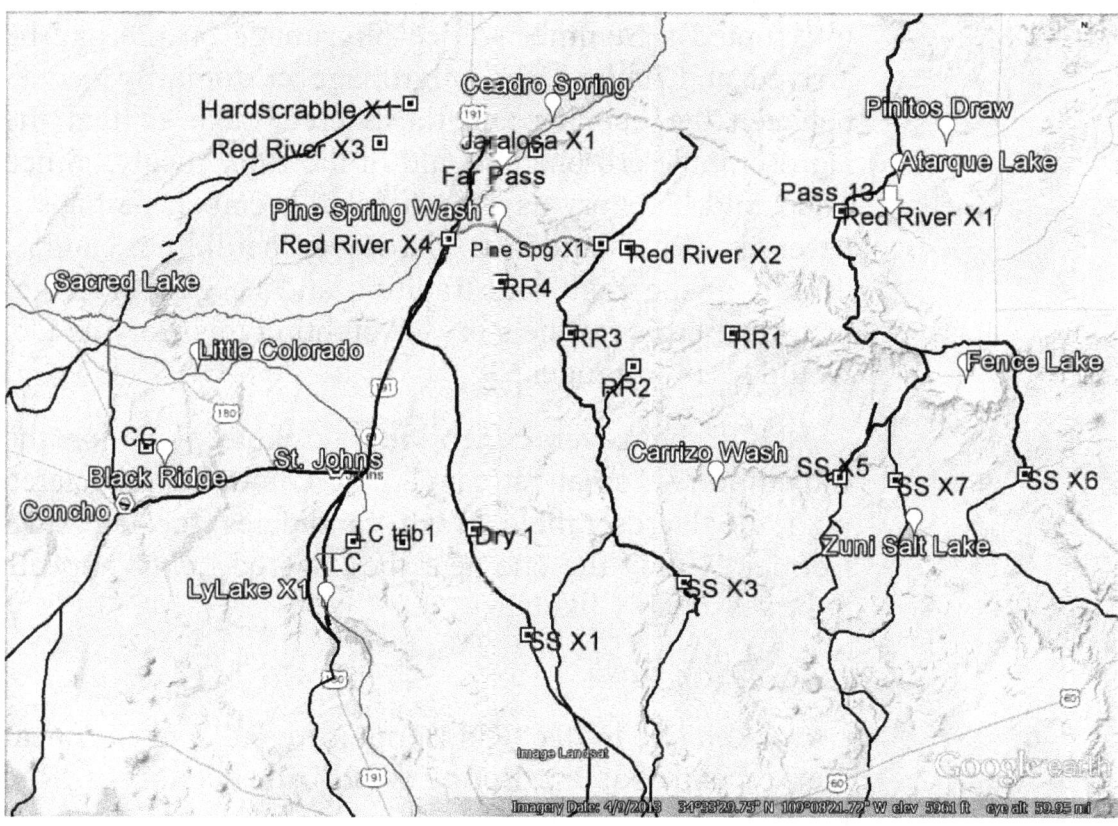

Figure 10.1. Satellite image showing locations of candidate "Rio Bermejo" crossings and candidate "small stream" sites. Modern highways are included for reference. Google Earth Imagery.

Little Colorado River just below the confluence with the Zuñi River and is labeled "Sacred Lake" on Figure 10.1. It can be expected that there would have been a well-worn trail between the Sacred Lake and the pueblos of Cíbola. A river crossing near this lake would be the correct distance from the identified possible "Rio Bermejo" sites at Hardscrabble Wash. It is possible to imagine that Coronado might have described the Little Colorado at this location as a "small stream" if he were comparing it to large rivers in Mexico or even to the "swollen" Rio de las Balsas which they had previously crossed using rafts.

4. LaddTN, p192

Edward J. Ladd has conjectured[4] that Coronado interrupted a Summer soltice pilgrimage on the day he arrived at Cíbola. The pilgrimage customarily occurs between the pueblos and the Sacred Lake so that the Hardscrabble crossings would fit the story nicely. Since Ladd told his story as a Zuñi tribal member, perhaps it deserves serious attention. However, he did not claim it as part of the Zuñi oral tradition and he gave no other historical basis for the story. Weighting this story as fact would seem imprudent.

Of the several identified possible sites for the Expedition's "small stream" that could be associated with the Hardscrabble Wash candidates for the "Rio Bermejo", only the one near the "Sacred Lake" appears to be reasonably likely.

Pine Spring Wash:

Relative to the "Rio Bermejo" candidate sites near the west end of of Pine Spring Wash, in the vicinity of "Red River X4", two candidate locations for the "small stream" crossing were identified. One is at Concho Creek in the immediate vicinity of Concho, Arizona. To Concho there was apparently a good route following the alignment of present-day Highway 61 through St. Johns, Arizona and then west through the Black Ridge mountains. That route would have been approximately 31 miles and would have required the Expedition to travel at the rate of about six leagues per day for the two days required from the "small stream" to the "Rio Bermejo". St. Johns, on the Little Colorado River, is about midway along this route and would have made a good camp place for the intervening night.

The second of these two candidate sites is in the vicinity of Lyman Lake on the Little Colorado south of

St. Johns. This site is labeled "LyLake X1" on Figure 10.1. The distance from the "Red River X4" location is about 26 miles by staying east of the Little Colcrado, or about 30 miles by following the route of Highway 180/191 south of St. Johns. The St. John's crossing of the Little Colorado would again be the logical camp site for the first night.

The location labeled "SS X1" on Figure 10.1 is situated on a presently dry stream bed about 3 miles north of the Springerville Generating Plant. This site is within an acceptable distance from any point along the western portion of the identified section of Pine Spring Wash. It has an apparently easy access to the stream bed, but the Expedition may not have needed to cross at this point. They could have followed it downstream for almost another ten miles along a seemly apparent trail.

Now, starting from the *east* end of the identified portion of Pine Spring Wash, at the location labeled "Pine Spg X1" on Figure 10.1, a candidate "small stream" crossing was found on Agua Fria Creek. That site is labeled "SS X3" and is about six miles south of the confluence of Agua Fria Creek with Carrizo Wash. This location is about 27 miles from "Pine Spg X1" along a likely route between the two sites.

Of the entire portion of Pine Spring Wash identified as possible "Rio Bermejo" crossing locations, there appear to be only three short stretches that would offer a southward route not severely blocked by a steep escarpment. These are the west and east ends, which have already been discussed, and a possible pass up the escarpment about two-thirds the distance from the west end toward the east end. The natural route south from that middle crossing appears to join the route from "Pine Spg X1" to "SS X3" and therefore contributes no new candidates for the "small stream".

The candidate "small stream" sites offered by the supposition that Pine Spring Wash was the "Rio Bermejo" of the Coronado Expedition chroniclers are:

1. Concho Creek near Concho, Arizona
2. Lyman Lake, Arizona
3. A dry creek north of Springerville Generating Plant (SS X1), Arizona
4. Agua Fria Creek, 6 miles south of Carrizo Wash (SS X3), New Mexico.

Pinitos Draw and Jaralosa Draw:

There are two sites lying along Pinitos Draw and two others nearby along Jaralosa Draw that have been identified in the previous chapter as possible "Rio Bermejo" crossing sites. These are Atarque Lake, Red River X1, Pass 13 and a location about two miles southwest Atarque Lake. These four sites all lie within a two-mile radius which is well within the uncertainty in the expected "2 days" travel between the Rio Bermejo and the "small stream". The four, then, will be considered one site for the present purpose.

Inspection of the topographic maps and the satellite imagery again has revealed four distinct possible candidate sites for the "small stream" crossing with a reasonable route from the Pinitos Draw sites. Three of these "small stream" sites lie along Carrizo Wash in the vicinity of the Zuñi Salt Lake and are labeled "SS X5", "SS X6" and "SS X7" on Figure 10.1. The fourth site is labeled "RR1" and is located just to the southwest of the Zuñi Plateau. Other sites a short distance down Carrizo Wash to the west of "SS X5" also appear to have some merit. However, the natural path northward from any of these sites seems to cross very rugged terrain so these latter sites are considered unlikely candidates.

The four viable "small stream" candidate sites associated with the "Rio Bermejo" candidates in the Pinitos Draw and Jaralosa Draw region near Atarque Lake are:

1. SS X5 in Carrizo Wash
2. SS X6 in Carrizo Wash
3. SS X7 in Carrizo Wash
4. RR1 just down off the Zuñi Plateau.

Summary of "small stream" Candidates

The locations identified in this chapter as possible "small stream" crossings are based on the possible "Rio Bermejo" locations identified in the previous chapter. Those, in turn were based on the supposition that Coronado's route went through either Pass 8 and Camp 8 or through Pass 2 and Camp 2. These were the only two passes and associated campsites that were deemed to have a reasonably high probability of being the actual "bad pass" and "last camp" of Coronado's Expedition. This results in only the following sites identified as possible locations for Coronado's "small stream".

For Pass 8 and Camp 8:

1. Little Colorado River near Zuñi Sacred Lake via Hardscrabble Wash
2. Concho Creek via "Red River X4" and St. Johns
3. Lyman Lake via "Red River X4" and St. Johns
4. Dry creek north of Springerville Generating Plant (SS X1)
5. Agua Fria Creek, 6 miles south of Carrizo Wash

(SS X3).

For Pass 2/Camp 2:

6. SS X5 on Carrizo Wash northwest of Zuñi Salt Lake
7. SS X6 on Carrizo Wash northeast of Zuñi Salt Lake
8. SS X7 on Carrizo Wash north of Zuñi Salt Lake
9. RR1 just southwest off the Zuñi Plateau.

The chroniclers also recorded the fact that this "small stream" was found near the northern edge of a forested region. That information, however, is difficult to apply in trying to locate this stream in modern times. It is widely accepted that the climate was much colder and wetter in 1540 than it is today, so the forest margins could be expected to have retreated significantly between 1540 and the present. Also, what is now dry stream beds may have been live streams at that time.

The above list of candidate "small stream" sites is based on the distance between them and the candidate "Rio Bermejo" sites as well as on the existence of seemingly reasonable routes between the two streams. It can reasonably be hoped that some of the multiplicity of candidates will be eliminated by developing a knowledge of the routes approaching these candidate "small stream" sites from the south. The next known place on the reverse tracking of the Coronado Expedition is the "Rio Frio". If any of the above sites cannot be associated with a possible "Rio Frio" one day's journey to the south or southwest, it can be dropped off the list of "small stream" candidate sites. The search for the Rio Frio will occupy the following chapter.

Chapter 11

Search for the Rio Frio

1. F&Fdocs30, p513

2. F&Fdocs22, p291

3. F&Fdocs19, p256

Juan Jaramillo, a member of Coronado's Advance Party, recorded that it took a one-day journey[1] from the "Rio Frio" to the "small stream" on the north bound trip. He also said that on the return, south bound, trip it took the Expedition five days to travel from Cíbola (presumably, but not certainly, the "first pueblo") to the Rio Frio. These two statements are consistent with the four-day travel time between Cíbola and the "small stream" given by the author[2] of the "Traslado de las Nuevas". See Appendix C for additional details about this portion of the journey.

From Coronado's letter[3] of August 3, 1540 to the Viceroy, it is understood that the Expedition was suffering from a shortage of food by the time they had reached the Rio Frio. Just one day later, at the "small stream" the Spaniard Espinosa and two Moors died from eating poisonous plants gathered for food. It would seem unlikely that the Expedition could travel a full six leagues per day under these circumstances.

A search was made for candidate "Rio Frio" crossing sites that lie about 4 to 6 leagues (10.5 to 15.8 miles) from each of the candidate "small stream" crossing sites. This search was conducted with the aid of satellite imagery and topographic maps using two criteria. The first of the two criteria is that "Rio Frio" candidate sites must lie at the proper distance from the referenced "small stream" site and the second is that there must be a reasonable route leading generally both northward and southward from them. A summary of the results of the search is presented below while the candidate "Rio Frio" locations are indicated on Figures 11.1 and 11.2. They are denoted by markers labeled "RFx", where the "x" represents sequential numbers. The locations of the "small stream" candidates from the previous chapter are also included on Figures 11.2 for reference and are used below to organize the current search results.

Little Colorado River Near the Sacred Lake

RF1:

This site is a crossing of Jeff Lake Draw about ten miles east-northeast of Snowflake, Arizona. It has a rocky bed, making it a good crossing for people and livestock and is presently crossed by a modern road linking the towns of Snowflake and Concho. There appears to be a good route, which is indicated on Figure 11.1, between RF1 and the Sacred Lake on the Little Colorado River. The distance between the sites is about 18.5 miles along the indicated route. The logical route southward from RF1 would follow the route of the present highway to Snowflake and then turn south to Show Low via highway 77 or continue on the highway from Snowflake southwest to Heber (and perhaps Payson) via highway 277.

RF2:

This site lies just to the north of Concho Lake along Concho Creek south of the town of Concho, Arizona. The route southward from the Little Colorado River crossing near the Sacred Lake follows modern road alignments to Concho as indicated on Figure 11.1 for about 13.5 miles. A reasonable route southward from RF2 follows State Road 61 southwest to Show Low and on to Globe. Alternately, this route could have turned south at Little Ortega Lake about 5.5 miles southwest of this "Rio Frio"

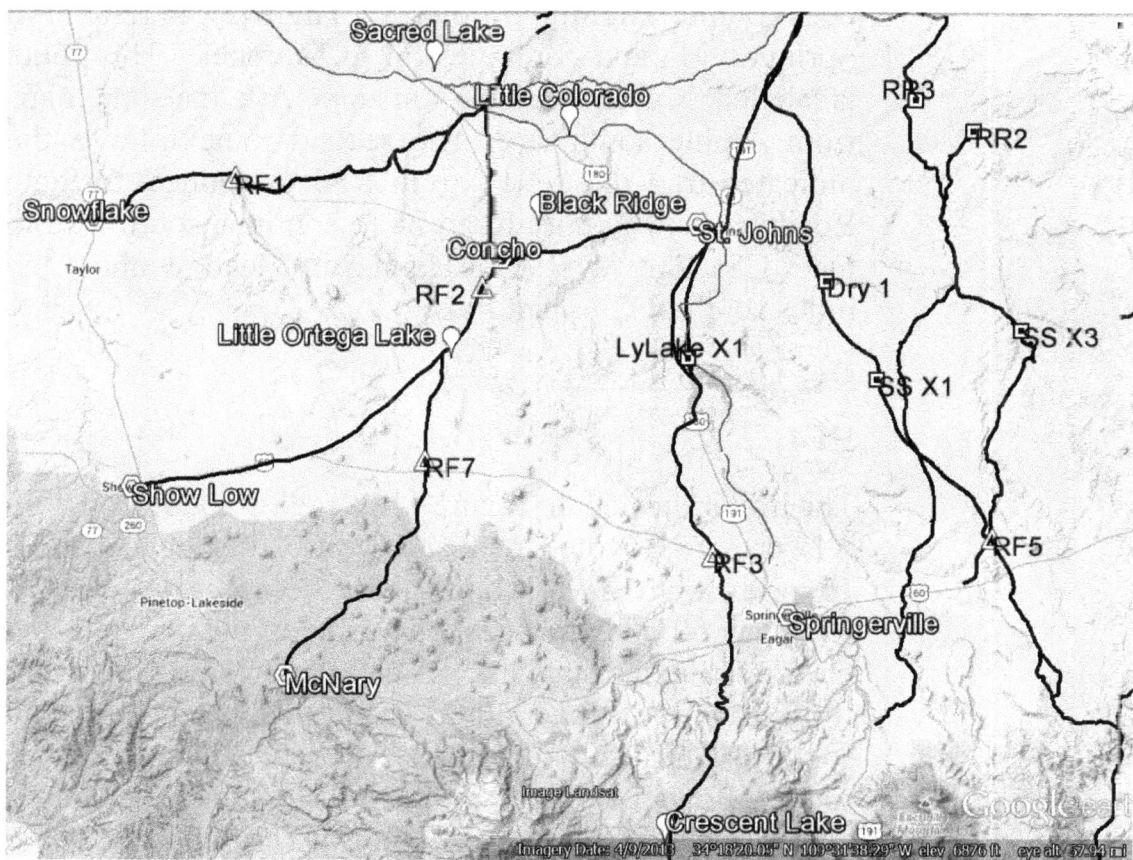

Fig 11.1 Locations of candidate sites for the "small stream" and "Rio Frio" in the western part of the Cíbola region. Google Earth image.

candidate site to go to Vernon and then on to McNary and Ft. Apache.

Lyman Lake

RF3:

RF3 is located at Becker Lake along Carnero Creek near US Highway 60 about six miles northwest of Springerville, Arizona. It lies about 16 miles south of the "LyLake X1" small stream candidate site. Two apparently reasonable routes southward from RF3 have been found. The first follows US Highway 191 south to Springerville and continues on to Morenci. This route is labeled "Coronado Trail" on some Arizona state maps from Alpine southward. The second route follows the indicated trail due South from RF3 to connect to State Road 261 and County Road 24 to continue southward to meet US Highway 191 at Hannagan Meadow about ten miles south of Crescent Lake.

Dry Creek, SS X1

RF4:

The trail indicated on Figure 11.2 leading south from "SS X1" crosses Coyote Creek at this site. It is located about 15 miles south of SS X1 and about 1.5 miles north of US Highway 60 midway between Springerville, Arizona and the New Mexico state line. A clear path leads southward from RF4 via "road 4002" to US Highway 191 and south to Nutrioso and Alpine, Arizona. From there, the route follows US Highway 191 to Morenci, Arizona, or, alternatively, it follows US Highway 180 toward Silver City, New Mexico.

RF5:

This site in Cow Springs Draw is very near the state line between Arizona and New Mexico about 14 miles south-southeast of site SS X1 and about 2.5 miles north of US Highway 60 along North Stateline Road. There are two obvious pathways leading southward from RF5. One leaves the site to the southwest to follow US Highway 60 and then joins the path south from RF4 to Nutrioso, Arizona. The second leaves RF5 to the south-southeast and follows trails to meet South Stateline Road which it then follows to Bill Knight Gap. From there it follows Bill Knight Gap Road southward to Luna, New Mexico.

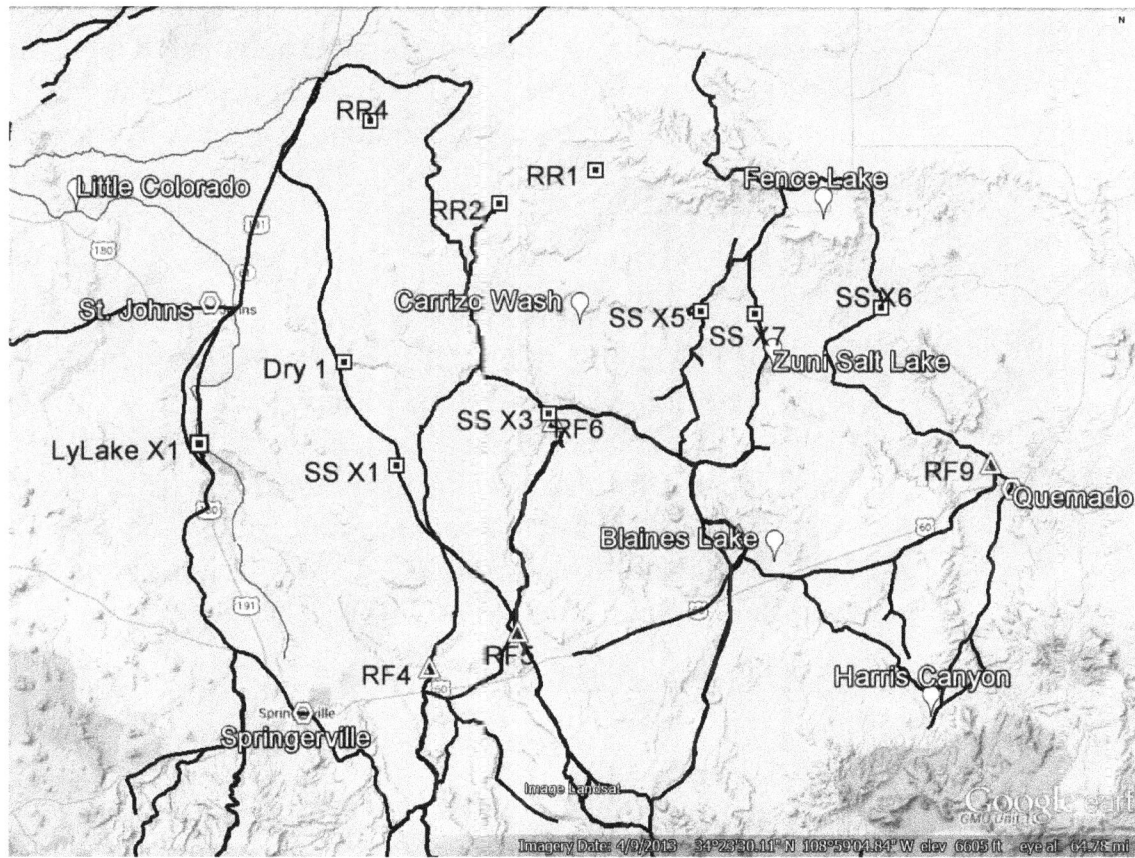

Fig. 11.2. Locations of candidate sites for the "small stream" and the "Rio Frio" in the eastern portion of the Cíbola region. Google Earth imagery.

RR1: (southwest of Zuñi Plateau)

RF6 (SS X3):

RF6 is the same location as SS X3 on Agua Fria Creek. This site is, itself, also a candidate "small stream" relative to the "Red River X4" Rio Bermejo candidate. This site lies in New Mexico about 10.5 miles northeast of the SS X1 site and about 12 miles south of the RR2 site. A good route southward follows County Road A001 (North Stateline Road) to the site of RF5 and then proceeds to Luna, New Mexico as described above (see paragraph

Search for the Rio Frio

for RF5). Since no reasonable routes were found between the Atarque Lake "Rio Bermejo" sites and the RR1 "small stream" site or between RR1 and RF6, it seems unlikely that RF6 would be a viable candidate for the "Rio Frio".

Concho Creek

RF7:

This site lies along Sepulveda Creek about 0.75 miles north of US Highway 60. It is on the Midway Junction Road (Vernon-McNary Road) leading north to Little Ortega Lake on State Road 61 and is about 15 miles from the Concho Creek candidate for the "small stream" site. A most likely southward route would follow the present Vernon-McNary Road from RF7 to McNary, Arizona and then follow State Road 73 to Ft. Apache.

SS X3: Agua Fria Creek

RF5:

This site lies about 16 miles south of SS X3 and is also a candidate relative to SS X1. See the discussion about this candidate "Rio Frio" site under the SS X1 (Dry Creek) entry above.

SS X5: on Carrizo Wash

RF8:

RF8 is another site on Agua Fria Creek and lies about 15 miles upstream southeast from the RF6 candidate site and about four miles north, downstream, from Blaines Lake. From SS X5 to RF8 there is an easily discernible trail found on the imagery (except for about a three-mile section) that is indicated on Figure 11.2. The route southward from RF8 would likely head southwest to US Highway 60 and turn south to Luna via Bill Knight Gap Road.

SS X6: on Carrizo Wash

RF9:

This site is located on Largo Creek about two miles north, downstream, from Quemado, New Mexico. From SS X6 a likely route lies along County Road 37 (Hubbell Draw Road) going southwest to US Highway 601 and then heading southeast toward Quemado to reach RF9. From RF9 the route would go to Quemado and then follow State Highways 32 and 12 south to Apache Creek, New Mexico. Alternatively, the route could head southwest from Quemado on US Highway 60 to join with Old Highway 32 and take that highway alignment south to meet State Highway 32 at Harris Canyon to continue on to Apache Creek.

Pass	Camp	Rio Bermejo	Small Stream	Rio Frio
Pass 8	Camp8	Hardscrabble X1	Sacred Lake	RF1 (Jeff Lake Draw)
				RF2 (Concho Lake)
		Red River X3	Sacred Lake	RF1 (Jeff Lake Draw)
				RF2 (Concho Lake)
		Red River X4	Concho Creek	RF7 (Sepulveda Ck)
			Lyman Lake X1	RF3 (Becker Lake)
			SS X1 (Dry)	RF4 (Coyote Creek)
		Pine Spgs X1	SS X3 (Agua Fria Ck)	RF5 (Cow Spgs Draw)
Pass 2 or Pass 4	Camp 2	Atarque Lake and vicinity	SS X5 (Carrizo Wash)	RF8 (Agua Fria Ck)
			SS X6 (Carrizo Wash)	RF9 (Largo Creek)
			SS X7 (Carrizo Wash)	RF8 (Agua Fria Ck)

Search for the Rio Frio

SS X7: on Carrizo Wash at State Road 601 crossing

RF8:

This site lies on Agua Fria Creek near Blaines Lake. The route from SS X7 to RF8 follows State Road 601 south to join with County Road A7 just north of Zuñi Salt Lake. The route continues along A7 for about 10 miles before turning south about 10 miles east of the SS X3 site as shown on Figure 11.2. The route southward from RF8 goes to Luna, New Mexico as discussed under in the SS X5 paragraph, above.

Summary of Results

The search for the "Rio Frio" in this chapter has provided a rationale for eliminating one of the nine "small stream" candidates found in the previous chapter. Eight additional sites were found that appear to be viable candidates for the Expedition's "Rio Frio". The next step in this investigation will lead to the "Arroyo de la Barranca" from which Coronado approached the Rio Frio.

Table 11.1 presents the relationships among the various candidate sites investigated to this point for the places between the "bad pass" and the "Rio Frio" known to have been visited by the Coronado Expedition on its way to Cíbola.

Chapter 12

Arroyo de la Barranca

Thanks to Juan Jaramillo it is known that the Advance Party of the Expedition to Tierra Nueva under command of the Captain General Francisco Vásquez de Coronado went to a stream they called "Arroyo de la Barranca." But all Jaramillo says is that it took two days to get there from the "Rio de las Balsas" and it would take another one day to reach the "Rio Frio". He offers no description of the place except for the name itself. The word "*arroyo*" usually signifies a small stream or stream bed that has been cut into a channel somewhat below the surrounding landscape. The word "*barranca*" usually refers to a cliff, but it could also signify a system of ravines or small canyons. This "Arroyo de la Barranca" might, then, be expected to be a stream running near a cliff or, perhaps, running in the bottom of a small canyon.

Search for the Arroyo de la Barranca

Starting from each of the locations previously identified as possible candidates for the "Rio Frio", a search of the satellite imagery and topographic maps has been made to locate candidate sites of the Arroyo de la Barranca. As usual, one requirement of this search was that a passable trail route exist between the "Rio Frio" candidate site and the proposed candidate site for "Arroyo de la Barranca". These sites are indicated in Figure 12.1 with "RFx" signifying the "Rio Frio" sites and with "ABx" signifying the "Arroyo de la Barranca" sites. Possible routes between the sites are also indicated on

Figure 12.1. It should be noted that the routes shown do not necessarily mark an actual path of the Expedition, but merely assure that a passable route was available to them. These indicated paths also serve as a reasonable means of establishing the distance likely to have been traveled between the sites.

RF1 (Jeff Lake Draw) and RF2 (Concho Lake)

An imagery and map search found no likely candidate sites for the Arroyo de la Barranca within a one-day journey from either of these two "Rio Frio" candidate sites. Both of these sites are therefore eliminated from consideration as possible "Rio Frio" candidates.

RF3 (Becker Lake)

AB3a:

This "Arroyo de la Barranca" candidate site lies southwest of Springerville, Arizona at the junction of Rosey Creek and Benny Creek very near the Greer Lakes. It is about 16.5 miles from RF3 along the route indicated on Figure 12.1.

AB3b:

This site is on the West Fork of the Little Colorado River about 1.2 miles north of Greer, Arizona and about 1.2 miles south of the AB3a site. It is about 16.8 miles from RF3 via "shortcut" indicated on Figure 12.1.

AB3c:

The site identified as AB3c is about twelve miles southeast of Springerville, Arizona and about 18 miles from RF3. It lies about 0.8 mile northeast up a side canyon off US Highway 180 and is deemed too far off the presumed trail to RF3 as well as being a bit too far distant from RF3.

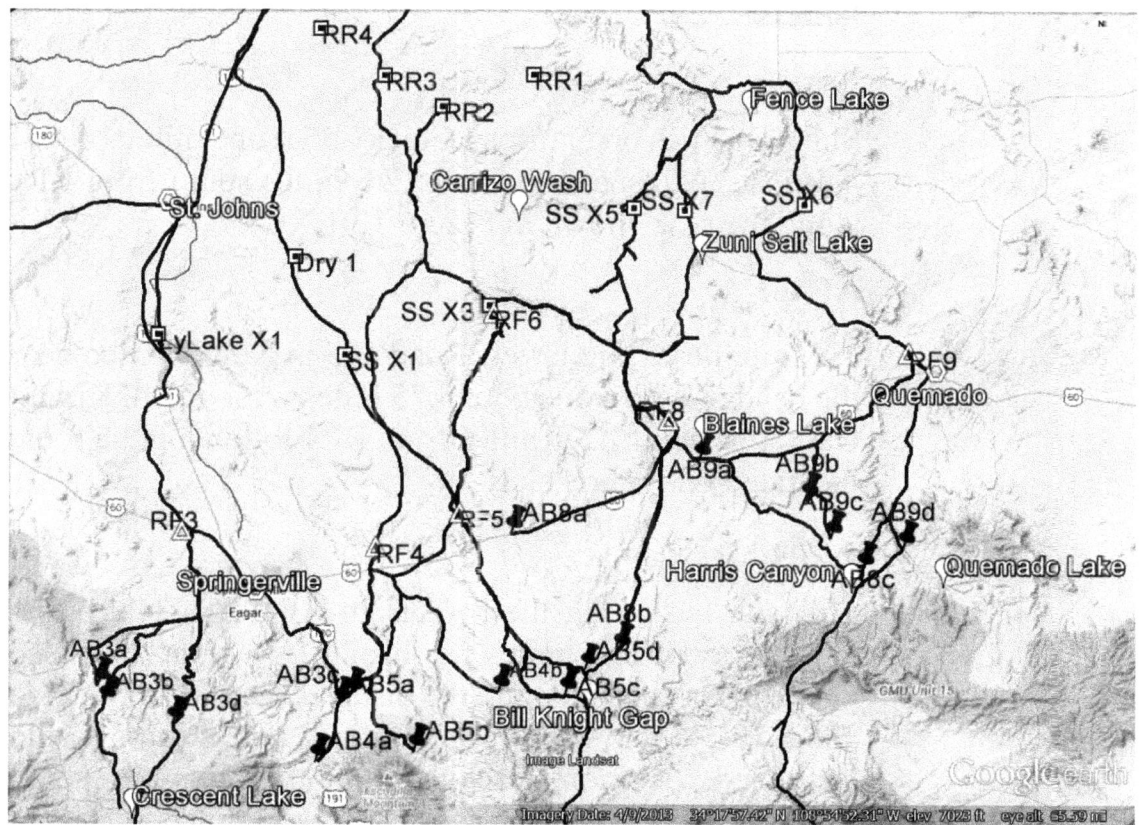

Figure 12.1. Topographic map of region with possible sites for the "Rio Frio" and the "Arroyo de la Barranca" indicated along with possible pathways between them. Google Earth image.

Therefore, this site is judged to be an unlikely candidate (relative to the RF3 site) for the Arroyo de la Barranca. However, this site will later prove to be a candidate relative to both RF4 and RF5.

AB3d:

This site is located at the head of a long canyon which is a tributary of the South Fork of the Little Colorado River and lies about 16 miles south of RF3 along State Road 261.

RF4 (Coyote Creek)

AB4a:

Site AB4a lies on Nutrioso Creek about one mile north of Nutrioso, Arizona and about 17.5 miles south from RF4 along the path shown in Figure 12.1.

AB4b:

This site lies along Forest Road 205 in New Mexico near the head of a canyon about 5.75 miles west of Bill Knight Gap. It is about 15.5 miles from RF4 following the route indicated on Figure 12.1.

AB5a:

This site lies along the path from RF4 to AB4a, but is located about four miles north of AB4a along Nutrioso Creek in Arizona, making the distance from RF4 to AB5a about 13.5 miles, a short day's march. This route would have the Expedition marching *along* the stream for about five miles before making camp. But Jaramillo talks about the distance "between" one stream (the Rio de las Balsas) and this stream (the Arroyo de la Barranca). This would seem strange language to use with respect to marching along the stream unless he was actually referring to the distance between *camp sites* at each stream instead of the streams, themselves.

AB3c:

Site AB3c also lies in Arizona along the path from RF4 to AB4a and lies about one mile northeast of AB5a, making the distance from RF4 to AB3c about 12.5 miles. This would seem to be an abnormally short day's march but not so unreasonably short that the site should be eliminated from consideration.

AB5b:

This site lies along Stone Creek Road in Arizona about one mile south of Skunk Flat Tank and about 17 miles from RF4 on the middle route to Luna, New Mexico indicated on Figure 12.1.

RF5 (Cow Springs Draw about three miles north of US Highway 60 at the state line)

AB5a:

AB5a lies along Nutrioso Creek about 5 miles north of Nutrioso, Arizona. (See entry for this site under RF4, above.) The distance from RF5 is about 18 miles along the shortest route indicated on Figure 12.1.

AB5b:

This site lies along Stone Creek Road in Arizona about one mile south of Skunk Flat and is about 21.5 miles from RF5. This is much too far for a one-day march so that AB5b can be eliminated as an "Arroyo de la Barranca" candidate with respect to RF5 (but not with respect to RF4).

AB5c:

This site lies in New Mexico along Forest Road 205 about 1.5 miles west of Bill Knight Gap along an arroyo within a broader stream bed. At this point the shallow margins of both the stream bed and the arroyo afford a convenient crossing. The distance from RF5 is about 16 miles.

AB5d:

At this New Mexico site, Bill Knight Gap Road crosses Cow Springs Draw at the mouth of a barranca just below the point at which several canyons join Cow Springs Draw. From RF5 to this site is about 15.5 miles along the indicated route.

AB3c:

This site is up a side canyon northeast of AB5a (see description under RF3, above). This site is along the indicated route from RF5 to AB5a but AB3c is about 17 miles from RF5.

RF7 (Sepulveda Creek N of Vernon)

No likely candidates for an "Arroyo de la Barranca" were found within a one-day march from the RF7 candidate site for the "Rio Frio".

RF8 (Agua Fria Creek near Blaines Lake)

AB8a:

This site is in Cow Springs Draw west of RF8 and lies very close to US Highway 60 in New Mexico. The distance from RF8 is about 14.5 miles along a path that closely follows the alignment of Highway 60.

AB8b:

This site in New Mexico lies to the south of RF8 along Forest Road 19 at an arroyo draining multiple hills and side canyons. The distance from RF8 is about 16.5 miles.

AB8c:

At this site, about five miles west of Quemado Lake and about 13 miles south of Quemado, New Mexico, multiple barrancas and hills drain into this one stream, Agua Fria Creek. About ten miles downstream, northwest, from this site, the route goes through an impressive pass between two mesas. This latter feature may have been reason enough for a name like "Arroyo de la Barranca". This site is about 19 miles southeast of RF8 which would have required a seven-march day. AB8c seems a bit far out of the way if the Expedition had taken the indicated trail from the south, but this site cannot be ruled out for that reason. In addition, it would not have been necessary, nor apparently desirable, for the Expedition to cross the stream at this location to reach RF8. It should be noted that Jaramillo did not specifically state that they *crossed* the stream here, but the implication[1] is strong. It is considered unlikely that AB8c (on the way to RF8) would have been the "Arroyo de la Barranca" of the Expedition.

1. F&Fdocs30, p513

RF9 (Largo Creek)

AB9a:

The site AB9a lies on Agua Fria Creek at a unique place where seven arroyos meet in a radial pattern. It is located just upstream south of Blaines Lake just north of US Highway 60 southwest of Quemado, New Mexico, about 18 miles from RF9.

AB9b:

This site is near the head of Agua Fria Creek which is fed by many barrancas within three of four miles above this location. This site appears to afford an easy crossing of the arroyo and is about 14 miles from RF9 along the route indicated on Figure 12.1.

AB9c:

This site, too, lies on Agua Fria Creek and is situated at the mouth of an arroyo about three miles downstream from AB8c. About ten miles further downstream the route goes through an impressive arroyo that could easily warrant the name "Arroyo de la Barranca." AB9c lies about 17 miles from RF9 along the same route that leads from RF9 to AB9b.

Arroyo de la Barranca

AB9d:

This site lies along Lark Creek about three miles downstream, northwest from Quemado Lake, New Mexico. Several side canyons feed into this stream in the vicinity of AB9d. It lies along State Road 32 and the distance from RF9 to AB9d is about 15 miles.

AB8c:

This site was discussed under the paragraph for RF8. It lies about 16 miles south of RF9.

Summary of Arroyo de la Barranca Sites

Considerations for the possible locations of the Arroyo de la Barranca have led to the elimination of three of the previously recognized candidates for the "Rio Frio". At present, the five remaining candidates are: RF3, RF4, RF5, RF8 and RF9.

Based on the search results presented in this chapter, the following locations are deemed to be reasonably probable candidates for the "Arroyo de la Barranca" of Jaramillo's account of the journey of the Coronado Expedition.

AB3a: Southwest of Springerville, Arizona

AB3b: North of Greer, Arizona

AB3c: North of Nutrioso, Arizona (to RF4 and RF5 but not to RF3)

AB3d: South-southwest of Eagar, Arizona

AB4a: North of Nutrioso, Arizona

AB4b: West of Bill Knight Gap, New Mexico

AB5a: North of Nutrioso, Arizona

AB5b: South of Skunk Flat Tank, Arizona (to RF4

but not to RF5)

AB5c: West of Bill Knight Gap, New Mexico

AB5c: Junction of Bill Knight Gap Road and Cow Springs Draw, New Mexico

AB8a: Cow Springs Draw at Highway 60, New Mexico

AB8b: On Bill Knight Gap Road, New Mexico

AB8c: Eight miles west of Quemado Lake, New Mexico (to RF9 but not to RF8)

AB9a: South of Blaines Lake near Highway 60, New Mexico

AB9b: Head of Agua Fria Creek, New Mexico

AB9c: South-southeast of AB9b, New Mexico

AB9d: Northwest of Quemado Lake, New Mexico

These seventeen sites are certainly not all equally probable "Arroyo de la Barranca" candidates based on subjective interpretations of Jaramillo's description, but all have some features that could be taken as fitting his description. All of these candidate sites will be tentatively accepted with the hope of eliminating some of them during the next step in of the investigation. Those eliminations will be based on the lack of reasonable routes to the south or the lack of likely associated candidates for the "Rio de las Balsas" at the appropriate distances.

Chapter 13

Rio de las Balsas

1. F&Fdocs30, p513

Juan Jaramillo recounts that "two short days" before reaching the "Arroyo de la Barranca" from the southwest, the Advance Party had crossed a river on rafts[1] (*balsas*) because, he says simply, "it was swollen." They had approached this river from the south and had named it "Rio de las Balsas". This raft crossing would have been on, or soon after, June 26, 1540 on the Julian calendar (or July 6, 1540 on the modern Gregorian calendar). Since it appears that the Expedition was normally traveling at about 6 leagues per day (16 miles per day), it can be expected that the distance between the "Rio de las Balsas" and the "Arroyo de la Barranca" would be somewhat less than 32 miles. Jaramillo gives no reason for traveling "short" days, but one might conjecture that there was a good camp site not quite a full normal day's march from one or both of these places.

The satellite imagery and topographic maps have been searched in attempting to find likely candidates for the "Rio de las Balsas" crossing site. The first step in this process was to determine probable routes from each of the candidate "Arroyo de la Barranca" sites that lead southward for approximately two days' travel. The second step was then to find possible river crossing locations that might be candidates for the "Rio de las Balsas" site. A discussion of the results of this search is now presented for each of the surviving "Arroyo de la Barranca" candidate sites.

AB3a: Southwest of Springerville, Arizona

RB1a:

This site is located where Forest Road 24 crosses the East Fork of the Black River, about 0.75 mile above its confluence with the West Fork of the Black River. The route southward from AB3a to this site takes the trails indicated on Figure 13.1 to State Highway 261 near Crescent Lake (a likely place for the first night's camp at 15.3 miles) and then goes south for about 13.6 miles. That would put the "Arroyo de la Barranca" and the "Rio de las Balsas" about 29 miles apart. Alternatively, the Expedition could have taken a route with a "Rio de las Balsas" crossing on the West Fork of the Black River about 0.75 mile to the west of RB1a. However, for a northward approach to the Rio de las Balsas, that would have entailed crossing both the West Fork and the main flow of the Black River. For this reason, as well as not finding any likely river crossings in the appropriate vicinity, this latter alternative is deemed very unlikely.

The northbound route from RB1a to the AB3a "Arroyo de la Barranca" candidate site is "nearly" northwest except for the final five or six mile portion which is to the northeast. This could be considered to be in agreement with Jaramillo if a copyist's error is presumed in transcribing "northeast" for "northwest." The route from RB1a southward is almost due south in full agreement with Jaramillo's statement. RB1a is considered to be a viable candidate for the Expedition's "Rio de las Balsas" crossing site.

There appear to be no probable routes through the mountains leading to AB3a from the southwest which leads one to conclude that RB1a will be the westernmost candidate for the "Rio de las Balsas" crossing site.

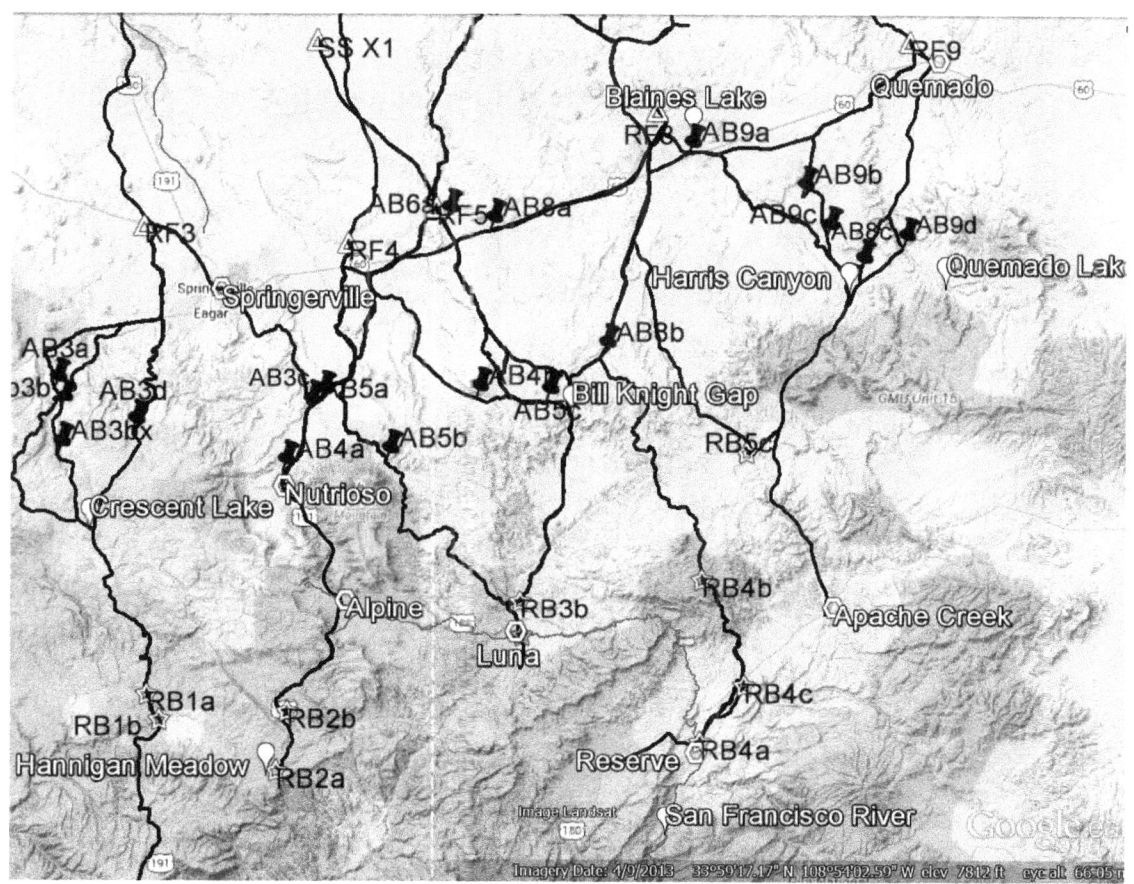

Fig 13.1. Locations of the "Arroyo de la Barranca" and "Rio de las Balsas" candidate sites determined from the descriptions and distances given by the Coronado Expedition chroniclers.

RB1b:

This site is a crossing of Beaver Creek a mile east, upstream, of its confluence with the Black River and lies about two miles south of RB1a. RB1b is about 31 miles south of the AB3a "Arroyo de la Barranca" candidate site and is considered a viable candidate for the "Rio de las Balsas" crossing site. The two sites, RB1a and RB1b, are both on the likely route indicated on Figure 13.1 and lie too close to each other to be discriminated on the basis of this distance analysis. Also, both streams drain sizable regions of mountainous terrain so either could have been "swollen" at the time the Expedition passed through.

AB3b: North of Greer, Arizona

RB1a:

This is the same site discussed in the AB3a paragraph, above. The AB3b site is about 1.5 miles from the AB3a site, so almost everything that applies to the former also applies to this site. AB3b lies about 0.5 mile off the proposed path from RB1a to AB3a but is situated in a broader valley and would have probably made a better camp site than AB3a. AB3b is also about 0.5 mile closer to RB1a so that the distance between them would be about 28.5 miles. The vicinity of Crescent Lake would have made a likely first night camp site for the Expedition before reaching AB3b from RB1a.

RB1b:

This site, also, was discussed in the paragraph about AB3a, above.

AB3c: North of Nutrioso, AZ (to RF5 but not to RF3)

RB2a:

The RB2a site lies where US Highway 191 crosses the head of the westward flowing Beaver Creek. The route to this site from AB3c takes the indicated trail 6.25 miles to Nutrioso, goes south on US Highway 180/191 for the 9.1 miles to Alpine and then continues south on US Highway 191 for about 14 miles for a total distance of about 29.5 miles. This site is located at the northern margin of Hannagan Meadow which is a high mountain meadow that constitutes a local high region. The streams flow down to the east and to the west out of this meadow, so it is difficult to imagine that any of the creeks could have been "swollen" to the extent of requiring rafts to cross. This site is therefore considered unlikely to be the Expedition's "Rio de las Balsas" even though the associated "Arroyo de la Barranca" lies to the northeast and the route south lies almost due south.

RB2b:

This site is where US Highway 191 crosses Campbell Blue Creek and lies about 25 miles south of AB3c and about four miles north of RB2a. Campbell Blue Creek flows eastward and drains a significant mountainous area extending from about four miles west of RB2b. It is conceivable that this creek could have been "swollen" at the time the Coronado Expedition would have crossed it. RB2b is considered a viable candidate for the Expedition's "Rio de las Balsas" crossing.

AB3d: South-southwest of Springerville, Arizona

RB1a:

RB1a could also be a possible "Rio de las Balsas" candidate relative to AB3d as well as one relative to AB3a and AB3b as discussed previously. However, the distance between RB1a and AB3d is only about 21 miles. This would imply two extremely "short" days of travel, but it must be considered a viable candidate since there is no reference for Jaramillo's meaning of "short".

RB1b:

This is the location where County Road 24 crosses Beaver Creek, about a mile above its confluence with the Black River and about 8.5 miles downstream from RB2a. It lies about two miles south of RB1a and is about 23 miles from AB3d along the same route as RB1a. Again, this would imply two short days of travel, but RB1b will also be considered a viable candidate with respect to AB3d (as well as with respect to AB3a and AB3b).

AB4a: North of Nutrioso, Arizona

RB2a:

This site was discussed previously under the paragraph for the "Arroyo de la Barranca" candidate site AB3c. It lies about 24 miles from AB4a, but is considered an unlikely candidate for the "Rio de las Balsas" because of its location near the headwaters of the Beaver Creek.

AB4b: West of Bill Knight Gap, New Mexico

RB3a:

This site is at Luna, New Mexico where the indicated route crosses the San Francisco River. From AB4b the route goes east along State Line Road to Forest Road 19 (Bill Knight Gap Road) and then follows that road all the way to Luna. The river crossing, RB3a, is about 23 miles from AB4b and both of the "short days" would have included significant mountainous terrain. It seems that the region around Hulsey Lake, about half way from Luna to Bill Knight Gap, would have afforded both water and pasture for a good first night's camp. RB3a will be accepted as a viable candidate site.

AB5a: North of Nutrioso, Arizona (to RF4 or RF5)

RB2a:

Site RB2a has been discussed previously under AB3c. AB5a lies about one mile along the route from AB3c to RB2a, so the distance between AB5a and RB2a is about 28 miles which would be a reasonable distance for two "short days" of travel.

RB2b:

Site RB2b also has been discussed previously under AB3c. AB5a lies about one mile along the route from AB3c to RB2b, so the distance between AB5a and RB2b is about 24 miles.

AB5b: Skunk Flat Tank, AZ (to RF4 but not to RF5)

RB3a:

This site is at Luna, New Mexico and lies about 20 miles from AB5b. The path is continuous mountain terrain along Stone Creek Road south from AB5b to Jenkins Creek Road and then to Forest Road 19 about two miles north of Luna. The route then continues along Forest Road 19 and picks up the indicated trail at Luna to RB3a.

AB5c: West of Bill Knight Gap, New Mexico

RB3a:

This site at Luna, New Mexico lies along the route from AB4b to Luna and is about 18 miles from AB5c. This distance is much shorter than even two "short" days' travel and effectively eliminates AB5c as a candidate for the "Arroyo de la Barranca" site since no other candidate "Rio de las Balsas" sites were found within the proper range of AB5c.

AB5d: Bill Knight Gap Rd and Cow Spgs Draw, NM

RB3a:

This is the site at Luna, New Mexico. The distance between AB5d and RB3a is also about 18 miles which is much shorter than even two "short" days' travel. This effectively eliminates AB5d, also, as a candidate for the "Arroyo de la Barranca" site since no other candidate "Rio de las Balsas" sites were found within the proper distance of AB5d, either.

AB8a: Cow Springs Draw at Highway 60, NM

No reasonable pathways were found leading southward to any likely "Rio de las Balsas" crossing sites.

AB8b: On Bill Knight Gap Road, New Mexico

RB3a:

This is the same site discussed previously of the Forest Road 19 (Bill Knight Gap Road) San Francisco River crossing near Luna, New Mexico. Distance from AB8b to RB3a is about 21.5 miles along Bill Knight Gap Road.

RB4a:

This is the site of the State Highway 12 crossing of the San Francisco River at Reserve, New Mexico. This site is about 36 miles from AB8b traveling along the routes of Forest Roads 306 and 49 and is much too far (for "two short days" travel) to be a candidate for the "Rio de las Balsas" crossing.

RB4b:

This site is a crossing of a side feeder creek flowing into Largo Creek along the same route that leads from AB8b to RB4a. The distance from AB8b is about 21 miles which may not be too short for a travel of "two short days".

RB4c:

RB4c is the location where the modern Forest Road 49 crosses Largo Creek just before joining State Highway 12. This site lies about 30 miles from AB8b. This crossing appears to be easily avoided by taking the alternative path just north of State Highway 12 as indicated on Figure 13.1. The Expedition would have almost certainly taken this alternative instead of risking a very dangerous and unnecessary raft crossing if this stream were swollen. This site is considered an unlikely candidate for the "Rio de las Balsas" crossing.

AB9a: South of Blaines Lake near Highway 60, NM

RB5a:

This site lies along Forest Road 306 about 8.6 miles south of AB8a where the road crosses a creek. It is about 24 miles from AB9a along the route leading south to Reserve, New Mexico.

RB5b:

This site lies along a southeastly section of Forest Road 23 (Hardcastle Gap Road) where it crosses Apache Creek about 2.3 miles west of the junction of Forest Road 23 and State Highway 32. The route to RB5b leaves AB9a to the southwest before turning south to meet Hardcastle Gap Road. The distance between RB5b and AB9a is about 24 miles along this route. Access to RB5b from the south would need to be along State Highway 32 in order to require crossing Apache Creek at this location heading northwest. The next of the Expedition's "places" along this "south" path would be the "Rio San Juan". However, no viable candidate for the "Rio San Juan" along the required route was identified, so RB5b must be considered as an unlikely candidate for the Expedition's "Rio de las Balsas".

RB5c:

RB5c is just downstream, south from RB5b and could be considered the same crossing location. For convenience this site designation will be assigned to the eastern alternate route leaving AB9a to the southeast. In order to require a stream crossing here requires that the Expedition would have been approaching RB5c from the southwest along Forest Road 216 from its junction with Forest Road 49. The eastern alternate route would then proceed northeast along the route of State Highway 32 to meet the indicated route to AB9a near Harris Canyon. Along this route the distance to AB9a is about 28.5 miles.

AB9b: Head of Agua Fria Creek, New Mexico

No candidates were found for the "Rio de las Balsas" within acceptable distances from AB9b.

AB9c: South-southeast of AB9b, New Mexico

RB5d:

This site is on the Tularosa River at Apache Creek where State Highway 32 meets State Highway 12. It is about 28 miles from AB9c, but it could serve as a crossing only if the Expedition had come up from the southeast along the route of Forest Road 94. This route from the southeast is considered to be too far east to make RB5d a viable candidate for the Expedition's "Rio de las Balsas". It is expected, rather, that the Expedition would have come to the vicinity of the town of Apache Creek from the southwest (if they came this way, at all) along the route of State Highway 12. This would not have required a river crossing here. Therefore, RB5d is not considered to be a viable candidate site.

AB9d: Northwest of Quemado Lake, New Mexico

RB5d:

This site is on the Tularosa River at Apache Creek where State Highway 32 meets State Highway 12 and is about 28.5 miles from AB9d. See the entry under AB9c for reasons that this site is not considered a viable candidate for the "Rio de las Balsas".

Summary of Results

Based on the lack of viable candidate "Rio de las Balsas" sites within the specified distances from them, nine of the seventeen previously accepted "Arroyo de la Barranca" candidates have been eliminated. The updated list of the eight accepted "Arroyo de la Barranca" candidates is now

AB3a: Southwest of Eagar, Arizona

AB3b: North of Greer, Arizona

AB3c: North of Nutrioso, Arizona

AB3d: South-southwest of Springerville, Arizona

AB4b: West of Bill Knight Gap, New Mexico

AB5a: North of Nutrioso, Arizona

AB8b: South of RF8 on Bill Knight Road, NM

AB9a: South of Blaines Lake on Highway 60, NM

There were also eight sites found to be viable candidates for the Expedition's "Rio de las Balsas" crossing. Acceptance of these sites was based on the distances from the eight surviving candidates for the "Arroyo de la Barranca."

RB1a: At the confluence of the East Fork and the West Fork of the Black River, Arizona (relative to AB3a, AB3b and AB3d)

RB1b: A mile above the confluence of the Black River and Beaver Creek, Arizona (relative to AB3a, AB3b and AB3d)

RB2a: Where US Highway 191 crosses Beaver Creek, Arizona (relative to AB5a)

RB2b: Where US Highway 191 crosses Campbell Blue Creek, Arizona (relative to AB3c and AB5a)

RB3a: San Francisco River at Luna, New Mexico (relative to AB4b)

RB4b: Forest 205 west of Bill Knight Gap, New Mexico (relative to AB8b)

RB5a: Forest Road 306 crossing of [unknown] creek, New Mexico (relative to AB9a)

RB5c: Forest Road 23 crossing of Apache Creek, New Mexico (relative to AB9a)

This investigation will next consider the southward path to the "Rio San Juan" in an attempt to discover Coronado's trail to Cíbola by reversing his progress.

Chapter 14

To the Rio San Juan

According to Juan Jaramillo's account, the Advance Party of the Coronado Expedition approached the Rio de las Balsas from the south with a march of "two full days" after leaving the Rio San Juan. They had arrived at the San Juan[1] on the evening before Saint John's Day, 1540 – the evening June 24 on their Julian calendar or July 4 on the current Gregorian calendar.

In this instance Jaramillo seems a bit unsure about the time of travel from one river to the next, but nevertheless, the current search for the Rio San Juan will be based on his "two full days" memory. The only additional information Jaramillo supplies is that the terrain between the two rivers was "somewhat broken". With this information, an attempt was conducted to extend possible pathways southward from each of the "Rio de las Balsas" candidate sites identified in the previous chapter to possible candidates for the "Rio San Juan". This search utilize satellite imagery and USGS topographic maps.

Jaramillo's subjective description of the land along this portion of the route as "somewhat broken" is difficult to interpret precisely so that information will not be used to discriminate between possible routes. His "two full days" of travel can probably be taken to translate into about 32 miles or perhaps a bit more. Jaramillo uses three terms to express a day's march: a "day", a "short day" and a "full day". It is thought that a normal day's march was about six leagues (or about 16 miles) but the distance traveled in

1. F&Fdocs30, p513

a "short day" or a "full day" is a matter of conjecture.

Four of the identified "Rio de las Balsas" candidate sites depend on southern access along US Highway 191 in eastern Arizona. However, this route is a high mountain road and has no possible "San Juan" river crossings south of the four sites for at least 50 miles. There are two other possible routes leading southward from the four sites, one to the west along Upper Eagle Creek Road, and one to the east along the Blue River, but neither of these routes seems to be a reasonable means of reaching any of the four sites. Therefore these four sites can be eliminated as viable candidates for the "Rio de las Balsas" crossing:

> *RB1a: At the confluence of East Fork and West Fork of the Black River, Arizona*
>
> *RB1b: A mile above the confluence of the Black River and Beaver Creek, Arizona*
>
> *RB2a: Where US Highway 191 crosses Beaver Creek near Hannigan Meadow, Arizona*
>
> *RB2b: Where US Highway 191 crosses Campbell Blue Creek, Arizona*

Routes leading toward the south from the remaining four viable "Rio de las Balsas" candidate sites will be addressed for each site, individually.

RB3a: San Francisco River at Luna, New Mexico

SJ1a:

This site is a road crossing of the San Francisco River about three-quarters of a mile below its confluence with Deep Creek. The site lies about eight miles northwest of Mogollon, New Mexico and about 31.6 miles from RB3a along the present route of US Highway 180.

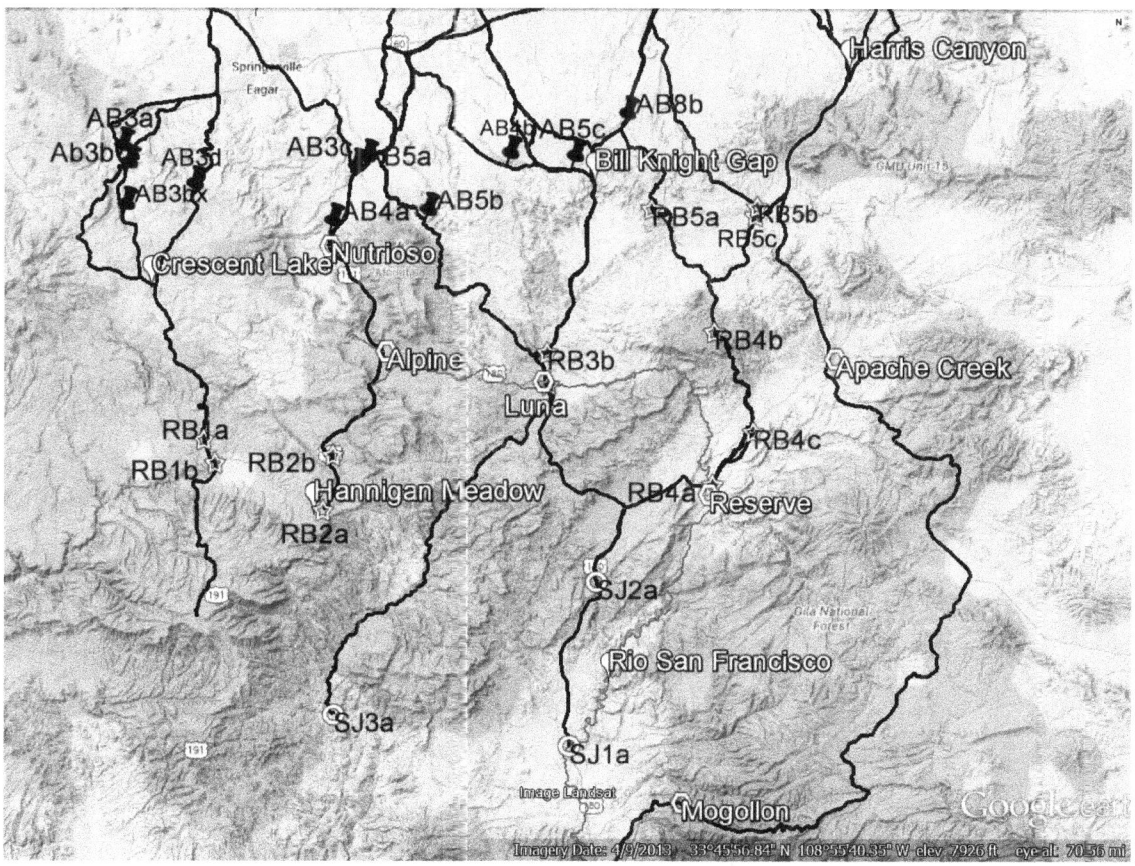

Fig 14.1. Location of candidate sites for the Rio de las Balsas (RBxx) and the Rio San Juan (SJxx) showing probable or possible routes between them.

SJ3a:

This site could lie at any of several side canyons feeding into the Blue River in eastern Arizona between KP Creek and Strayhorse Canyon. The Blue River is a major river in that region and joins the San Francisco River about 20 miles south of SJ3a. These side canyons range from about 31 miles to 35.5 miles from RB3a. The route to them is along Forest Road 216, following the Blue River, going southwest from Luna, New Mexico. While these sites are within the proper distance from RB3a, Jaramillo's statement that it was a two day journey "between streams" (referring to the Rio San Juan and the Rio de las Balsas) would seem strange language to describe a march *along* a river. Also the direction of march from any of these side canyons to RB3a would be to the northeast while Jaramillo states that the direction was "to the north". These SJ3a sites are considered to be non-viable candidates for the Expedition's "Rio San Juan".

RB5a: Forest Road 306 creek crossing, New Mexico

SJ2a:

This site is where US Highway 180 crosses Cottonwood Canyon at the confluence with Saliz Canyon. It lies about 33.7 miles from RB5a.

RB5c: FR 23 crossing of Apache Creek, New Mexico

SJ2a:

The location of this site is where US Highway 180 crosses Cottonwood Canyon at the confluence with Saliz Canyon. The distance between RB5c and SJ2a is about 33 miles via Forest Road 216 southwest from RB5c to Forest Road 49 to State Highway 12 and passing through Reserve, New Mexico.

There is another probable Indian trade route leading southward from "Rio de las Balsas" candidate sites RB5c and RB5d. It is indicated by the easternmost route depicted on Figure 14.1. This route follows Bursum Road between Glenwood and Mogollon, New Mexico most of the way to the two RB5 sites. However, no candidate "Rio San Juan" candidate site was located along this route within the proper distance from either of those two sites. This route is, therefore, eliminated from consideration. The next probable Indian trade route lies to the east of Silver City, New Mexico and goes up the Mimbres River valley. It then continues up Black Canyon through the Forest Service's Beaverhead Work Camp and along the western edge of the San Augustine Plains. There it meets Bursum Road on the path discussed previously. This latter route has a possible "Rio San Juan" site near the Beaverhead Work Camp, but lies too far east to be considered a viable route of the Coronado Expedition.

Summary of Routes

Five possible routes for the Expedition to have taken on its north bound journey between the "Rio San Juan" and the "Rio de las Balsas" have been identified. The western-most route generally follows US Highway 191 in Arizona and the next most westerly route follows the Blue River in Arizona and New Mexico. Both of these routes have been judged to be unlikely paths for the Expedition. The eastern-most route follows the Mimbres River in New Mexico before continuing northward to the San Augustine Plains. The second-most easterly route departs from US Highway 180 to follow Bursum Road through Mogollon, New Mexico on it northward course. Both of these eastern routes have also been eliminated due primarily to a lack of associated "Rio San Juan" candidate sites.

This leaves only one viable route for the Expedition in this portion of its journey. This one remaining route generally follows US Highway 180 in western New Mexico through the Mangas Trench as far north as the junction of US Highway 180 and State Highway 12. At that point the possible route splits, one branch going northwest to site RB3a at Luna, New Mexico and the other branch going northeast toward Reserve, New

Table 14.1 Candidate Sites and Connecting Paths

Pueblo	Pass	Camp	Rio Bermejo	Small Stream	Rio Frio	Arroyo de la Barranca	Rio de las Balsas	Rio San Juan
Hawikuh			Hardscrbl X1					
				Sacred Lake	✱			
Chalo:wa	8	8	Red River X3					
				Concho Creek	✱			
Kechiba:wa			Red River X4			AB3a ✱		
				Lyman Lake X1	RF3	AB3d ✱		
Kwakin'a ✱						AB3b ✱		
				SS X1	RF4	AB5a ✱		
						AB4b		
				SS X5			RB3a	SJ1a
					RF8	AB8b		
				SS X7			RB4b	
			Atarque Lake					
Halona:wa							RB5a	SJ2a
				SS X6	RF9	AB9a		
Kyakima	2 or 4	2					RB5c	
Mats'akya						AB5a ✱		
			Pine Spgs X1	SS X3	RF5			
						AB3c ✱		

Mexico. This more eastern branch later splits again with one branch going northwest to RB5a and RF8 and with the other branch going northeast to RB5b and RF9.) Along this route, two possible locations for the Expedition's "Rio San Juan" were identified.

> **SJ1a:** US Highway 180 crossing of Rio San Francisco about eight miles northwest of Mogollon, New Mexico.

> **SJ2a:** US Highway 180 crossing of Cottonwood Canyon about 18 miles south of Luna, New Mexico.

The more southern of the two sites, "SJ1a" is located at a Rio San Francisco crossing and is associated with "Rio de las Balsas" candidate sites along both branches of the route north. The more northern of these two "Rio San Juan" sites, labeled "SJ2a" is at Saliz Canyon and is associated only with the eastern branch of the route leading to the RB5a and RB5c "Rio de las Balsas" candidate sites.

Based on these two accepted candidates for the "Rio San Juan" site, five of the previously accepted eight "Rio de las Balsas" candidates can now be eliminated. The three sites remaining as viable candidates for the Expedition's "Rio de las Balsas" are:

RB3a: San Francisco River at Luna, New Mexico

RB5a: Forest Road 306 crossing of [an unknown] creek, New Mexico

RB5c: Forest Road 23 northeasterly crossing of Apache Creek, New Mexico.

Table 14.1 presents a graphical summary of all the candidate sites considered viable at this point in the investigation starting with the pueblos at Cíbola. The arrows in this chart indicate that pathways were found between sites while the "X" indicates that viable candidate sites and/or reasonable paths further in the progression were not found.

Note that there is only one path indicated that would lead from the "Rio San Juan" to any of the three pueblos in the western group at Cíbola. This path goes through SJ1a, RB3a, AB4b, RF4, SS X1, Red River X4, Camp 8 and Pass 8. The eastern group of three pueblos has one double-branched path leading northward from SJ1a and one single-branched path leading northward from SJ2a. From SJ1a this path would go through either RB3a or RB4b to AB8b to RF8 to either SS X5 or SS X7 to the Atarque Lake vicinity to Camp 2 to Pass2 (or Pass4). The path from SJ2a would go through either RB5a or RB5c to AB9a to SS X6 to the Atarque Lake vicinity to Camp 2 to

Pass 2 (or Pass4).

There were, of course, a multitude of paths which were readily available to the Expedition. The chroniclers of the Coronado Expedition have offered only meager descriptions of sites and imprecise information on the distances between sites, but this investigation has resulted in only two possible approach routes to Cíbola. The validity of this result, of course, is not an absolute certainty, but unless additional information comes to light, little further refinement of this portion of the route is expected to be made (except, perhaps, for a better discernment of actual trails).

The investigation of Coronado's route to the south of the Rio San Juan will continue in the following chapter with a study of the possible paths between the "Deep Canyon" to the Rio San Juan.

Chapter 15

The Deep Canyon

Both of the primary chroniclers of the Coronado Expedition, Juan Jaramillo and Pedro de Castañeda, mention a "deep canyon" on the route prior to reaching the Rio San Juan. According to Jaramillo's account[1] the Expedition reached the Rio San Juan from the "nearly" southwest in three days' travel from a place he described as a "deep arroyo and canyon" where they found water and pasture "for the horses". Pedro de Castañeda[2] describes this place as "a river in a very deep canyon". This is one of the very few places for which Castañeda offers even a hint of a description. It might be surmised that the "deep canyon" was an extraordinary experience. Jaramillo gives no other description of the terrain or conditions between the "deep canyon" and the Rio San Juan, so once again only the distance and direction are available to guide the search.

The documentation of Jaramillo's account used for this investigation is an English translation of a transcript of a copy of his original (or more likely a scribe's original). It is unknown how many times and by how many scribes that copies were made in the process leading to the transcript and translation used in this study. This copying and re-copying process very likely resulted in errors and one of the more likely of the errors is the interchange of "northeast" and "northwest". Therefore, Jaramillo's documented statement that the Expedition traveled "northeast" between the "deep canyon" and the Rio San Juan could actually have originally read that they traveled northwest, instead.

1. F&Fdocs30, p513

2. F&Fdocs28, p395

Because of this, the direction will be ignored and the present investigation will depend primarily on only the distance information. But this also presents something of a difficulty because Jaramillo expressed some uncertainty in this specific instance, saying that it took three days "I think" to go from the "deep canyon" to the Rio San Juan. However, for other travel times for which there is some corroboration, Jaramillo's memory has been correct so the present search for the "deep canyon" will tentatively be based on the "three days" period.

A study of the satellite imagery and topographic maps of the region shows that the most probable route for the Expedition's journey was along the Mangas Trench between SJ1a or SJ2a and points southward. High, rugged mountains flank either side of this route all the way to the south end of the Big Burro Mountains, about 25 miles south of Silver City, New Mexico. There are very few places along that portion of the Mangas Trench that afford a reasonable route through the mountains to the west or southwest. Only four of these routes lie in the region of current interest (i.e., in a region that may contain candidate sites for the "Deep Canyon").

State Highway 78

Continuing to trace the Coronado Expedition's route in reverse, one possible route would follow US Highway 180 south from either SJ1a or SJ2a as far as the junction with State Highway 78 where it would turn to the west. This route has two branches. One branch follows Highway 78 all the way into Three Way, Arizona where it meets US Highway 191. The other branch turns southward off Highway 78 in the vicinity of Mule Creek, New Mexico, and winds its way to Apache Creek.

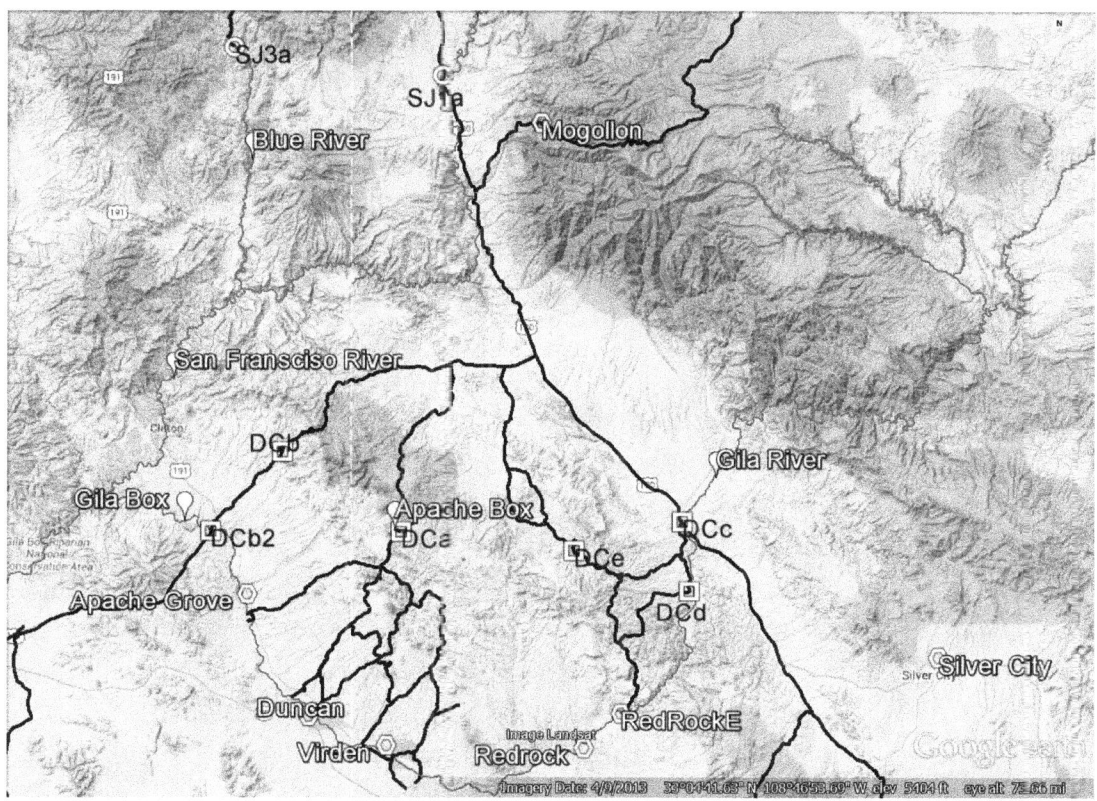

Fig 15.1. *Location of the candidate sites for the Expedition's "Deep Canyon" site. The two center sites have been judged to be improbable locations. Google Earth image.*

DCb:

On the first branch, there is a candidate "Deep Canyon" site, labeled "DCb" on Figure 15.1, where the road crosses Mule Creek in Arizona. (There are two different streams named "Mule Creek" in this vicinity, one in Arizona and one in New Mexico, and both are crossed by Highway 78. It is the one in Arizona that is of current concern.) The site "DCb" is about 52 miles (a long three-day march) from SJ1a and about 64 miles (a reasonable four-day march) from SJ2a.

The Deep Canyon

DCb2:

A second "Deep Canyon" candidate site, labeled DCb2, is also on this route and is located at the Gila River near the town of Three Way, Arizona. This site is about 60 miles from SJ1a which is too far for a three-day march but which would be a reasonable distance for a four-day march.

DCa:

The second branch turns south from Highway 78 onto Y6 Road and follows Brushy Mountain Road to Apache Creek. From that point, it follows the creek bed, ranch roads and trails through a very spectacular "Deep Canyon" candidate site, called "Apache Box" labeled DCa on Figure 15.1. There the route turns southward to join Bitter Creek Road about 14.5 miles north of Virden, New Mexico. From SJ1a to DCa is a distance of about 51 miles, a long three-day march.

Highway 180 to Cliff

DCc:

Continuing southbound along US Highway 180 from the State Road 78 junction, there is another possible candidate "Deep Canyon" site just south of Cliff, New Mexico. This site, labeled DCc, is where Highway 180 crosses the Gila River and lies about 43 miles south of SJ1a (a short, but not unreasonably short, three-day march) and about 56 miles south of SJ2a (a reasonable four-day march). The route to the south of this site would almost certainly have continued down the Mangas Trench. There may be a pathway though the mountains following the Gila River, but this country is very rugged and is cut by many side canyons so that the likelihood of an Indian trade route along the river is extremely remote.

H Bar Y Ranch Road to Redrock

DCe:

This route turns south off State Highway 78 about 2.5 miles west of its junction with US Highway 180 and continues past the H Bar Y ranch headquarters. It then follows the path of ranch roads and eventually meets Bald Knoll Road about eleven miles west of Cliff, New Mexico. The "deep canyon" candidate site DCe lies on the southern continuation of this route about 45 miles from SJ1a or about 58 miles from SJ2a. DCe lies a reasonable three-day travel from SJ1a or a reasonable four-day travel from SJ2a, and since Jaramillo's "three days, I think" is imprecise, one is obliged to consider both possibilities. This route continues southward to cross the Gila River at Redrock, New Mexico.

McCauley Road and Bald Knoll Road to Redrock

DCd:

Another plausible route leaves US Highway 180 at Cliff, New Mexico at site DCc and proceeds southward along McCauley Road and Bald Knoll Road to join the path from DCe to Redrock. Along this route, DCd is about six miles from DCc or about 49 miles from SJ1a and about 62 miles from SJ2a. Again, these are reasonable three-day or four-day journeys and both DCd and DCe will tentatively be accepted as viable candidates for the "deep canyon" of the Expedition's accounts.

Considerations and Confidence

Based on distances from the "Rio San Juan" candidate sites, six candidates for the "Deep Canyon" site mentioned by Juan Jaramillo and Pedro de Castañeda have been found. Each of these will now be investigated in more detail to develop some level of confidence that they could, indeed, be the site visited by the Expedition on its journey northward.

DCa:

This is a very deep and narrow section of a canyon called the Apache Box through which Apache Creek flows. (This is a different "Apache Creek" from the one encountered previously. That one joins the Tularosa River along State Highway 12 northeast of Reserve, New Mexico.) DCa lies in western New Mexico about 17 miles north of Virden. It has good trails leading to it from the south and away from it to the north. The Expedition's march would have been upstream where the canyon widens to provide bottom land pasturage for the horses and livestock about four miles from the point of entry to the canyon.

This site seems to fit Jaramillo's and Casteñeda's descriptions very well, but there are several problems with its location.

1. To reach this canyon, the Expedition would have had to cross the Gila River about one day previously and there is no mention of the Expedition's having done so. The chroniclers of the Expedition seem to have been meticulous in recording the rivers and the distances between them, so this lack of a mention of a necessary river crossing is a serious problem. However, it is possible that the flow of the Gila was low enough for the Expedition to not consider it a major river and, therefore, to not take note of it.

2. The narrowness of the canyon and the likelihood of high water would make this a dangerous passage. The Expedition would probably have been passing through this canyon during mid- to late- June, 1540.

The Rio de las Balsas, a little to the north and several days later, was flooding when the Expedition reached it, so the region could have been getting seasonal rains and Apache Creek could well have been running high. Even if this canyon were on a normal trade route, it is somewhat questionable that the Expedition would have been guided that way by the local Indians during the rainy season. On the other hand, Apache Box lies along the upper reaches of Apache Creek so this may not have been a concern.

3. The route leading away from DCa would have taken the Expedition almost due north whereas Jaramillo said they went to the northeast.

DCb:

State Highway 78 crosses Mule Creek and Black Jack Canyon just a few miles west of the Arizona - New Mexico state line. This crossing appears to match Jaramillo's description of the "Deep Canyon" fairly well in that the canyon can be described as "deep" and has a significant area of flat bottom land which probably supported grass for pasture. It does not, however, seem to match Casteñeda's description of being "very deep" and probably cannot be considered "extraordinary". Also, it suffers the same difficulty as DCa of being within about a one-day march from the Gila River when no such river is mentioned by the Expedition's chroniclers. On the positive side, it should be noted that the route northward lies to the northeast – in agreement with Jaramillo's account.

DCb2:

This site is the Gila River crossing at Three Way, Arizona. The river course could easily be described as

The Deep Canyon

a deep canyon with a fairly broad, flat bottom and has some reasonable natural crossing access routes within about one-quarter of a mile of the present bridge over the river. While this site fits Jaramillo's description, it lies about a four-day march from the Rio San Juan candidate site, SJ1a, instead of his "three days, I think" journey. Accepting the possibility of a four-day journey from one river to the next seems preferable to accepting a three-day journey with its inherent "missing river" problem. For this site, also, it should be noted that the route northward lies to the northeast – in agreement with Jaramillo. Therefore, this site will be considered a viable candidate for the Expedition's "Deep Canyon" location. DCb2 is one of the two "Deep Canyon" candidate sites that does not suffer the "missing river" problem.

DCc:

This site is another possible crossing of the Gila River. The site, labeled DCc on Figure 15.1, is about 1.25 miles south of Cliff, New Mexico. Another likely crossing point in the immediate vicinity lies two miles upstream near the town of Gila, New Mexico where State Highway 211 crosses the Gila River. This latter site is above the confluence of Bear Creek with the Gila River, and would have entailed crossing Bear Creek also. The choice of which site to use may well have depended on the flow rate of the streams when the Expedition arrived there. During the rainy season it might be preferable to cross two smaller streams than to cross the one combined flow below their confluence.

This canyon has a large flat bottom which probably supported lush vegetation in 1540. The primary difficulty with this site is that the canyon is not extremely deep. It is only about a hundred feet deep, but that may have seemed enough to be called "deep" compared to the many smaller arroyos they probably crossed on their way northward. This site, at either crossing location, is about 43 miles from SJ1a (a rather short 3-day march) and about 55 miles from SJ2a (a rather short 4-day march). The DCc site will tentatively be considered to be a somewhat viable location for the Expedition's "Deep Canyon" crossing, in spite of it not being a "very deep canyon". The route northward leads to the northwest – perhaps in agreement with Jaramillo if the previously noted confusion of "northeast" and "northwest" is considered. DCc is the second of the two "Deep Canyon" candidate sites that does not suffer the "missing river" problem.

DCd:

The DCd site could be described very much the same as DCc except that the canyon here is slightly deeper and is walled by hills so that Castañeda's "very deep" description might be more appropriate. The distances from DCd to SJ1a and SJ2a would be reasonable three-day and four-day travels. This site is considered a viable candidate "Deep Canyon" location.

DCe:

This site is where the trail indicated on Figure 15.1 crosses Sycamore Canyon. At about 150 feet deep here, this canyon might easily be described as "deep" or even as "very deep" compared to the arroyos and canyons the Expedition would have encountered to this point on its northbound journey. The route northward lies to the northwest – perhaps in agreement with Jaramillo. DCe is considered to be a viable candidate "Deep Canyon" location even though it also suffers the "missing river" problem.

Summary

The information known about the "Deep Canyon" and the routes between it and the "Rio San Juan" is insufficient to eliminate any of the six "Deep Canyon" candidate sites found by the imagery and map search. Acceptance of some of these sites is based on either a three-day travel or a four-day travel and/or a lack of knowledge of whether the Expedition was traveling fast or slow. The search for the sites themselves was based on a very subjective interpretation of Jaramillo's "arroyo in a deep canyon" and Casteñeda's "stream in a very deep canyon". Terrain features were found that seemed to reasonably fit those descriptions of the "Deep Canyon".

Both of the previous candidates for the "Rio San Juan", SJ1a and SJ2a, also remain viable with the latter of these dependent upon a four-day journey to DCc instead of Jaramillo's "three days, I think" journey.

Chapter 16

Chichilticale

In the reverse tracing of the Coronado Expedition, the next place mentioned by the chroniclers is "Chichilticale," but precisely what they mean by that name is unclear. Juan Jaramillo[1] describes the location of Chichilticale as being at "the foot of a mountain range", but it appears he is saying that the mountain range, itself, is called Chichilticale. Pedro de Castañeda[2] says that "in the vicinity" of Chichilticale they found a building made of "reddish or bright red earth" and that it was "large and clearly seemed to have been strong." Castañeda, too, seems to apply the name to the entire mountain range and not just to a pueblo building structure. He also says that after leaving Chichilticale[3] (presumably, the mountain range), it took "three days" to reach the "Deep Canyon". The only thing that Jaramillo says about that part of the journey is that they were traveling toward the "northeast" and crossed a mountain range[1], but, uncharacteristically, gives no travel time.

The search for the location of Chichilticale using the satellite imagery and topographic maps began at the "Deep Canyon" candidate sites found in the previous chapter. This search included two objectives. First, a search for the western slopes of a mountain range at a distance of about 48 miles or more from the "deep canyon" sites was conducted. Alternatively, a search for a possible site of the "building" at a distance of about 48 miles from the "Deep Canyon" site was undertaken while requiring the presence of a mountain range between the two sites. This

1. F&Fdocs30, p513

2. F&Fdocs28, p417

3. F&Fdocs28, p395

Chichilticale 195

alternate search was included to cover the possibility that the chroniclers were actually referring to the building site instead of the mountain range. Such searching revealed several candidate sites for Chichilticale:

Chi0:

The Chi0 site is located west of Soldiers Farewell Hill about 47 miles from DCc via Separ Road south from State Highway 90 at White Signal, New Mexico. This distance would have required a nominal three-day travel.

Chi1:

This site is southwest of the Big Burro Mountains between Knight Peak and Hornbrook Mountain about 48 miles from DCc via US Highway 180 and Mangas Valley Road to State Highway 90 or about 44 miles from DCc via Redrock Road and Thompson Canyon.

Chi2:

The Chi2 site lies on the west slope of Summit Hills,

> a) about 52 miles from DCc via McCauley Road and Game Department Road, staying west of the Gila River from Cliff, New Mexico to Redrock, New Mexico and then following State Highway 464 to Fuller Road.

> b) about 46 miles from DCd via McCauley Road and Game Department Road staying west of Gila River from Cliff, New Mexico to Redrock, New Mexico and then following State Highway 464 to Fuller Road.

> c) about 48 miles from DCe east via Bald Knoll Road and south via Game Department Road to the Gila River crossing at RedRock and then southwest

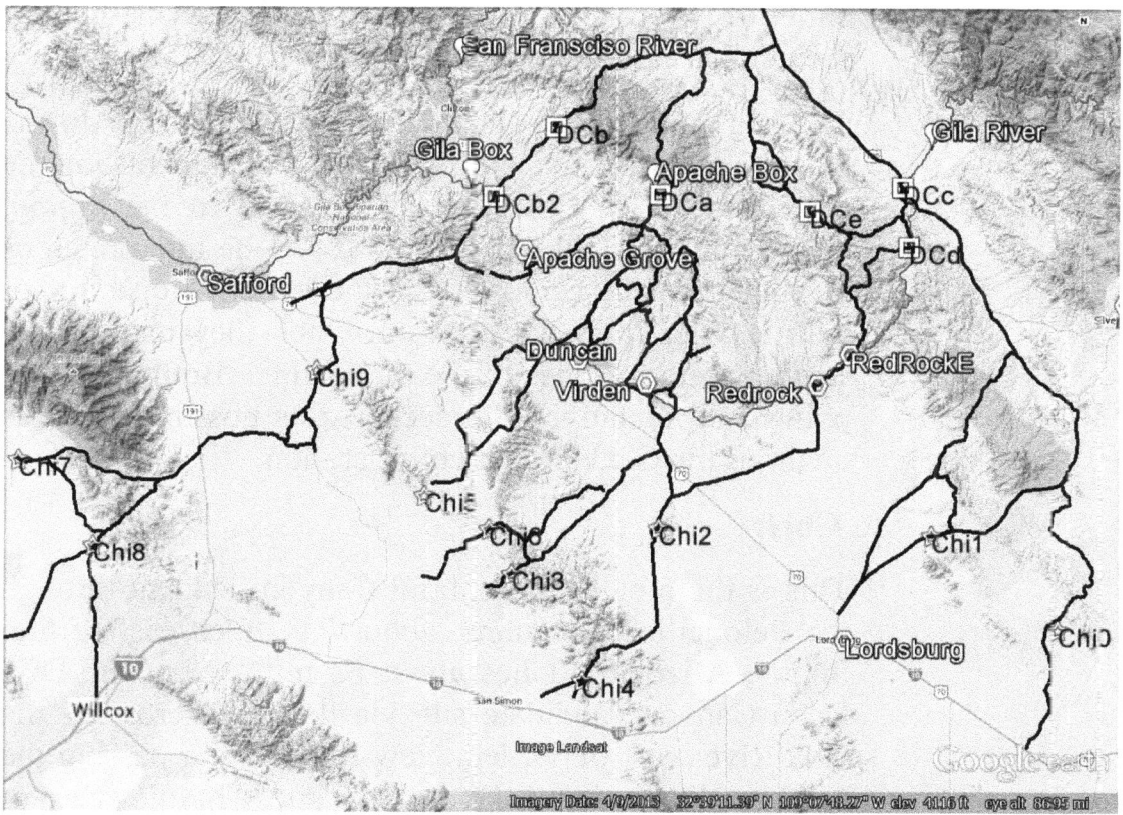

Fig 16.1. Satellite Image showing locations for the "Deep Canyon" and "Chichilticale" candidate sites. Google Earth image.

via Redrock Road and Fuller Canyon Road.

All three of these routes could have required three days.

Chi3:

This site is near Orange Butte, a peak in the western part of the Peloncillo Mountains in far eastern Arizona. It lies about 53 miles from the DCa Deep Canyon candidate site via the far eastern route from that site as shown on Figure 16.1. About 8 or 9 miles northeast of the Chi3 site, across the Peloncillo Mountains, is a reasonable campsite from which it would be about three days' travel to DCa via either of two routes, crossing the Gila River one mile or three miles east of Virden, New Mexico.

The beginning point of the "three days" journey to the Deep Canyon is not clear from the documents of the Expedition. If "Chichilticale" referred to the *region*, then leaving Chichilticale could easily be interpreted as leaving from the camp site on the eastern slopes rather than leaving from the place at which they had arrived on the western slopes of the mountains. Both departure points will tentatively be accepted as possible and this qualifies the Chi3 site for consideration.

Chi4:

This is the mouth of Doubtful Canyon, leading through the Peloncillo Mountains, about 7.5 miles east of San Simon, Arizona. It lies about 62 miles from the DCa Deep Canyon candidate site via the route crossing the Gila River east of Virden, New Mexico and passing the Chi2 candidate site. Like the Chi3 site, Chi4 lies west of a mountain range which the Expedition would have had to cross before starting the count of the "three days" it took to get to the DCa site.

Chi5:

This site is located at the southern end of the Whitlock Mountains in Arizona just west of Park Lake. There are two branches to the route between Chi5 and the DCa "deep canyon" site. Chi5 lies about 41 miles from the DCa site via the Gila River crossing northwest of Duncan, Arizona and via the eastern branch indicated on Figure 16.1 from there southward. This branch route goes through the northern part of the Peloncillo Mountains and appears to be a rather difficult path. This makes the rather short distance of 41 miles seem quite reasonable for a three-day journey. Along the western-most branch indicated on Figure 16.1 leading to the Duncan-Virden valley, Chi5 is about 44 miles from DCa. This route avoids the rough mountainous terrain by staying west of the Peloncillo Mountains for most of the way. Accepting Chi5 as a candidate Chichilticale site would require one to interpret the chroniclers' "three days" as starting when they left the Chi5 site.

Chi6:

The Chi6 site lies just west of the Peloncillo Mountains about midway between the Chi3 site and the Chi5 site. It lies about 55 miles from DCa via the eastern Virden, New Mexico Gila River crossing via the northern branch of the route through the Lazy B ranch. The acceptance of this site as a candidate Chichilticale site is based on the Expedition's crossing the Peloncillo Mountains before starting the "three day" journey to DCa. There appears to be a good camp site with probable water and pasture about 9 miles along this route toward the Lazy B.

Chi7:

This site is on the southwest flank of Mount Graham in southeast Arizona just south of Fort Grant in the Sulphur Springs Valley. It is about 67 miles from DCb2 on the Gila River. A one-day travel would have taken the Expedition across that part of the Mount Graham range, putting itself within a three-day journey from the DCb2 site via the westernmost route shown on Figure 16.1.

Chi8:

The Chi8 site is also on the southwest flank of Mount Graham in southeast Arizona in the Sulphur Springs Valley and lies about ten miles southeast of the Chi7 site. Again, a one-day travel would have taken the Expedition across the Mount Graham range at that location, putting itself within a three-day journey from the DCb2 along the same path that it would have been taken from Chi7.

Chi9:

This site is at the northwest tip of the Whitlock Mountains about 15 miles southeast of Safford, Arizona. It lies about 47 miles from the "Deep Canyon" candidate, DCa in the Apache Box, along the route crossing the Gila River at Apache Grove, Arizona. This is the northernmost of the routes leading southward from DCa to the Rio Gila as indicated on Figure 16.1.

Likelihood of Site Candidates

Inspection of the satellite imagery and topographic maps has resulted in ten candidate sites for the "Chichilticale" mentioned by the Coronado Expedition's chroniclers, Juan Jaramillo and Pedro de Castañeda. These ten sites were determined using only the distance from "Deep Canyon" candidate sites and the fact the Chichilticale was described as either being at the foot of a mountain or, perhaps, the mountain itself.

It must be pointed out, however, that the distances along the indicated possible paths are approximate and that shortcuts could easily have been possible. For instance, the large southeasterly loop on the path from Chi7 and Chi8 to the Gila River could have been eliminated by a shortcut bypassing the entire loop. This could then put the "Deep Canyon" site DCb back into consideration or, alternatively, it might put the locations of Chi7 and Chi8 about eight miles further toward the south or southwest. This latter condition would possibly put either of those two sites well into the Sulphur Springs Valley. This, in turn, would likely have yielded a better chance of the builders of the old pueblo to have found a supply of the "reddish or bright red" clay needed for its construction as reported[2] by Casteñeda.

A valley location for Chichilticale would also be more consistent than a mountain location with the fact that the Melchoir Diaz and Juan de Zaldivar entrada wintered there in 1539-1540. That expedition would have needed ample supplies of both water and pasture for their horses. Such supplies would certainly have been more plentiful in the valley than in the smaller canyon bottoms found in the mountainous terrain.

Not all of the ten "Chichilticale" candidate sites are equally probable from the viewpoint of a reverse tracing of the Expedition's route. Each of the identified possible sites will now be evaluated.

Site Evaluations

Chi0 and Chi1

Candidate sites Chi0 and Chi1 are both predicated on the DCc "Deep Canyon" site, but that site, as mentioned previously, is highly unlikely to have been described as "deep" and almost certainly would not be called "very deep" by anyone. Therefore, the sites Chi0 and Chi1 are considered to be unlikely candidates for the Expedition's "Chichilticale".

Chi2

While candidate site Chi2 was originally discovered relative to the DCc site and would therefore be excluded from consideration, it was later also accepted relative to the "Deep Canyon" sites DCd and DCe. The Chi2 site is, then, considered a viable candidate for the "Chichilticale" site.

Chi3, Chi4, Chi5, Chi6 and Chi9

Candidate sites Chi3, Chi4, Chi5, Chi6 and Chi9 are all predicated on the DCa "Deep Canyon" site at Apache Box. The routes to these sites from DCa take different paths to the various crossing points of the Gila River as depicted on Figure 16.1. Sites Chi3, Chi4, Chi6 and Chi9 lie too far from DCa for a three-day journey, so they require one to interpret the chroniclers' wording to mean that the Expedition crossed the intervening mountains before starting the count of the three days to DCa. The site Chi5, on the other hand, lies well within a three-day journey from DCa using either of the two noted routes, so the count of the three-day journey would have started when they left the Chi5 site. As noted previously, either interpretation of the start point for the three-day journey is reasonable, depending upon whether the chroniclers meant "Chichilticale" to refer to the site itself or to the associated mountain range. All five of these sites are considered viable candidates for the Expedition's "Chichilticale".

Chi7 and Chi8

The candidate sites Chi7 and Chi8 are predicated on the DCb or DCb2 "Deep Canyon" candidate sites as discussed previously. While the DCb2 (Gila River crossing site at Three Way, Arizona) could easily be described as a "deep" canyon, the DCb (Black Jack Canyon crossing) site cannot readily be so described. However, a short distance upstream from the crossing, Black Jack Canyon does indeed become "deep" and even further upstream it becomes spectacularly deep and impressive. There is even a "scenic overlook" observation area on the modern highway along the canyon. It is, of course, possible that both Juan Jaramillo and Pedro de Castañeda described features of the canyon not observed until some time after the crossing, so the DCb site cannot be dismissed out-of-hand. It follows, then, that the Chi7 and Chi8 sites need to be interpreted as indicating a general local area, even more so than the other "Chichilticale" candidate sites. With this caveat, both Chi7 and Chi8 are considered viable candidates for "Chichilticale".

Acceptable Candidates

At this point, a low probability has been assigned to only two of the ten identified "Chichilticale" candidate sites. Chi0, just west of Soldier's Farewell Mountain, and Chi1, between Knight Peak and Hornbrook Mountain, were judged unlikely based, primarily, on the low probability of the "Deep Canyon" candidate DCc, a Gila River crossing near Cliff, New Mexico.

The possibility of eliminating others of the "Chichilticale" candidates can be investigated based on additional information the chroniclers have supplied regarding that location. They say that "Chichilticale" lies at the end of the region of "spiny" plants, that the mountainous country begins there and that the route from there to the "Deep Canyon" runs to the northeast. An inspection of Figure 16.1 shows that all of the eight surviving candidate sites are associated with paths leading generally to the northeast. All these sites also are situated at or near the northern or northeastern boundary of the Sonoran Desert which is notorious for its spiny flora. The statement about the mountainous country beginning at Chichilticale is so subjective and imprecise that all of the candidate sites could be considered as meeting that condition. In short, there is no reasonable cause to remove any of the eight remaining candidates from consideration. These eight sites are designated Chi2 through Chi9 on Figure 16.1. They are all located in a relatively small rectangular region measuring about 30 miles by 60 miles extending from just within New Mexico westward into southeastern Arizona.

One final consideration should be noted before moving on to other portions of the possible route of Coronado's Expedition. The lack of any mention of crossings of the Gila River (with the exception of the DCc and DCb2 sites) has already been noted, whereas the chroniclers appear to have been diligent in recording other rivers. If this lack of mention is interpreted as an indication that the Expedition crossed no river there, only the DCc and DCb2 "Deep Canyon" sites would remain as viable candidates. Subsequently, only the Chi7, Chi8 and Chi9 sites would be viable candidates for "Chichilticale."

However, the rivers noted by the chroniclers tend to be those of major flow, with only five "rivers" being named in what is now Arizona and New Mexico. These are the Rio Nexpa (the first one encountered flowing northward and mentioned, perhaps more for its relationship to the trail than for its flow), the Rio San Juan (encountered on St. John's Day, 1540), the Rio de las Balsas (which was swollen and had to be crossed on rafts), the Rio Frio (named for it cold water) and the Rio Bermejo (named for its bright red color). In addition to these five rivers, the Expedition would certainly have come upon numerous smaller streams which may not have warranted naming or even noting as anything special. The Gila River may well have fallen into this latter category. The author has experienced this river in this locale to be bone dry at the same time of year, so it is conceivable that the flow could have been too low for the Expedition to bother recording. As a result, the other possible Gila crossings cannot be ignored or eliminated.

Summary

At this point in the investigation, the site DCc has rather certainly been eliminated as a "Deep Canyon" candidate. Consequently the "Chichilticale" candidate sites Chi0 and Chi1 are also eliminated. One caveat remains and should be well understood. The site locations indicated on Figure 16.1 and the trails depicted are not intended to represent hard-and-fast pinpointed geographical locations. There exist many possible variations on the indicated routes with subsequent variations on distances between the indicated points. The pathways indicated do, however, represent reasonable routes that approximate likely possible paths both in routing and in length.

At this point of the investigation of Coronado's route, the list of the five remaining viable candidates for the "Deep Canyon" includes DCa, DCb, DCb2, DCd and DCe.

There are also eight surviving "Chichilticale" candidates: Chi2, Chi3, Chi4, Chi5, Chi6, Chi7, Chi8 and Chi9.

The next step in this investigation will be to consider the "Rio Nexpa" and the specific point along that river where the Expedition changed direction of march from northward along the river to northeast toward "Chichilticale".

Chapter 17

Dogleg on the Rio Nexpa

The Advance Party of the Coronado Expedition under the direct command of Captain General Francisco Vásquez de Coronado reached Chichilticale after a two-day march[1] from the "dogleg" on the "Rio Nexpa". They had been on a generally north-oriented route since leaving Culiacan and had followed this "rivulet" of the Rio Nexpa downstream toward the north for two days before departing from it "to the right" and toward the "northeast" at this "dogleg" point. Jaramillo[1] is the only source for information about this portion of the journey. The reverse tracing of the Expedition's route continued with a search of the satellite imagery and topographic maps for a north-flowing river about two days' distance (32 miles) southwest from the eight surviving Chichilticale candidate sites, Chi2 through Chi9.

The five "Chichilticale" candidates Chi3, Chi4, Chi5, Chi6 and Chi9 lie much too close to the present Rio San Simon for that river to be considered as the "Rio Nexpa". Also, they all lie much too far from the Rio San Pedro. However, they all do lie about the correct distance from the Surphur Springs Valley, but there are several features about that valley that don't fit the requirements for its being the "Rio Nexpa". Aravaipa Creek is, indeed, a northward flowing stream, but it drains only the northern portion of Surphur Springs Valley. Also, it is too far north to have been on the routes passing through these five "Chichilticale" candidate sites. The central part of the Surphur Springs Valley drains into the Wilcox Playa via a

1. F&Fdocs30, p513

southerly flow beginning just south of the headwaters of Aravaipa Creek. Only about twelve miles of the central part of the Valley immediately south of the Wilcox Playa drains northward. South of that point, the Valley drains southward into Mexico as part of the Rio Yaqui drainage. Since these five "Chichilticale" candidate sites fail to meet the "Rio Nexpa" proximity requirements, all five can be eliminated from consideration.

That leaves only three "Chichilticale" sites as viable candidates: Chi2, Chi7 and Chi8. The Chi7 site can also be eliminated as a probable candidate. The San Pedro River is the only candidate river that meets the "two days" distance requirement, but no reasonable path from Chi7 to that river was found. A path of that length would necessitate crossing the Galiuro Mountains in a very rugged region. Such a route would have been extremely unlikely since a more direct, less rugged and shorter route was available by going to the Chi8 site from the Rio San Pedro. Chi7 is therefore a very unlikely candidate for the Expedition's "Chichilticale". Only two sites, Chi2 and Chi8, remain as viable Chichilticale candidates.

The Dogleg Candidates

The results of the imagery and map search for possible locations of the "dogleg" on the Expedition's route yielded the following candidate sites laying along a possible "Rio Nexpa".

Dog1:

This site is located along the San Simon River about 7.3 miles southeast of San Simon, Arizona and lies about 28 miles south-southwest of the Chi2 site. The position of this site as indicated on Figure 17.1 could well be misplaced a significant distance because any possible traces of a path in the valley have been obliterated by modern agricultural

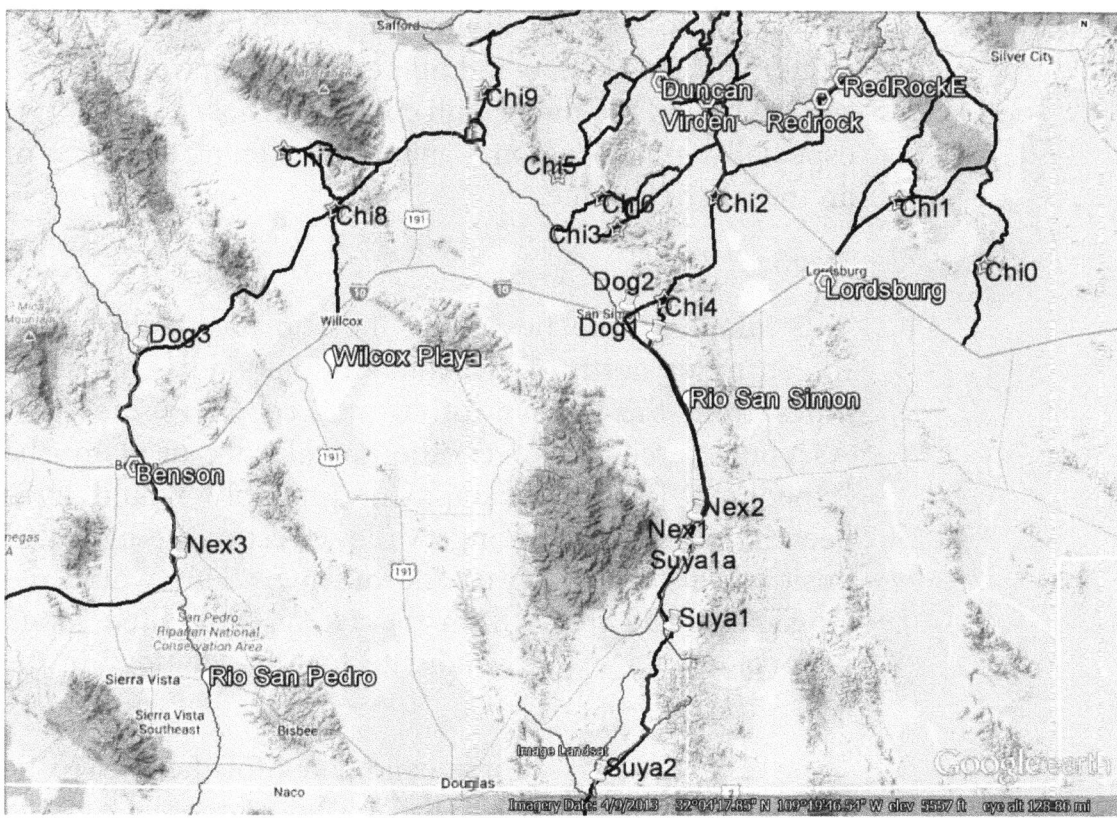

Fig 17.1. Image showing nominal locations of the candidate sites for the dogleg on the "Rio Nexpa", the candidate Indian village sites, and the ten "Chichilticale" candidate sites.

activity. Also, there is only a faint trace of any pathway along the indicated route south of the modern Interstate 10 Highway. Much of the indicated path follows present-day roads leading out of Doubtful Canyon and ranch roads running on paths that seem reasonable for the Expedition.

Dog2:

The Dog2 candidate site also lies on the San Simon River, but is only about two miles east of the town of San Simon, Arizona. A well discernible trail marks the route all the way from Chi2 to the valley where, again, agricultural activity has obliterated it. The trail through Doubtful Canyon and into San Simon was probably used by the Butterfield Stage Line and numerous wagon trains in the second half of the nineteenth century. Discernable trails, especially in this region, cannot be taken as evidence of an Indian trade route.

Dog3:

This "dogleg" site lies along the Rio San Pedro about fifteen miles north of Benson, Arizona and is about 38 miles from the Chi8 position marked on Figure 17.1. As conjectured, however, the actual spot used by the Expedition for an encampment probably would have been in the Sulphur Springs Valley, west of the indicated position, instead of up on the hillside. This would put Dog3 about 32 miles from the actual Chi8 site. Dog3 is considered a viable candidate for the "dogleg" in the route.

There are only three candidates for the site of the "dogleg" on the "Rio Nexpa". Two of these lie along the Rio San Simon and are associated with the Chi2 "Chichilticale" candidate while the third lies along the Rio San Pedro and is associated with the Chi8 "Chichilticale" candidate site. The two sites along the San Simon are separated from the San Pedro site by approximately 70 miles with the Chiricahua Mountains lying between them.

The Indian Village on the Rio Nexpa

Jaramillo reported, on the northbound journey, that after a two-day travel upstream (south) from the dogleg they had come upon an Indian settlement[1] where "just a few Indians came out to see the general with gifts of little value…" He also says that this settlement is where the Expedition came upon the Rio Nexpa. The candidate sites for this Indian village are indicated on Figure 17.1

and are labeled Nex1, Nex2 and Nex3. Each is a two-day journey along the river south of the associated "dogleg" candidate. Nex1 and Nex2 lie at, or very near, Rodeo, New Mexico in the southern part of the San Simon Valley near the head of the San Simon River. Nex3 lies along the Rio San Pedro about nine miles south of St David, Arizona, south of Benson and about 32 miles south of the Dog3 site. That distance presumes a path following the river in the valley, but it is possible that the Expedition followed the river on a shorter path higher up out of the valley and bypassing some of the major twists and turns. If this were the case, then, the candidate site Nex3 would move a bit further south and might be placed near the site of the ruins of the 1775 Spanish presidio Santa Cruz de Terrenate which lies about 10.5 miles south of St David.

Summary

This analysis has resulted in three viable candidate sites for the Rio Nexpa "dogleg" in the Expedition's route: Dog1, Dog2 and Dog3. There are also three viable candidate sites for the un-named Indian village on the Rio Nexpa: Nex1, Nex2 and Nex3, each associated with an individual candidate for the dogleg site.

In addition, six of the eight "Chichilticale" sites which had been deemed "viable" in the previous chapter have now been eliminated. There are remaining only two viable "Chichilticale" candidate sites: Chi2 and Chi8.

As a consequence of eliminating all but two of the "Chichilticale" candidates, the DCa "Deep Canyon" candidate was also eliminated. There are now only four of those sites remaining: DCb and DCb2, associated with Chi8, and DCd and DCe, associated with Chi2.

Chapter 18

The Three Sites of San Gerónimo

The Indian settlements of Suya, Señora and Los Corazones (each referred to as San Gerónimo) were the three sites of the Coronado Expedition's midway supply base, in reverse order of establishment (see Chapter 5). Determining their locations with respect to the "dogleg" in the Expedition's route will be the next step in the investigation of possible routings of Coronado's 1540 entrada.

Juan Jaramillo says that the Expedition had passed through an Indian settlement called "Ispa" about "four days" before reaching the un-named poor village on the Rio Nexpa. The only other information he gives about the route from Ispa to the "dogleg" is that it went through "unsettled land." Ispa, itself, Jaramillo says, was "probably one day's journey" from the *Arroyo de Señora* (where the second settlement of San Gerónimo would later be established). Somewhat uncharacteristically, Jaramillo provides a reasonably detailed description of the Arroyo de Señora. He says that the Expedition arrived there by[1]

1. *F&Fdocs30, p513*

> ...*going through a sort of small pass and, very near this stream, to another valley formed by the same stream ... It is also irrigated and [is inhabited] by more Indians than the others. ... This valley probably extends about six or seven leagues, a little more or less. ... There are mountain ranges that are little vegetated on both sides [of the valley].*
>
> *From here we traveled beside this same stream,*

crossing it at the bends it makes, to another Indian settlement called Ispa.

Jaramillo does not mention any Indian village or location called "Suya", but Pedro de Castañeda states[2] that there are 40 leagues (105 miles) between the Indian village of Suya (the third and final San Gerónimo site) and "Señora" (obviously referring to Arroyo de Señora). Castañeda, however, makes no mention of an "Ispa" or of Jaramillo's "un-named settlement on the Rio Nexpa" anywhere along the route. The unknown author of the *Relación del Suceso*[3] reports that Señora "was the best of all the settled places" and that it was located ten leagues (26 miles) upstream from the first site of San Gerónimo at the Indian settlement the Spaniards called "Los Corazones". Based on these unequivocal distances, Suya, then, was 50 leagues north of Los Corazones.

From Los Corazones the poor settlement at the Rio Nexpa is "about four days" from Ispa plus the "probably one day's journey" from Señora to Ispa plus the 10 leagues from Los Corazones to Señora. Taking these Jaramillo-supplied distances at face value, the Rio Nexpa site would be about five days travel (30 leagues or 79 miles) plus the ten leagues (26 miles) or about 40 leagues (105 miles) from Los Corazones. This would place Suya about 10 leagues north of the Rio Nexpa site and very close to the "dogleg" point. However, none of the chroniclers mention or imply the existence of an Indian settlement at the "dogleg", so this positioning of Suya seems unlikely. A very reasonable resolution of this problem can be made by allowing Jaramillo's "about four days" to be "five days" or a little more. This would put the "Rio Nexpa" site very close to 50 leagues from Los Corazones and would place the "Suya" site coincident with the "Rio Nexpa" site. If this is correct, it marks one of the very

2. F&Fdocs28, p416

3. F&Fdocs29, p497

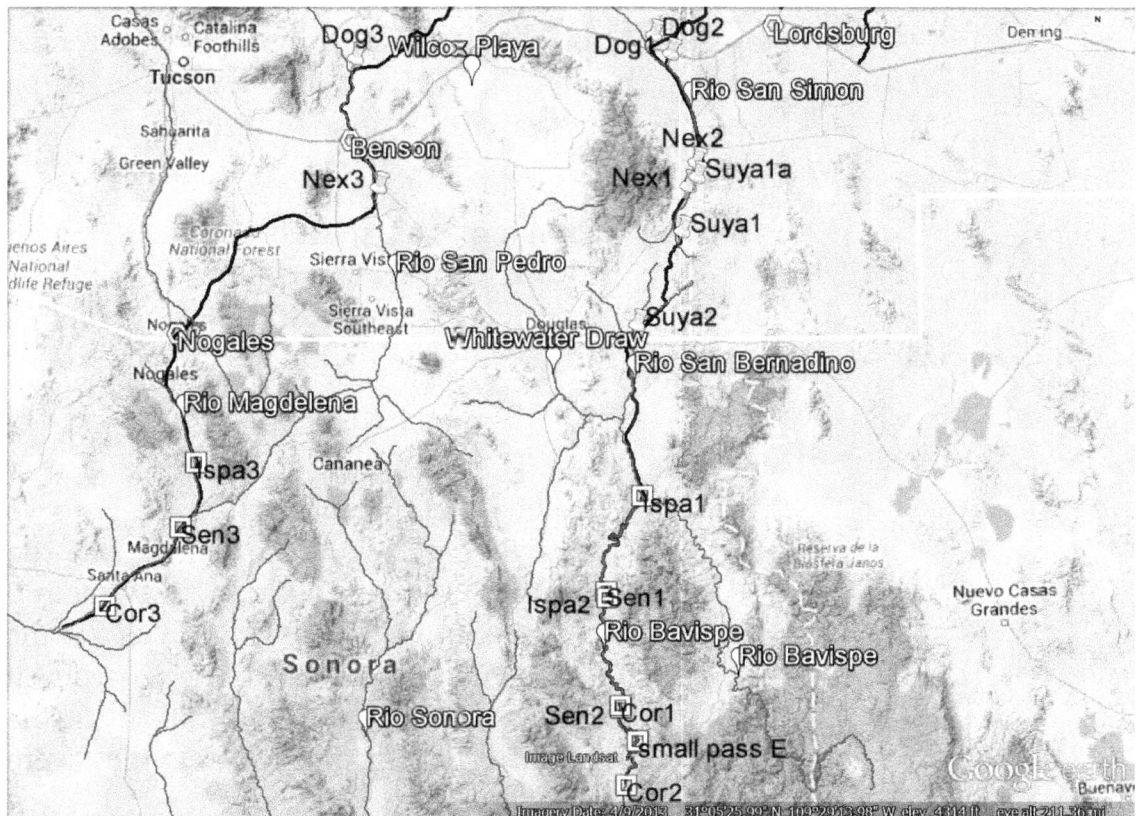

Fig 18.1. Image showing the two sets of candidate sites for Suya, Ispa, Señora, and Los Corazones on probable routes of the Coronado Expedition of 1540.

few times Jaramillo and Castañeda apply different names to any feature or place. (But note that Jaramillo did not actually apply any name to this Indian village – he simply named the river).

Since all the distances involved are uncertain, it is not possible to determine with much confidence the positions of the four (or perhaps only three) settlements south of the un-named settlement on the Rio Nexpa. This portion of the investigation relied on searching for places with the geographical features described by the eyewitnesses. The distances which are known with confidence were used as aids in this search. The imagery and map search for candidate locations of the expected sites between the un-named settlement on the Rio Nexpa and Los Corazones was based on identifying reasonable possibilities for:

1. **Suya:** San Gerónimo was moved to this location because it afforded an abundant food supply and good pasturage. This implies a probable location in a relatively large, fertile valley with an adequate water supply.

2. **Ispa:** This site is known to be in a river valley. It was by-passed when the Expedition moved its base to Suya which might imply that the valley was too small, too poor or too close to Señora. No information about the dimensions of this valley is given by the chroniclers. To the south of this valley the Expedition "traveled beside this same stream, crossing it at the bends it makes[1]". This seems to imply that they were marching along the banks of the river.

3. **Señora:** This site lies along the same river as does Ispa, but in a different valley. The "Señora" valley ("the best of all the settled places") is about 105 miles south of Suya and about 16 miles south of Ispa. The valley at Señora is expected to be about six or seven leagues (16 or 18 miles) long and is situated between two barren mountain ranges. Also expected is a "sort of small pass" just south this valley.

4. **Los Corazones:** This was the site of the first Spanish settlement of San Gerónimo and was chosen because of its food supply and its friendly Indian inhabitants. It is located about 10 leagues (26 miles) south of Señora along the same river. No information about the dimensions of this valley is given by the chroniclers.

It seems that this sequence of three rather closely spaced, habitable valleys that supported Ispa, Señora and Los Corazones *along a single river* would be sufficiently unique to be discovered by an imagery and map search. Note that the *Relación del Suceso's* distance from Los Corazones to Señora, Castañeda's distance from Señora to Suya and Jaramillo's village of Ispa and its distance from Señora have been accepted in order to establish the search criteria.

Candidate Sites

It will be convenient to discuss the current search results individually relative to the two surviving candidates for the Chichilticale site, Chi2 and Chi8.

Candidates Derived from Candidate Chi2

As seen in the previous chapter, there are only two "dogleg" candidate sites and only two "Rio Nexpa" (i.e., the unnamed Indian settlement on the Rio Nexpa) candidate sites predicated on Chi2. Since the distance between the "Rio Nexpa" and "Suya" is unknown, it is not expected to be able to resolve the locations of the "dogleg" and "Rio Nexpa" to any finer detail than that already presented.

Suya1 and Suya1a

These site are in the upper (southern) part of the San Simon River drainage. The site labeled "Suya1" on Figure 18.1 is based on a distance of 50 leagues (132 miles) along the indicated route from the Los Corazones candidate "Cor1". While this "Suya1" is located along the river, it does not appear to have ever been a site that would support a large population and probably would not have appealed to the Spaniards as a place to establish their third settlement of San Gerónimo. A much more probable site would have been somewhere between the locations of "Nex1" and "Nex2" very close to the present town of Rodeo, New Mexico. Rodeo is located about 147 miles from Los Corazones. This distance is about twelve percent farther than the 50 leagues expected, but this is probably well within the precision of the Expedition's distance measurements. Based on a later acceptance of the Cor1 "Los Corazones" candidate site, it appears that "Suya" and "Rio Nexpa" are one and the same and that the site is located in the close vicinity of Rodeo, New Mexico. That approximate location is labeled "Suya1a" on Figure 18.1.

Ispa1

This Ispa1 valley lies at the confluence of the Rio San Bernadino, flowing south from Suya2, with the Rio Bavispe where it makes its 180-degree bend around the north end of the Sierra San Diego. This Ispa1 valley extends perhaps twelve miles north to south and lies about 40 miles south of Suya2. The Rio Bavispe is a tributary of the Rio Yaqui which it joins farther to the south.

Jaramillo says that it took "about four days" from Ispa to the Rio Nexpa. If "about four" is taken to actually be "five", then his travel time would agree remarkably well with the 80 miles found for that interval. This "five days" between Ispa and the Rio Nexpa would also imply that Suya and the Rio Nexpa site were the same, as already concluded in the discussion of Suya1 and Suya1a, above. It seems, then, that Jaramillo's memory of this portion of the journey was a bit faulty.

Sen1

This is a candidate site for "Señora" ("the best of all the settled places") and now lies at the bottom of the reservoir, "Presa La Angostura". This reservoir extends

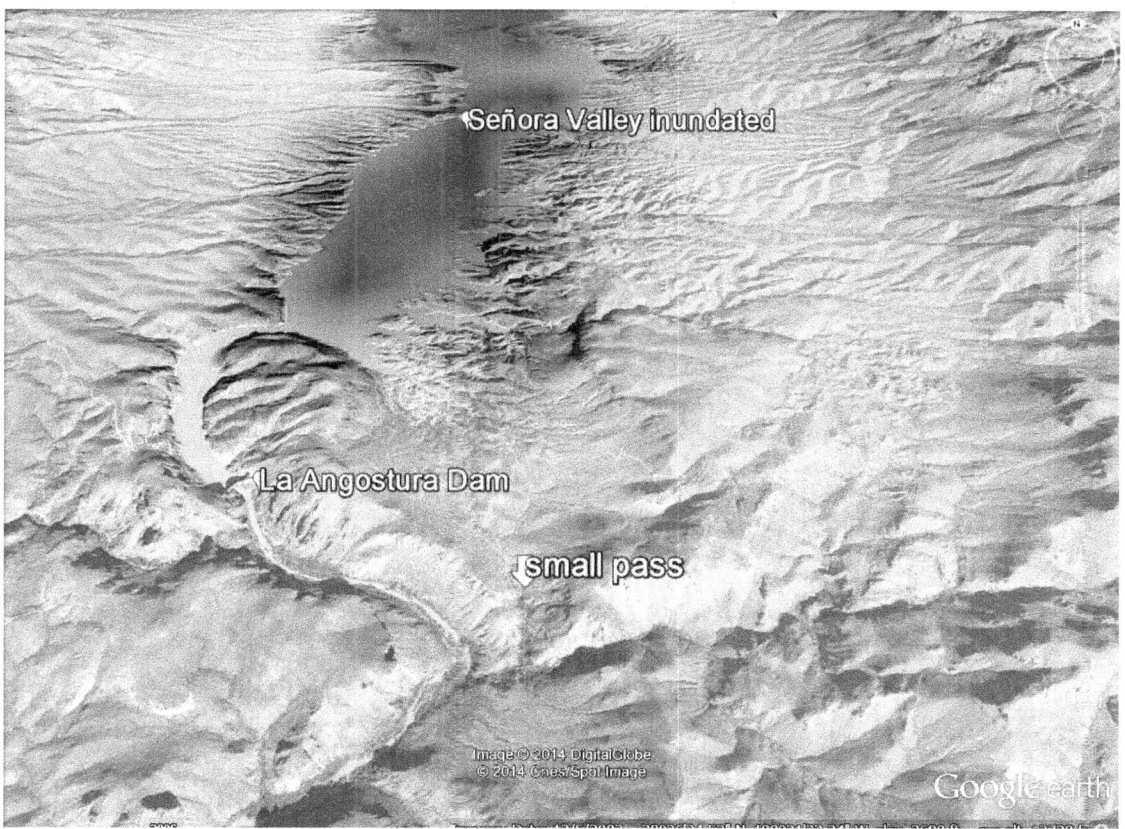

Fig 18.2. Image showing the main course of the Rio Bavispe (forming a reservoir) and a possible "sort of small pass" (center of picture) just south of the Sen1 candidate site for the Señora Valley.

about 17 miles along the valley, in good agreement with Jaramillo's "six or seven leagues (16 or 18 miles)". From the south end of the Ispa1 valley to the north end of this Señora valley is about 16 miles. This agrees well with Jaramillo's "probably one day's journey", assuming that is what he meant by "from the last valley to this one". Another distinguishing feature of this valley is shown in Figure 18.2. This shows a relatively short (about one-half mile long) gap leading into the southern end of this valley. It is close to, but not part of, the main flow of the river and is very adequately described[1] by "*a sort of small pass and, very near this stream, to another valley formed by the same stream"*. This valley is considered very likely to be the Expedition's "Arroyo de Señora". It is not possible to be more about the locations of the Indian village and the Spanish settlement of San Gerónimo within this valley are unknown.

Cor1

This valley is a candidate for the site of Los Corazones where the Spaniards of the Coronado Expedition established the first settlement of San Gerónimo in 1540 and where, presumably, Cabeza de Vaca had visited in 1536. The valley here has a length of about six miles, north to south, and the modern town of Villa Hidalgo is located in it. From the south end of the Sen1 valley to the north end of this valley is about 26 miles in excellent agreement with the "ten leagues" given by the unknown author of the *Relación del Suceso*[3]. The probable location within this valley of neither the Indian village of Los Corazones nor the Spanish settlement of San Gerónimo is known. The vicinity of Villa Hidalgo served as the reference for the 50 leagues (132 miles) distance to locate Suya1 near Rodeo, New Mexico.

A separate and distinct valley is located about 28 miles along the Rio Bavispe south of Cor1 and is also a candidate for the valley of "Los Corazones". This valley is labeled "Cor2" on Figure 18.1 and has the following candidate sites associated with it.

Suya2

This candidate site is shown on Figure 18.1 to be located in Arizona where Cottonwood Wash crosses the international boundary between the USA and Mexico. It lies at the western edge of the San Bernardino National Wildlife Refuge and its position is based on the "Cor2" candidate for "Los Corazones" found below. The location has an uncertainty of a few miles due to the uncertainty in the position of the site of "Cor2" within its valley. The position indicated for Suya2 lies about 39 miles from the Nex1 candidate site for the "Rio Nexpa" settlement.

Ispa2

This is the same site described as "Sen1" above. The distance from this valley to the "Sen2" valley (which is coincident with the Cor1 valley) is about 26 miles. This doesn't agree very well with Jaramillo's "probably one day's journey" but he could have been mistaken about this.

Sen2

This valley has been described above as Cor1 and lies about 19 miles north of the Cor2 valley. The distinguishing "sort of a small pass" might now apply to one of several possible places along the river channel between this valley and the Cor2 valley. None of these possible places, however, appears to have any feature that would be described as a pass "very near this stream". The distance between some point in one valley to some point in the other could easily be the expected "10 leagues". The length of this "Sen2" valley is about 6.5 miles whereas Jaramillo said that the length of the "Señora" valley was about six of seven leagues (16 or 18 miles).

Cor2

This is the valley of the modern town of Huásabas and is about 12 miles in length. This valley lies about 19 miles down the Bavispe River south from the valley of Sen2.

This second set of candidate sites for the locations of Suya, Ispa, Señora and Los Corazones does not fit the chronicler's descriptions nearly as well as the first set. The disagreements are sufficiently important to consider Suya2, Ispa2, Señ2 and Cor2 unlikely candidates for the Expedition's settlements.

Candidates Derived from Candidate Chi 8

From the previous chapter there is only one candidate site remaining for each of the "dogleg" and "Rio Nexpa" locations associated with the Chi8 "Chichilticale" candidate: Dog3 and Nex3. Since knowledge of the distance between the "Rio Nexpa" and "Suya" is uncertain, this part of the imagery and map search was based on trying to locate a reasonable sequence of the Suya, Ispa, Señora and Los Corazones sites along a plausible route, as before.

To begin, note is taken of something that Jaramillo[1] said about the approach to the settlement on the Rio Nexpa:

> *From here {Ispa} one travels in about four days [through] unsettled land to another stream we understood to be called Nexpa.*

This language strongly suggests that the Expedition was not traveling along the Rio Nexpa on its journey north from Ispa. Therefore a search for a reversed-itinerary route toward the southward that did not follow along the Rio San Pedro was conducted. Such a route was found going west from the "Rio Nexpa" candidate, Nex3 and then southwest to Nogales, Arizona and then southward toward Magdalena, Sonora, Mexico. The candidate Expedition sites for Ispa, Señora and Los Corazones on this route are all along the upper (northern) reaches of the Rio Magdalena.

Suya3

Suya3's position was determined by distance along the route indicated on Figure 18.1 starting from Cor3, the candidate site for Los Corazones. This site is then coincident with the Nex3 site on the San Pedro River south of Benson, Arizona.

Ispa3

This candidate site near the village of Agua Caliente, Sonora is located on Mexico Highway 15 about 30 miles south of the international border at Nogales. It is in a region where many large arroyos feed into the river from both the east and the west, which would have made a route in the valley the only reasonable path for the Expedition's journey.

Sen3

This site lies at the town of San Ignacio, about 16 miles south of Ispa3, which agrees with Jaramillo's "probably one day's journey", and about 108 miles from Nex3. The valley along this part of the river is about 17 miles in length and much of it can be well described by Jaramillo's words "there are mountain ranges that are little vegetated on both sides [of the valley]".

Cor3

The site of this candidate for Los Corazones lies very near the village of Ejido El Claro, about eight miles southwest of the city of Santa Ana, Sonora. It is about 26 miles along the Rio Magdalena from Sen3 and about 134 miles from Nex3, agreeing well with the expected 50 leagues (132 miles). This location well fits Jaramillo's description[4] of its being in a "hot lowland".

4. F&Fdocs30, p512

Summary

Two potential routes of the Coronado Expedition for the portion of the journey between Los Corazones and Chichilticale were found. The first of these routes passes through the Suya candidate, Suya1a, near Rodeo, New Mexico and crosses the border near San Bernadino before going to the candidate sites of Ispa, Señora and Los Corazones along the Rio Bavispe; Ispa1, Sen1 and Cor1. The second route passes through Suya3, south of Saint David, Arizona and crosses the border at Nogales before continuing through Ispa3, Sen3 and Cor3 along the Rio Magdalena in Mexico. Both of these routes resulted in identifying "Suya" with the appropriate candidate for the "Rio Nexpa", Jaramillo's un-named Indian village on the Rio Nexpa, even though that was not specified as one of the search requirements.

Before leaving the portion of the Expedition's route between Los Corazones and Chilchilticale, note that the suggested routing disagrees with that of many other authors. The most popular routing identifies Los Corazones with the modern town of Ures, Sonora, and continues upstream along the Rio Sonora. That routing then follows the Rio San Pedro into Arizona, but does not locate the "dogleg" or Chichilticale.

It may be possible to ignore the implication in Jaramillo's statement that the Expedition was not traveling along a river when they came to the settlement on the Rio Nexpa and then to conjecture that they had come up the Rio Sonora valley. Even though that route has been suggested by several authors, such an interpretation cannot be justified from the present viewpoint of a reverse tracing of the route.

Chapter 19

To Arroyo de los Cedros

The chroniclers of Coronado's Expedition to Cíbola in 1540 supply very sparse geographical information on the portion of the route between Los Corazones and the Arroyo de los Cedros. And this represents approximately one-quarter of the entire distance between Culiacan and Cíbola. The little information known about this section of the route comes primarily from Juan Jaramillo's account[1] and Coronado's letter[2] to the Viceroy.

1. F&Fdocs30, p512
2. F&Fdocs19, p255

Jaramillo says

From here {Arroyo de los Cedros} we went to the river called Yaquimí, which is probably approximately three days' travel from this [stream]. [The route was] by way of a dry arroyo, traveling on the route about another three days. The dry arroyo, however, probably lasts only about one league. [There] we reached another stream where some Indians were settled who had shelters of thatch and planted fields of corn, beans, and squash. Having departed from here, we went to the stream and place called Los Corazones... This is probably about two days' journey.

It is possible to interpret this in several different ways, but the most consistent seems to be that the Expedition traveled from the Arroyo de los Cedros to the Rio Yaquimí in about three days, with no other information given about that interval. Leaving the Rio Yaquimí, the Expedition passed through a dry arroyo somewhere during the three-day journey to "another stream" and continuing from there, reached Los Corazones in about another two days. Fortunately, Jaramillo supplies us with a clue that might help in identifying the Arroyo de los Cedros.

> *From here* {the Rio Sinoloa} *the general ordered ten of us horsemen to double the daily journeys, by [traveling] light, until we arrived at the Arroyo de los Cedros. From there we were to go through an opening which the mountains formed to the right of [our] route and to see what was in those [mountains] and behind them.*

In his letter, Coronado tells Viceroy Mendoza about some of the difficulties encountered in the vicinity of the Rio Yaquimí prior to reaching Los Corazones.

> *... we all cheerfully traveled along a very difficult trail that could not be traversed without either [ourselves] preparing one or restraightening the track that was there. ... among other things the father* {Marcos de Niza} *said and attested was that the route was excellent and flat and that there was only one insignificant grade half a league long. The truth is that there are mountains. And even if the trail is well repaired it cannot be traversed without great danger of the horses rolling there.*

> *... a great number of the livestock Your Lordship sent as provisions for the armed force remained behind at this [point of the] journey, because of the roughness of the rock. The lambs and wethers lost their hooves because of the [roughness of the] ground. And I left the greater part of those I had brought from Culiacan at the Yaquimí River because they could not travel. ...* {Later} *The rest were left behind dead because of that cliff, even though they*

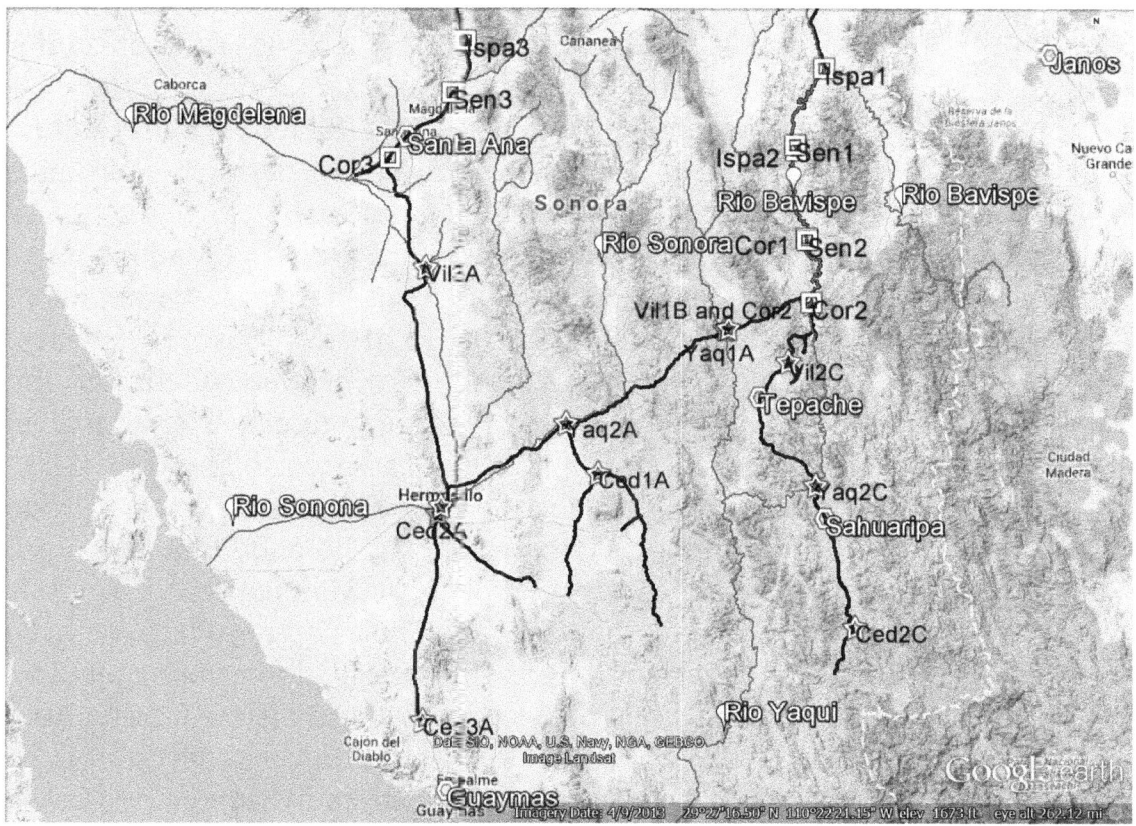

Fig 19.1. Image showing locations of the candidate sites for Los Corazones, the Indian village, the Rio Yaquimí and the Arroyo de los Cedros. Google Earth image.

had traveled no more than two leagues and had rested there several days.

From this it is understood that the Expedition was traveling though mountains over a rough and rocky trail. It also appears that there was a dangerous cliff about two leagues (5.2 miles) beyond the Rio Yaquimí. This location of the cliff is a reasonable interpretation of Coronado's letter but is not certain. The cliff could be anywhere between the Rio Yaquimí and Los Corazones. Perhaps this cliff is where the horses were also in danger of rolling.[2]

In addition to the meagerness of the information afforded by the chroniclers, there is another major problem with this part of the Expedition's journey. A disagreement of about 30 leagues (80 miles) exists among the various sources of information about the distance between Culiacan and Los Corazones. In his letter[3] of 1539 to King Carlos V of Spain, Viceroy Mendoza states the distance as 120 leagues, but the unknown author of the *Relación de Suceso* in 1540 says it is 150 leagues[4] and adds that it was half way between Culiacan and Cíbola. At the time Mendoza wrote his letter late in 1539, the only Spaniards that had been so far north as Los Corazones were Alvar Nuñez Cabeza de Vaca's group (Cabeza de Vaca, Dorantes, Castillo and Dorantes' black slave, Estevan) and (probably) Marcos de Niza. It is almost certain that Cabeza de Vaca's group had not been noting and recording the distances along their route and it is possible that de Niza had taken a different route from that taken by Coronado. Mendoza's knowledge of the geography would have been extremely limited.

3. F&Fdocs4, p48

4. F&Fdocs29, p497

On the other hand, the author of the *Relación de Suceso* had traveled the route with Coronado's Advance Party which was (presumably) measuring and recording the distances involved. Castañeda says that the total distance from Culiacan to Cíbola was 300 leagues[5] which would put Los Corazones 150 leagues from Culiacan (if, indeed, it was half way). It seems most probable that the 150 leagues would be the more accurate of these two estimates of the distance between Culiacan and Los Corazones. However, as will be discussed later, Jaramillo's reported 20 days' travel (120 leagues) between the "Culiacan valley" and Los Corazones and Castañeda's 10 leagues from San Miguel de Culiacan ("Culiacan") to the Culiacan valley would result in about 136 leagues from Culiacan to Los Corazones, about midway between

5. F&Fdocs28, p388

the other two estimates.

A third fundamental problem presents itself on the portion of the Expedition's journey from Culiacan to Los Corazones. Castañeda says that the Advance Party left Culiacan[6] traveling "at a fairly rapid pace", but he gives no indication of just what that pace was nor of any results of that faster pace. It is reasonable to conjecture that Coronado increased the pace in order to travel farther than normal on each day. The nominal order of march seems to have been six one-league marches with a rest period between each. It is known that two men were assigned to measure the distances, so it is probable that one-league marches would remain the standard and that a faster pace would likely have allowed the Advance Party to make more than six such marches during the daylight hours.

6. F&Fdocs28, p392

Since they were traveling this section of the route during May, the days would have been relatively long and they could probably have made seven (or even eight) marches per day. This would have increased the distance traveled per day from the nominal 16 miles to about 18.4 miles (or even 21 miles). Whereas the nominal 16 league per day rate resulted in identification of reasonable sites on the route north of Los Corazones, one might expect to find camp sites spaced relatively farther apart on the route south of there. As a guide to locating the various candidate sites on this southern half of the Expedition's route, a nominal seven leagues per day travel rate was used.

Since Jaramillo's account is the only detailed information known, the imagery and map search was based on his information. A search for sites with the following characteristics was made while being aware of a possible lapse in Jaramillo's memory and a probable

To Arroyo de los Cedros

rate of travel exceeding seven leagues per day.

Village

An Indian settlement two days' travel south of Los Corazones.

Dry Arroyo

A dry arroyo approximately 2.5 miles long and located somewhere between the Indian settlement and the Rio Yaquimí.

Rio Yaquimí

A river or river crossing about three days' travel from the Village. The terrain before and after this river will be rough and there may be a cliff along the trail north of the river.

Arroyo de los Cedros

An arroyo about three days' travel from the Rio Yaquimí. At this place there is a pass leading eastward through the mountains.

Candidate Sites

Search Results based on the "Cor2" candidate

Even though the Cor2 site is considered a weak candidate for Los Corazones, it was included in the present search for the sake of completeness. Two likely routes southward from Cor2 were found. The first of the routes goes though the following possible candidate sites.

Vil2B

This site is a candidate for the Indian settlement reached two days travel south Los Corazones at the Cor2 candidate location. It lies about 30 miles southwest from the Cor2 site along the route indicated on Figure 19.1 at the town of Moctezuma along the Rio Moctezuma.

Dry Arroyo 1

There appears to be a "dry arroyo" about 12 miles further southwest from Vil2B along the indicated route as well as a modern settlement named "Rancho Arroyo Seco" (Dry Arroyo Ranch) in that same vicinity.

Yaq2A

This candidate for the "Rio Yaquimí" site lies at the modern town of Ures, Sonora which is about 62 miles southwest of Vil2B. This would be a long three-day journey.

Ced2A

This is a candidate for the Arroyo de los Cedros and is located at the modern city of Hermosillo, Sonora about 46 miles (a nominal three-day journey as expected from Jaramillo's account) southwest of Yaq2A along the modern highway Mexico 14. This location is where the Rio Sonora is joined by an extensive network of other streams and arroyos, but does not have "mountains" close by to the east.

This set of candidate sites seems to fit Jaramillo's description fairly well with the exception of the missing mountains and with one partial day added to Jaramillo's account. Another major problem is that this candidate for the Arroyo de los Cedros lies about 370 airline miles (140 leagues) from Culiacan but the Expedition traveled from one to the other *on the ground* in about only 14 days (see the next chapter). This would have required an average travel rate in excess of 12 leagues per day. This is highly improbable, so this set of sites is judged unlikely to be the places visited by the Coronado Expedition.

The second of the two likely routes leading south from Cor2 goes through the following places.

Vil2C

This site lies along the Rio Bavispe in a valley about a mile long and a quarter of a mile wide and is about 30 miles from Cor2 by the path indicated in Figure 19.1.

Dry Arroyo 2

There appears to be a portion of the path between Tepache and Divisaderos that would well fit Jaramillo's description of the "dry arroyo". There are also several places between here and the Yaq2C site that could easily be described as "cliff". These are not a vertical drops but are fairly steep slopes.

Yaq2C

This candidate site for the Rio Yaquimí lies at the confluence of the Rio de Aros and the Rio Bavispe. It lies about 48 miles from the Vil2C site which is consistent with Jaramillo's "three days" of travel.

Ced2C

This candidate for the "Arroyo de los Cedros" site lies about 46 miles south of the Yaq2C site which would require a three-day journey, as Jaramillo said it did. It lies in mountainous terrain and has a very distinctive and inviting pass leading eastward.

This set of candidate sites seems to fit the descriptions reasonably well. However, if these are indeed the sites that the Advance Party of the Expedition visited, then another dilemma presents itself. Ced2C is about 285 straight-line miles (108 leagues) from Culiacan and would have required a travel rate of about 8 leagues per day for the fourteen days required to travel from one place to the other. Although relatively high, this rate is considered to be within the realm of possibilities, so this set of candidate sites will not be eliminated on this basis.

Search Results based on the "Cor1" candidate

The "Cor1" candidate site is about 10 leagues (26 miles) north of the "Cor2" site. Any route to the south from Cor1 and passing through Ures, Sonora (labeled Yaq2A) *toward the west* would put the resulting candidate site for the Arroyo de los Cedros even farther away from Culiacan than it was for the Cor2 site. This route can therefore be ruled out as a possibility even without searching for the intermediate sites. However, a route from Cor1 through Ures and turning south there yields the following candidate sites.

Vil1B

This site for the Indian village is located in the 10-mile long Huásabas valley south of the Villa Hidalgo valley where the Cor1 site is located. Vil1B is indicated on Figure 19.1 at the town of Huásabas (coincident with the Cor2 site) about 27 miles south of Cor1, but the actual site could be anywhere in the valley. This would agree with Jaramillo's travel time of "probably two days" between the Indian village and Los Corazones.

Yaq1A

This site is a candidate for the "Rio Yaquimí" reached prior to arriving at the Indian village at the Vil1B candidate location. It is coincident with the Vil2B site and lies about 56 miles southwest from the Cor1 site along the route indicated on Figure 19.1 at the town of Moctezuma. This distance agrees with that given by Jaramillo as "about another three days" travel.

To Arroyo de los Cedros

Dry Arroyo

The most probable "Dry Arroyo" candidate on this route lies immediately to the west of the indicated "Ced1A" location shown on Figure 19.1. This arroyo is a bit shorter than the expected length of about 2.5 miles but seems to fit Jaramillo's narrative "*[the route was] by way of a dry arroyo*" upon leaving the Arroyo de los Cedros.

Ced1A

This candidate for the Arroyo de los Cedros lies about 17 miles south of Ures along a modern paved road. It is about 136 miles from here to the Los Corazones "Cor1" candidate site which is in reasonable agreement with the 147 miles expected from Jaramillo's total of eight days travel time between these sites. There is an "*an opening which the mountains formed*" just to the east of this site, but there are also several other such openings along the probable trail leading to this site from the south. It is not clear why this particular site would have been singled out for exploration.

This set of candidate sites is considered viable from the viewpoint of the southward retracing of the Expedition's north-bound journey.

There is also another route indicated on Figure 19.1 that goes more directly southward from Cor1 and passes through Sahuaripa, Sonora. This route yields the following candidate sites.

Vil1B

This is the same site discussed under the first route leading south from Cor1.

Dry Arroyo 2

This is the same site discussed above under the second route leading south from Cor2.

No probable "Rio Yaquimí" site within a three day march from Vil1B was identified. However, if it is conjectured that Jaramillo's memory of a "three day" march was actually a "four day" march, then the candidate sites for Rio Yaquimí and the Arroyo de los Cedros would be the same as in the previous case for Cor2. In that case, we would, as before:

Yaq2C

This candidate site for the Rio Yaquimí lies at the confluence of the Rio de Aros and the Rio Bavispe. It lies about 78 miles from the Vil1B site which is about four days travel instead of Jaramillo's "three days" travel.

Ced2C

This candidate for the "Arroyo de los Cedros" lies in mountainous terrain along the present Rio de Guisamopa and has a very distinctive and inviting pass leading eastward. The site lies about 46 miles south of the Yaq2C site and about 150 miles from Cor1 site. This would require a three-day journey to Yaq2C and about an eight day travel to Los Corazones, both in agreement with Jaramillo at the assumed travel rate of seven leagues per day.

From the viewpoint of a south-bound imagery and distance analysis, this set of candidates sites is considered viable.

Search Results based on the "Cor3" candidate

Los Corazones candidate site, Cor3, is located on the Rio Magdalena about eight miles southwest of Santa Ana, Sonora and about fifteen miles upstream of the point at which the Rio Magdalena begins its turn toward the northwest. The likely associated candidate sites for the "Indian village", the "Rio Yaquimí", the "dry arroyo" and the "Arroyo de los Cedros" all lie along the route of present Mexico Highway 15.

Vil3A

This candidate site for the Indian village of the Expedition's route is located at the modern town of Querobabi in a valley along a stream that eventually joins the present Sonora River at Hermosillo, Sonora. It is about 36 miles (about 14 leagues) south of the Cor3 site and appears to be the only habitable location in the vicinity that lies along a reasonable trail route. This would imply that the Expedition was traveling at the rate of 7 leagues per day over this fairly unencumbered terrain.

Yaq3A

This Rio Yaquimí candidate lies along the present Sonora River at the city of Hermosillo, Sonora (coincident with the Ced2A site) near the confluence with the stream coming from the north and the Vil3A site. Yaq3A is about 74 miles (28 leagues) from Vil3A which is a bit far for a three-day march. It could be that Jaramillo's *about another three days* included a fourth day of travel. That would be consistent with a daily travel rate of 7 leagues per day.

Dry Arroyo 3

There are two places between Yaq3A and Ced3A that could reasonably fit the description of the "dry arroyo". One is about six miles south of the Yaq3A site at Hermosillo and the other is about 15 miles north of the Ced3A site. This latter site is the more probable and is labeled "Dry Arroyo 3" on Figure 19.1.

Table 19.1 Candidate Site Associations				
Sites	Los Corazones Candidate			
	Cor1	Cor2	Cor3	
Indian Village	Vil1B	Vil1B	Vil2C	Vil3A
Dry Arroyo	Dry Arroyo	Dry Arroyo 2	Dry Arroyo 2	Dry Arroyo 3
Rio Yaquimí	Yaq1A	Yaq 2C	Yaq 2C	Yaq3A
Arroyo de los Cedros	Ced1A	Ced2C	Ced2C	Ced3A

Ced3A

This site lies about 60 miles (23 leagues) south of Hermosillo (Yaq3A) and about 24 miles north of Guaymas, Sonora. It is just west of a range of mountains which has an "opening" that provides access to the east of this site. If this distance between "Ced3A" and "Dry Arroyo 3" had been travelled in "probably approximately" three days as Jaramillo says, then the Expedition's rate of travel would have been "probably approximately" 7.5 leagues per day.

This set of sites well fits the distances and descriptions given by the chroniclers and is considered to represent viable candidates for the locations visited by the Coronado Expedition.

Summary

From the search of imagery and maps viable candidates were found for the "Indian village", the "dry arroyo", the "Rio Yaquimí" and the "Arroyo de los Cedros" associated with each of the three "Los Corazones" candidate sites identified in the previous chapter. These are summarized in Table 19.1. In the process of developing these associations it was discovered that Coronado's "fairly rapid pace" on this part of the route was seven leagues per day. It appears that the

Advance Party maintained that pace until they reached Los Corazones, after which they apparently adopted the "normal" pace of six leagues per day.

Chapter 20

Into Culiacán

After mustering the Expedition at Compostela, Coronado traveled northward to the villa of San Miguel de Culiacán where he arrived on March 27, 1540. Here he reorganized the Expedition and split it into two parts. (See Chapter 2.) The Advance Party, under the direct command of Coronado, included Juan Jaramillo who recorded much of the existing information on distances traveled by the Expedition. This group left Culiacán on April 22 (Julian calendar), while the main body of the Expedition under the command of Tristán de Arellano, including the other primary source of Expedition information, Pedro de Castañeda, left about the middle of May.

1. F&Fdocs30, p512

In his account of this part of the journey[1] near Culiacán, Juan Jaramillo says that

> *at this villa {Culiacán} [the route] turns and goes approximately to the northwest*

and he goes on to say

> *Having left the valley of Culiacán, he {the Captian General, Francisco Vásquez de Coronado} went to a river called Petatlán, which is probably about four days' travel. ... From here, we went to another river called Sinaloa. From the one [river] to the other it is probably about three days' travel. From here the general ordered ten of us horsemen to double the daily journeys...until we arrived at the Arroyo de los Cedros. ...From the river Petatlan {Sinaloa} to this*

> *Arroyo [de los Cedros] there is probably another five days' travel.*

(The Flints' translation has this last river as "Petatlán", but from the context this appears to be a transposition error.)

Coronado, himself, in his letter[2] to the Viceroy has nothing at all to say about this portion of the trip, except to say that he left from the *provincia* of Culiacán on April 22, 1540. Castañeda, in telling about the northbound trip[3], says

2. F&Fdocs19, p254

3. F&Fdocs28, p416

> *...the general departed from the valley of Culiacán, continuing his travel at a fairly rapid pace. ...From Culiacán to there [Petatlán] it is twenty leagues.*

About Petatlán, itself, he says

> *Petatlán is a settlement of houses covered with a sort of matting made of reeds. [The houses] are congregated into pueblos. They extend all along a river from the mountains to the sea.*

While Castañeda mentions the Rio Sinaloa and several other rivers, he gives no information about their locations. In telling about the return trip a couple of years later, he says

> *Having left there [Petatlán]–with greater speed than previously, they sought to cross those thirty leagues which there are to the valley of Culiacán. There [the settlers] again gave them shelter...*

Here there are three different references to "Culiacán": The *villa* of Culiacán, the *valley* of Culiacán and the *provincia* of Culiacán. The location of the *villa* of Culiacán at the time the Expedition passed through has been identified[4] as a spot along the present Rio San Lorenzo about ten miles above its mouth on the Gulf of

4. F&Fdocs, p601

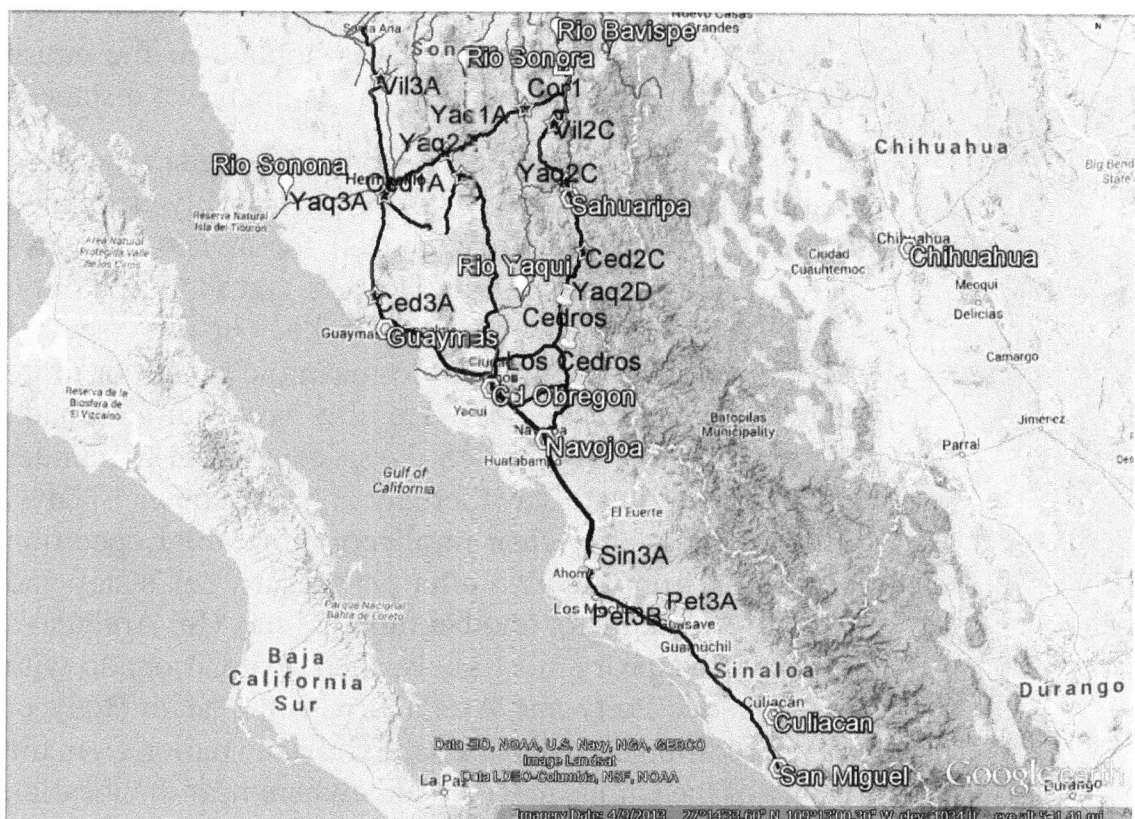

Fig. 20.1. Image showing candidate locations for sites between Culiacán and Los Corazones.

Califronia (the Sea of Cortez). The *valley* of Culiacán is more difficult to locate and is subject to some speculation. On the one hand, since there were settlers at the *valley* of Culiacán, that term and *villa* of Culiacán could have been used interchangeably for the same place. On the other hand, it is highly probable that the river valleys were named for the rivers flowing through them and, since the Rio Culiacán was well known to the Spaniards as the river where the original settlement of Culiacán was established in 1532, it is also highly probable that the chroniclers' "valley of Culiacán" referred to valley of that same river and not to the Rio San Lorenzo valley

Into Culiacán   241

in which the *villa* (San Miguel de Culiacán) was located. The term *provincia* probably was applied to the entire region surrounding the villa for some unknown distance.

It is possible to infer from Castañeda's account that the main body of the Expedition probably encamped in the valley of the Rio Culiacán for at least 30 days before departing the region. He says that the Expedition rested for "several days" at the villa, but this "several days" could hardly be taken to mean the month or more they stayed in the region. He also says that Coronado departed the *valley* after 15 days, leaving the remainder of the Expedition to stay there for at least another 15 days. This seems a fairly clear implication that the Expedition moved on from the *villa* after perhaps a week's stay and went to the *valley* for another month's stay (for Arellano's group). It appears most likely, then, that Coronado with the Advance Party and Arellano with the Main Body of the Expedition both departed the Culiacán region from the valley of the Culiacán River somewhere near the location of the present-day city of Culiacán, Sinaloa.

Another plausible interpretation of the same facts would have the Expedition staying at the villa of Culiacán for the entire four or five weeks and would have Coronado departing from the villa. In that case, the chronicler's terms "valley of Culiacán" and "villa of Culiacán" would refer to the same place. With either interpretation there is still an unresolved dilemma. Castañeda says that Petatlán was 20 leagues from "Culiacán" on the northbound journey but says it was 30 leagues from the "valley of Culiacán" on the return journey. Jaramillo says that it took "probably about four days" to cover that distance "at a fairly rapid pace". There are several plausible ways to reconcile this dilemma by allowing the possibility that Castañeda's "20 leagues" was simply a mistake or by allowing the possibility that Jaramillo's "probably four days" was actually *three* days.

> 1. Coronado leaves from the *valley* of the Rio Culiacán (near present-day Culiacán, Sinaloa) and goes *30 leagues* to Petatlán in four days at a rate of 7.5 leagues per day.
>
> 2. Coronado leaves from the *valley* of the Rio Culiacán (near present-day Culiacán, Sonora) and goes *20 leagues* to Petatlán in three days at a rate of 6.7 leagues per day.
>
> 3. Coronado leaves from the *villa* of San Miguel de Culiacán and goes *30 leagues* to Petatlán in four days at a rate of 7.5 leagues per day.
>
> 4. Coronado leaves from the *villa* of San Miguel de Culiacán and goes *20 leagues* to Petatlán in three days at a rate of 6.7 leagues per day.

With this small amount of information and inference and by accepting the first of these reconciliations as the most probable, the satellite imagery and topographic maps were searched for sites with the following characteristics.

Rio Sinaloa

This site would lie about 35 leagues (92 miles) from Culiacán and is expected to be at a crossing point of a sizable river "*probably another five days' travel*" south of the Arroyo de los Cedros. However, this travel time was reported by Jaramillo who was traveling at "*double the daily journeys*" with the group going to the Arroyo de los Cedros. This travel time, then, *could* represent about 60 or 70 leagues (160 or 184 miles), depending on whether the "doubled" rate was based on six or seven leagues per day. The rest of the Advance Party was presumably traveling

Into Culiacán

at the nominal "fairly rapid" rate of seven leagues per day.

Rio Petatlán

This river is *"probably about three days' travel"* (21 leagues or 55 miles) south of the Rio Sinaloa. This river valley is expected to have supported human habitation for a great portion of its run from "the mountains to the sea".

Culiacán

This site is in the valley of the Rio Culiacán about 10 leagues north of the 1540 site of the villa of Culiacán (San Miguel de Culiacán) and is expected to be about four days' travel (30 leagues or 79 miles) south of the Rio Petatlán.

Note that Coronado's "fairly rapid pace" leaving Culiacán may have averaged about seven and a half leagues per day based on covering the 30 leagues to the Rio Petatlán in four days.

Candidate Sites

The Expedition's chroniclers have supplied considerably more information concerning the southern part of this section of the route than about the path closer to the Arroyo de los Cedros. Therefore, the current search for candidate sites began at the valley of Culiacán and proceded toward each of the three Arroyo de los Cedros candidates found in the previous chapter.

Search Results based on candidate Ced3A

Pet3A

This "Rio Petatlán" candidate site lies along the present Rio Sinaloa about 84 miles northwest of the valley of Culiacán. This distance would have required a travel rate of about eight leagues per day which is within reason for a "fairly rapid pace", especially since this would have occurred on the first four days after leaving Culiacán.

Pet3B

This alternate "Rio Petatlán" candidate site lies along a stream about 72 miles northwest of the valley of Culiacán. This distance would have required a travel rate of about seven leagues per day which is also within reason for a "fairly rapid pace".

Sin3A

The Sin3A candidate site for the Expedition's "Rio Sinaloa" lies along Mexico Highway 15 where it crosses the El Fuerte River in the northern part of the modern Mexican state of Sinoloa. The Rio El Fuerte is the only river in its vicinity that lies within a reasonable distance from either of the two "Rio Petatlán" candidate sites. Sin3A lies about 48 miles from the Pet3A site and about 60 miles from the Pet3B site. With Jaramillo's "probably about three days' travel" between the two rivers, the Expedition would have travelled at a rate of about 6 leagues per day from Pet3A or a rate of about 7.6 leagues per day from Pet3B. Sin3A on the Rio Fuerte is considered a very likely candidate for the Expedition's "Rio Sinaloa".

Ced3A

This candidate site has already been established in the previous chapter from the viewpoint of reverse itinerary, but it now needs to be tested against a northbound Sin3A candidate location. The distance between Ced3A and Sin3A is about 220 miles (84 leagues) along the modern Mexico Highway 15. If Jaramillo's "probably another five days' travel" at a pace of "double the daily journeys" is taken to be equivalent to about ten days of usual travel, then the average travel rate would have been 8.4 leagues per day. This is not a totally unreasonable "fairly rapid pace", but if his "probably another five days' travel" is taken to be an equivalent *eleven* days, then the rate would have been 7.6 leagues per day, the same pace estimated for the journey between Culiacán and the Rio Petatlán. It appears that Jaramillo's "probably another five days' travel" time referred to travel at the doubled rate, but may have been one day short. In any case Ced3A cannot be eliminated as a possible candidate for the Arroyo de los Cedros.

Unless additional information is discovered in the future, the Expedition's travel rates or times or distances will probably never be known any more accurately than presented here. However, the reasonable estimates, interpretations and conjectures made above seem to be self-consistent and, therefore, the current set of candidate sites are considered to be viable locations for the Expedition's Arroyo de los Cedros, the Rio Sinaloa, the Rio Petatlán and the Culiacán departure point.

Search Results based on candidate Ced2C

No reasonable routes northward from Culiacán were found other than that discussed above as far as the "Rio Sinaloa" candidate Sin3A on the modern Rio El Fuerte. From there the likely route to candidate site Ced2C would follow Mexico Highway 15 to Navojoa, Sonora and then continue toward the northeast along the path shown on Figure 20.1. This route follows modern roadways almost all the way to Ced2C which is about 222 miles from the Sin3A site as measured along the indicated route. The same arguments can be made for the distance and travel rates to Ced2A as were made for the 220 league distance to Ced3A, above. On that basis the pathway indicated from Sin3A to Ced2C is considered to be a plausible route for the Coronado Expedition.

Search Results based on candidate Ced1A

To arrive at the Ced1A site the candidate sites from Culiacán to Sin3A would be accepted and the likely path would continue along the route toward Ced3A as far as Cuidad Obregon. From there the route would go almost due north to Ced1A. The distance from Sen3a to Ced1A along the indicated route is approximately 275 miles (105 leagues). At an average travel rate of 7.5 leagues per day, it would have taken 14 days for the Expedition to reach Ced1A from Sin3A whereas Jaramillo said it took "probably" ten days. This 275 miles is considered too great a distance to accept the indicated path to be a viable route and, at least tentatively, Ced1A can be eliminated as a viable candidate for the Expedition's "Arroyo de los Cedros".

Another Possibility

The above results were based on the supposition that Jaramillo's "five days travel" from the Rio Sinaloa to the Arroyo de los Cedros involved the "double the daily journeys" pace. If that supposition were to be abandoned and if his "five days" was, instead, intended to be the expected travel time for Coronado moving at the "fairly rapid pace" of about 7 or 8 leagues per day, then another possible candidate for the "Arroyo de los Cedros" could be found.

Los Cedros

On modern maps, about 120 miles (45 leagues) along the indicated path from Navojoa, there is a region called "Los Cedros" along the present Rio los Cedros. This place has both an *arroyo* (small stream) and an "opening in the mountains". It fits the description and is a reasonable distance for the "probably another five days' travel" (particularly for a six-day journey). This location is labeled "Los Cedros" on Figure 20.1.

Yaq2D

Another three days' travel (about 22.5 leagues or 60 miles) northward along this indicated route places a candidate for the "Rio Yaquimí" very near the present settlement of Nuri, Sonora. This site, labeled as "Yaq2D," is located in a fairly large valley along the southernmost of three streams that join to form the Rio Chico about 60 miles upstream (east) of that river's confluence with the Rio Yaqui. This appears to be an ideal place for Coronado to have left his flock of "lambs and wethers" to recover.

The distance between the Yaq2C site (determined by a reverse tracing of Coronado's route) and the Yaq2D site (determined from a northward tracing from the Expedition's "Rio Sinaloa") is about 33 leagues as measured along the indicated path. The chroniclers mention only one Indian settlement between the Arroyo de los Cedros and Los Corazones, but the most straight forward explanation of the "missing" 33 leagues is that someone in the chain of storytelling through the centuries simply combined two settlements and "lost" the distance between them. There is no compelling reason to accept "Los Cedros" and "Yaq2D" as candidate sites, but there is likewise no compelling reason to eliminate them. So these two sites will remain under consideration with the understanding that Cor1 (or perhaps Cor2) remains as the associated "Los Corazones" candidate site.

Summary and Discussion

The chroniclers of the Coronado Expedition mention only six places in the 150 to 180 leagues between Culiacán and Los Corazones and give extremely sparse information about any of them. In addition, the distances and/or travel times given by the chroniclers (for any reasonable rates of travel) do not tally correctly for the possible locations of Culiacán and Los Corazones. The tally is also not correct for the total distance between Culiacán and Cíbola. In both cases, the tallies seem to be in error by approximately 30 leagues (80 miles). This ten percent overall error would normally be considered small and totally acceptable for the methods of distance measurements employed by the Expedition. However, in this case the physical locations identified along the various possible paths resulted in that entire 30 league error being compressed into the portion of the route between the "Rio Sinaloa" and "Los Corazones".

The results of the previous chapter indicated two possible and viable routes leading south from candidate sites for the Expedition's "Los Corazones". To make reasonable connections with Culiacán along the routes indicated on Figure 20.1, it is necessary to make one of two suppositions:

1. Travel between the Rio Sinaloa and the Arroyo de los Cedros took five days at double pace or ten to eleven days at the "fairly rapid pace" of about an average 7.5 leagues per day.

2. Travel between the Rio Sinaloa and the Arroyo de los Cedros took 5 days at the "fairly rapid pace" of about 7.5 leagues per day and 33 leagues were "lost" between the Arroyo de los Cedros and Los Corazones.

With the first of these suppositions, the westernmost route (passing near Guymas) indicated on Figure 20.1 becomes viable as does the more easterly route passing through the Arroyo de los Cedros candidate site Ced2C. Under the second supposition, Ced2C is no longer a candidate but "Los Cedros" does become viable, so the eastern route indicated on Figure 20.1 remains acceptable. It cannot be determined, on the basis of the imagery and map search, which of these two routes was taken by the Coronado Expedition. However, it does appear that the eastern path through the Bavispe valley fits the known facts a bit better than the western route and requires less use of imagination.

If the eastern path is Coronado's actual route, it raises an interesting possibility. The western route bypasses almost all mountains until it reaches the Gila River in Arizona and it stays close to the coast for a much longer distance. Since Marcos de Niza was charged by the Viceroy to do just that, could this western route be the route he followed? If so, that would explain much of the difference in the conditions Coronado later complained about to the Viceroy as well as his apparent utter disgust with de Niza by the time they reached Cibola.

As a final note, it appears that Coronado and the Advance Party traveled an average 7.5 leagues per day all the way to Los Corazones after departing Culiacán. From the analysis on the northern half of the route, it appears that the Expedition traveled at the more "normal" rate of six leagues per day from Los Corazones to Cibola. These are nominal rates of travel, of course, and probably varied considerably from point to point depending on various factors. The condition of the men and animals, the location of the next desirable overnight camp site and the local terrain would have all affected the rate of travel.

Chapter 21

The Routes in Summary

In the previous chapters, detailed developments of the likely routes traveled by the Coronado Expedition's Advance Party on its way northward to Cíbola in 1540 have been presented. An analysis of satellite imagery and topographical maps was conducted starting in the vicinity of Zuñi Pueblo in western New Mexico. This choice was made for two reasons: first, it is almost certain that the pueblos of Cíbola were in this region and, second, the chroniclers provided much more detailed information for the northern part of the journey than for the southern part. This latter point made it more likely that places mentioned by the chroniclers could be found.

Using only the information provided by the members of the Expedition, it was possible to locate enough features on the ground to deduce possible routes that reasonably satisfy the chroniclers' accounts. That said, it is important to note that their descriptions of various places and features were, of course, their own personal observations, usually as recorded by a scribe and copied several times by other scribes through the centuries. These descriptions have now been interpreted subjectively by the author who attempted to fit present-day, observed geographical locations to those descriptions. This process is imprecise, at best, and it is recognized that different people going through the same process may derive different results.

Compounding those problems, in order to make

reasonable associations with the described sites it was sometimes necessary to take some liberties with the number of days of travel provided by Juan Jaramillo. This was justified by Jaramillo's repeated statement that he had trouble remembering such things when he was writing his account some twenty years after the Expedition's return. Another difficulty is that almost all of the "distances" were actually given by Jaramillo as time of travel and the chroniclers provided little knowledge of the rate of travel and provided no knowledge of how long they marched on any given day. The search of the imagery and maps was conducted using the distances as only a guide in locating candidate sites for the places visited by the Expedition. The results of the reverse-itinerary analysis have been presented with detailed arguments for any assumptions and exceptions made in deriving those results.

Two primary routes resulted from that search and are indicated on Figure 21.1. In this chapter a summary of those two routes will be presented. Some of the major alternate branch routes will also be included. Tables 21.1 through 21.4 present the sequence of places visited by the Expedition on its northbound journey. These Tables list the designated candidate site names and the distance between sequential sites as measured along the presented routes. Table 21.1 represents the western-most route depicted on Figure 21.1, while the other three Tables represent various routings that all utilize the eastern-most route for the southern part of the journey. Figure 21.1 presents these routes in graphical form beginning the journey in Culiacan and ending in the vicinity of Zuñi Pueblo.

Note that these routes stop short of any of the pueblos of Cíbola. The reason for this is that the analysis

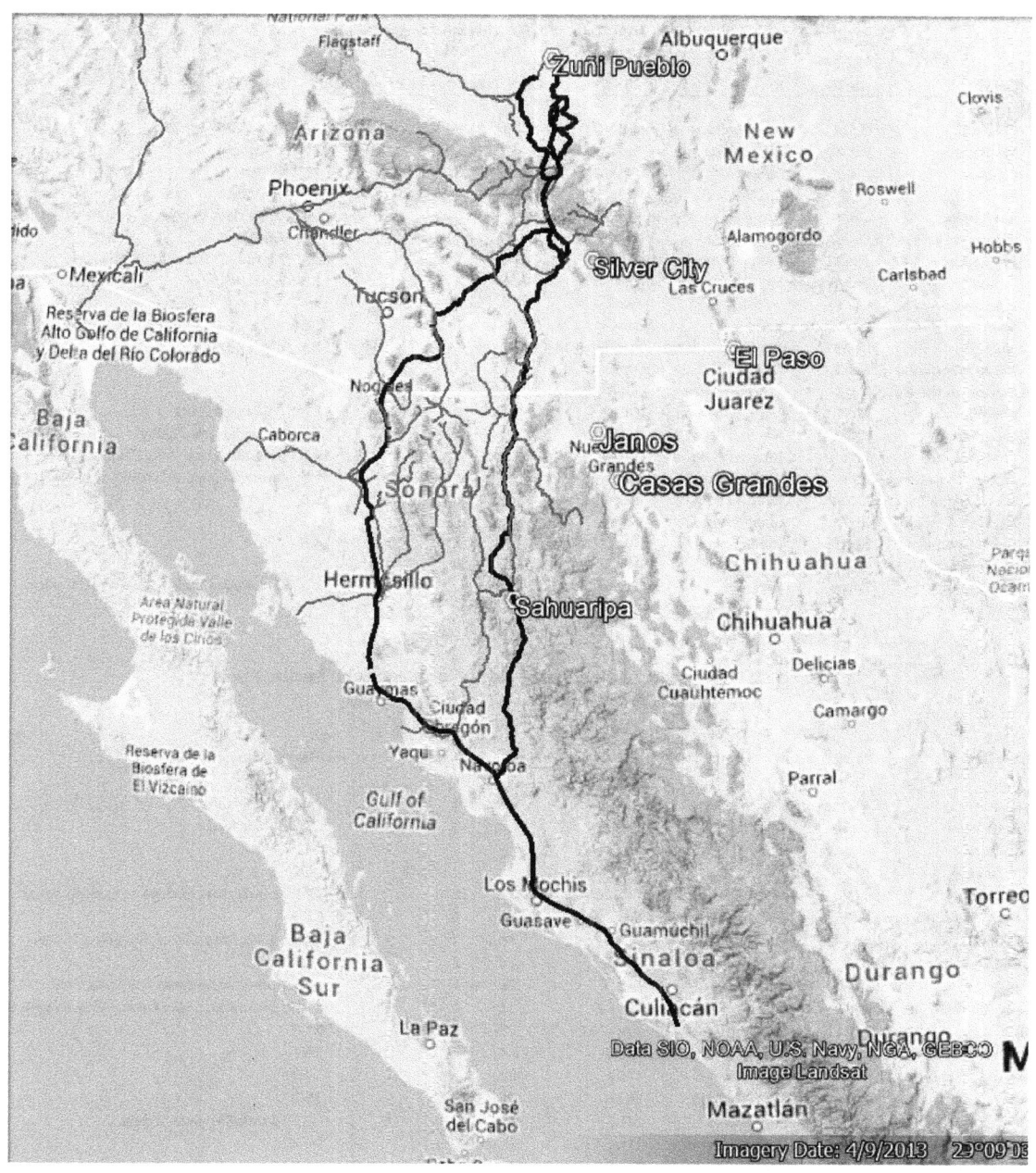

Fig 21.1. Satellite image showing the possible routes for the Coronado Expedition to Tierra Nueva in 1540.

Table 21.1 Coronado Trail to Cibola: Northbound Segments: **Western Route**

from	site ID	to	site ID	miles	days	branches miles	branches days	rate mi/day	comments
Culiacan	Culiacan	Rio Petatlan	Pet3B	72	4			18	6.8 lg/day
Rio Petatlan	Pet3B	Rio Sinaloa	Sin3A	60	3			20	7.6 lg/day
Culiacan	Culiacan	Rio Petatlan	Pet3A			84	4	21	8 lg/day
Rio Petatlan	Pet3A	Rio Sinaloa	Sin3A			48	3	16	6 lg/day
Rio Sinaloa	Sin3A	Arroyo de los Cedro	Ced3A	220	11			20	equiv days (5 days at double pace)
Arroyo de los Cedro	Ced3A	Rio Yaquimi	Yaq3A	60	3			20	7.6 lg/day.
Rio Yaquimi	Yaq3A	Indian Village	Vil3A	74	4			18.5	7 lg/day. Jaramillo gives 3 days
Indian Village	Vil3A	Los Corazones	Cor3	36	2			18	7 leagues/day
Los Corazones	Cor3	Señora	Sen3	26	unk			unk	
Señora	Sen3	Ispa	Ispa3	16	1			16	
Ispa	Ispa3	Rio Nexpa (Suya)	Nex3/Suya3	92	5			18.4	7 leagues/day
Rio Nexpa (Suya)	Nex3	Dogleg on the Nexp	Dog3	32	2			16	
Dogleg on the Nexp	Dog3	Chichilticale	Chi8	32	2			16	
Chichilticale	Chi8	Deep Canyon	DCb2	56.4	3			18.8	7.1 leagues/day
Deep Canyon	DCb2	Rio San Juan	SJ1a	60	4			15	Jaramillo gives 3 days
Rio San Juan	SJ1a	Rio de las Balsas	RB3a	31.6	2			15.8	Jaramillo gives 2 "full" days
Rio de las Balsas	RB3a	Arroya de la Barran	AB4b	23	2			11.5	Jaramillo gives 2 "short" days
Arroya de la Barran	AB4b	Rio Frio	RF4	15.5	1			15.5	
Rio Frio	RF4	Small Stream	SS X1	15	1			15	
Small Stream	SS X1	Rio Bermejo	Red River X	29	2			14.5	
Rio Bermejo	Red River X	Last Camp	Camp 8	16.8	1			16.8	
Last Camp	Camp 8	Bad Pass	Pass 8	1.5					Coronado: "half a league" (1.3 miles)
Total Distance				968.8					

Table 21.2 Coronado Trail to Cibola: Northbound Segments: **Eastern Route**
Eastern Branch A: (DCd & Dce) to SJ1a to RB3a

from	site ID	to	site ID	miles	days	branches miles	branches days	rate mi/day	comments
Culiacan	Culiacan	Rio Petatlan	Pet3B	72	4			18	6.8 lg/day
Rio Petatlan	Pet3B	Rio Sinaloa	Sin3A	60	3			20	7.6 lg/day
Culiacan	Culiacan	Rio Petatlan	Pet3A			84	4	21	8 lg/day
Rio Petatlan	Pet3A	Rio Sinaloa	Sin3A			48	3	16	6 lg/day
Rio Sinaloa	Sin3A	Arroyo de los Cedro	Ced2C	222	11			20.2	equiv days (5 days at double pace)
Arroyo de los Cedro	Ced2C	Rio Yaquimi	Yaq2C	46	3			15.3	
Rio Yaquimi	Yaq2C	Indian Village	Vil1B	78	4			19.5	7.4 lg/day. Jaramillo gives 3 days
Indian Village	Vil1B	Los Corazones	Cor1	28	2			14	
Los Corazones	Cor1	Señora	Sen 1	26	unk			unk	one league from Los Corazones
Señora	Sen 1	Ispa	Ispa 1	32	2			16	Jaramillo: 1 day from valley to valley
Ispa	Ispa 1	Rio Nexpa (Suya)	Suya1a1	79	5			15.8	
Rio Nexpa (Suya)	Suya1a	Dogleg on the Nexp	Dog1	29.4	2			14.7	
Dogleg on the Nexp	Dog1	Chichilticale	Chi2	28	2			14	
Chichilticale	Chi2	Deep Canyon	DCd	46	3			15.3	
Deep Canyon	DCd	Rio San Juan	SJ1a	48	3			16	Jaramillo gives 3 days
Chichilticale	Chi2	Deep Canyon	Dce			49	3	16.3	
Deep Canyon	Dce	Rio San Juan	SJ1a			43.5	3	14.5	Jaramillo gives 3 days
Rio San Juan	SJ1a	Rio de las Balsas	RB3a	31.6	2			15.8	Jaramillo gives 2 "full" days
Rio de las Balsas	RB3a	Arroya de la Barran	AB4b	23	2			11.5	Jaramillo gives 2 "short" days
Arroya de la Barran	AB4b	Rio Frio	RF4	15.5	1			15.5	
Rio Frio	RF4	Small Stream	SS X1	15	1			15	
Small Stream	SS X1	Rio Bermejo	Red River X	29	2			14.5	
Rio Bermejo	Red River X	Last Camp	Camp 8	16.8	1			16.8	
Last Camp	Camp 8	Bad Pass	Pass 8	1.5					Coronado: "half a league" (1.3 miles)
Total Distance				926.8					

Table 21.3 Coronado Trail to Cibola: Northbound Segments: Eastern Route
Eastern Branch B: (DCd & Dce) to SJ1a to RB4b

from	site ID	to	site ID	miles	days	branches miles	days	rate mi/day	comments
Culiacan	Culiacan	Rio Petatlan	Pet3B	72	4			18	6.8 lg/day
Rio Petatlan	Pet3B	Rio Sinaloa	Sin3A	60	3			20	7.6 lg/day
Culiacan	*Culiacan*	*Rio Petatlan*	*Pet3A*			84	4	21	*8 lg/day*
Rio Petatlan	*Pet3A*	*Rio Sinaloa*	*Sin3A*			48	3	16	*6 lg/day*
Rio Sinaloa	Sin3A	Arroyo de los Cedro	Ced2C	222	11			20.2	equiv days (5 days at double pace)
Arroyo de los Cedro	Ced2C	Rio Yaquimi	Yaq2C	46	3			15.3	
Rio Yaquimi	Yaq2C	Indian Village	Vil1B	78	4			19.5	7.4 lg/day. Jaramillo gives 3 days
Indian Village	Vil1B	Los Corazones	Cor1	28	2			14	
Los Corazones	Cor1	Señora	Sen 1	26	unk			unk	one league from Los Corazones
Señora	Sen 1	Ispa	Ispa 1	32	2			16	Jaramillo: 1 day from valley to valley
Ispa	Ispa 1	Rio Nexpa (Suya)	Suya1a1	79	5			15.8	
Rio Nexpa (Suya)	Suya1a	Dogleg on the Nexp	Dog1	29.4	2			14.7	
Dogleg on the Nexp	Dog1	Chichilticale	Chi2	28	2			14	
Chichilticale	Chi2	Deep Canyon	DCd	46	3			15.3	
Deep Canyon	DCd	Rio San Juan	SJ1a	48	3			16	Jaramillo gives 3 days
Chichilticale	*Chi2*	*Deep Canyon*	*Dce*			49	3	16.3	
Deep Canyon	*Dce*	*Rio San Juan*	*SJ1a*			43.5	3	14.5	*Jaramillo gives 3 days*
Rio San Juan	SJ1a	Rio de las Balsas	RB4b	39.8	2			19.9	Jaramillo gives 2 "full" days
Rio de las Balsas	RB4b	Arroya de la Barran	AB8b	21.2	2			10.6	Jaramillo gives 2 "short" days
Arroya de la Barran	AB8b	Rio Frio	RF8	16.8	1			16.8	
Rio Frio	RF8	Small Stream	SS X5	17.6	1			17.6	
Small Stream	SS X5	Rio Bermejo	Atarque Lak	29	2			14.5	
Rio Frio	*RF8*	*Small Stream*	*SS X7*			19.4	1	19.4	
Small Stream	*SS X7*	*Rio Bermejo*	*Atarque Lake*			27	2	13.5	
Rio Bermejo	Atarque Lak	Last Camp	Camp 2	14.5	1			14.5	Coronado: "half a league" (1.3 miles)
Last Camp	Camp 2	Bad Pass	Pass 2	1.3					
Total Distance				934.6					

Table 21.4 Coronado Trail to Cibola: Northbound Segments: Eastern Route
Eastern Branch C: (DCd & Dce) to SJ2a to (RB5a &, RB5c)

from	site ID	to	site ID	miles	days	branches miles	days	rate mi/day	comments
Culiacan	Culiacan	Rio Petatlan	Pet3B	72	4			18	6.8 lg/day
Rio Petatlan	Pet3B	Rio Sinaloa	Sin3A	60	3			20	7.6 lg/day
Culiacan	*Culiacan*	*Rio Petatlan*	*Pet3A*			84	4	21	*8 lg/day*
Rio Petatlan	*Pet3A*	*Rio Sinaloa*	*Sin3A*			48	3	16	*6 lg/day*
Rio Sinaloa	Sin3A	Arroyo de los Cedro	Ced2C	222	11			20.2	equiv days (5 days at double pace)
Arroyo de los Cedro	Ced2C	Rio Yaquimi	Yaq2C	46	3			15.3	
Rio Yaquimi	Yaq2C	Indian Village	Vil1B	78	4			19.5	7.4 lg/day. Jaramillo gives 3 days
Indian Village	Vil1B	Los Corazones	Cor1	28	2			14	
Los Corazones	Cor1	Señora	Sen 1	26	unk			unk	one league from Los Corazones
Señora	Sen 1	Ispa	Ispa 1	32	2			16	Jaramillo: 1 day from valley to valley
Ispa	Ispa 1	Rio Nexpa (Suya)	Suya1a1	79	5			15.8	
Rio Nexpa (Suya)	Suya1a	Dogleg on the Nexp	Dog1	29.4	2			14.7	
Dogleg on the Nexp	Dog1	Chichilticale	Chi2	28	2			14	
Chichilticale	Chi2	Deep Canyon	DCd	46	3			15.3	
Deep Canyon	DCd	Rio San Juan	SJ2a	60.4	3				Jaramillo gives 3 days
Rio San Juan	SJ2a	Rio de las Balsas	RB5a	37.5	2			18.7	Jaramillo gives 2 "full" days
Rio de las Balsas	RB5a	Arroya de la Barran	AB9a	23	2			11.5	Jaramillo gives 2 "short" days
Rio San Juan	*SJ2a*	*Rio de las Balsas*	*RB5c*			35.7	2	17.8	*Jaramillo gives 2 "full" days*
Rio de las Balsas	*RB5c*	*Arroya de la Barran*	*AB9a*			24.6	2	12.3	*Jaramillo gives 2 "short" days*
Arroya de la Barran	AB9a	Rio Frio	RF9	17.7	1			17.7	
Rio Frio	RF9	Small Stream	SS X6	19	1			19	
Small Stream	SS X6	Rio Bermejo	Atarque Lak	33	2			16.5	
Rio Bermejo	Atarque Lak	Last Camp	Camp 2	15	1			15	
Last Camp	Camp 2	Bad Pass	Pass 2	1.3					Coronado: "half a league" (1.3 miles)
Total Distance				953.3					

The Routes in Summary

was unable to specify with sufficient confidence which of the pueblos would have been the "first pueblo of Cíbola". However, there are three likely candidates for that distinction. For the western branch of the final approach on Cíbola depicted on Figure 21.1, either Hawikuh or Kechiba:wa appears equally likely. For any of the variations of the eastern branch of the final approach, only Kyaki:ma (Kiakima) appears likely. The analysis yields nothing more to help resolve which pueblo was the "first pueblo" or which path led to it. It is interesting to note that

Table 21.5 Locations of the Expedition's Places along Western Route

Coronado's Place	Modern Location	North Latitude	West Longitude
San Miguel de Culiacan	Rio San Lorenzo, 10 miles from coast[1]	24° 22.0'	107° 18.0'
valley of Culiacan	Culiacancito, Sinaloa	24° 49.5'	107° 31.9'
Rio Petatlan (Pet 3B)	Rio Surutato (?)	25° 29.3'	108° 17.6'
Rio Petatlan (Pet 3A)	Rio Sinaloa near Guasave	25° 27.8'	108° 27.2'
Rio Sinaloa (Sin 3A)	Rio Fuerte at San Miguel Zapotitlan	25° 57.4'	109° 3.0'
<routes split>	Navojoa	27° 5.2'	109° 26.8'
Arroyo de los Cedros (Ced3A)	23 miles N of Guaymas	28° 14.3'	111° 0.7'
Dry Arroyo (3)	3.3 miles N of Cieneguita	28° 26.3'	111° 2.9'
Rio Yaquimi (Yaq3A)	Rio Sonora at Hermosillo	29° 4.1'	110° 57.1'
Indian Village (Vil3A)	Rio Zanjón at Querobabi	30° 2.3'	111° 1.2'
Los Corazones (Cor3)	Rio Magdalena 6.3 miles SW of Santa Ana	30° 28.3'	111° 11.5'
small pass	4.6 miles SW of Santa Ana	30° 29.9'	111° 10.8'
narrow pass	4.2 miles NE of Santa Ana	30° 35.4'	111° 4.6'
narrow pass 2	2 miles W of Magdalena	30° 37.4'	110° 59.6'
narrow pass 3	6.1 miles NNE of Magdalena	30° 12.5'	110° 55.5'
Señora (Sen3)	Rio Magdalena at San Ignacio	30° 44.0'	110° 54.8'
Ispa (Ispa3)	Rio Magdalena 10.7 miles N of Imuris	30° 56.3'	110° 51.4'
Suya on Rio Nexpa (Nex3)	Rio San Pedro 14.3 miles SSE of Benson	31° 46.4'	110° 12.5'
Dogleg on Route (Dog3)	Rio San Pedro 15 miles N of Benson	32° 11.0'	110° 17.8'
Chichilticale (Chi8)	SSW Pinaleno Mts 15.3 mi N of Wilcox	32° 28.4'	109° 51.0'
Chichilticale (Chi8-alternate)	Sulphur Springs Valley 14 mi N of Wilcox	32° 26.8'	109° 55.5'
Deep Canyon (DCb2)	Gila River at Three Way	32° 56.1'	109° 14.2'
Deep Canyon (DCb)	Black Jack Canyon at Highway 78 crossing	33° 1.5'	109° 8.4'
Rio San Juan (SJ1a)	Rio San Francisco 8 miles NW of Mogollon	33° 27.1'	108° 55.6'
Rio San Juan (SJ2)	Cottonwood Can. 10.3 mi SW of Reserve	33° 37.2'	108° 53.7

Table 21.6 Locations of the Expedition's Places along Eastern Route

Coronado's Place	Modern Location	North Latitude	West Longitude
San Miguel de Culiacan	Rio San Lorenzo, 10 miles from coast[1]	24° 22.0'	107° 18.0'
valley of Culiacan	Culiacancito, Sinoloa	24° 49.5'	107° 31.9'
Rio Petatlan (Pet 3B)	Rio Surutato (?)	25° 29.3'	108° 17.6'
Rio Petatlan (Pet 3A)	Rio Sinaloa near Guasave	25° 27.8'	108° 27.2'
Rio Sinaloa (Sin 3A)	Rio Fuerte at San Miguel Zapotitlan	25° 57.4'	109° 3.0'
<routes split>	Navojoa	27° 5.2'	109° 26.8'
Arroyo de los Cedros (Ced2C)	Rio de Guisamopa 2 mi S of Guisamopa	28° 37.0	109° 6.1'
Rio Yaquimí (Yaq2C)	Rio Aros and Rio Bavispe confluence	29° 11.1'	109° 16.5'
Indian Village (Vil1B)	Rio Bavispe near Huásabas	29° 54.0'	109° 17.5'
Los Corazones (Cor1)	Rio Bavispe near Villa Hidalgo	30° 9.7'	109° 18.8'
Señora (Sen1)	Rio Bavispe under Gral Lázaro Cárdenas	30° 31.9'	109° 21.8'
Ispa (Ispa1)	Rio Bavispe at Rio Bate Pito confluence	30° 50.2'	109° 13.8'
Suya (Suya1a)	San Simon Valley 2.2 mi S of Rodeo	31° 48.2'	109° 2.3'
Dogleg in Route (Dog1)	Rio San Simon 7.3 mi SE of San Simon	32° 11.8'	109° 8.3'
Chichilticale (Chi2)	West flank of Summit Hills	32° 29.8'	108° 59.0'
Deep Canyon (DCd)	Gila River 1 mi W of Bill Evans Lake	32° 52.0'	108° 35.9'
Rio San Juan (SJ1a)	Rio San Francisco 8.5 mi NW of Mogollon	33° 27.1'	108° 55.6'
Rio San Juan (SJ2a)	Cottonwood Canyon at US Highway 180	33° 37.2'	108° 53.7'

Table 21.7 Locations of the Expedition's Places along Northern Route

Coronado's Place	Modern Location	North Latitude	West Longitude
Rio de las Balsas (RB3a)	Rio San Francisco at Luna	33° 49.0'	108° 57.0'
Rio de las Balsas (RB4b)	Largo Canyon at Spur Trail Draw	33° 52.1'	108° 45.3'
Rio de las Balsas (RB5c)	Forest Road 23 at Apache Creek	33° 59.0'	108° 42.4'
Arroyo de la Barranca (AB4b)	Forest Road 205 at head of Canovas Creek	34° 2.0'	109° 0.1'
Arroyo de la Barranca (AB8b)	Forest Road 19 at N end of Mangitas Flat	34° 4.4'	108° 51.8'
Arroyo de la Barranca (AB9a)	US Highway 60 at Agua Fría Creek	34° 15.5'	108° 46.2'
Rio Frío (RF4)	Coyote Creek at Upper Coyote Road	34° 10.5'	109° 8.5'
Rio Frío (RF8)	Agua Fria Creek 2.5 mi NW of Blaines Lake	34° 17.8'	108° 48.2'
Rio Frío (RF9)	Largo Creek 2 mi NW of Quemado	34° 21.6'	108° 31.7'
Small Stream (SS X1)	Dry stream 3 mi N of Springerville Gen	34° 21.7'	109° 10.6'
Small Stream (SS X6)	Carrizo Wash at Catron Co Rd A037	34° 30.3'	108° 38.8'
Small Stream (SS X7)	Carrizo Wash at NM St Rd 601	34° 30.1'	108° 47.1'
Rio Bermejo (Red River X4)	Pine Spring Wash at US Highway 191	34° 43.0'	109° 15.8'
Rio Bermejo (Atarque Lake)	Pinito Draw at Atarque Lake	34° 46.3'	108° 46.9'
Last Camp (Camp 2)	Mesa West of Galestina Canyon	34° 57.4'	108° 45.0'
Last Camp (Camp8)	Zuñi River 1.2 mi WSW of Venadito Draw	34° 51.6'	109° 4.7'
Bad Pass (Pass 2)	W wall of Galestina Can 1.3 mi E Camp 2	34° 57.4'	108° 43.6'
Bad Pass (Pass 8)	Zuñi River 1.3 mi NE of Camp 8	34° 51.7'	109° 3.4'

both Kiakima (which has an oral history indicating that Estevan visited there and was killed there) and Hawikuh (which Fredrick Hodge took to be the pueblo first visited by Coronado) are two of the three likely candidates derived from the present analysis.

Tables 21.5, 21.6 and 21.7 list the major places visited by the Coronado Expedition and the associated candidate sites identified along the various branches of the possible route. These tables describe the locations of the candidate sites and also give their Latitude and Longitude as derived from modern maps. The locations given are to be understood to be a "locality" rather than a precise point.

At a minimum, this work has shown that there are possible paths through this territory which satisfy, in a reasonable manner, the descriptions handed down by the members of the Expedition. It is very surprising that so few of the multitude of possible paths survived the scrutiny of this investigation. This suggests some hope that one of the routes described could be the actual route taken by the Coronado Expedition to Tierra Nueva in 1540.

It is to be hoped that a study of the existing archaeological evidence and significant additional field work will someday be able to verify (or refute) these results. It can also be hoped that additional Expedition documentation will come to light and that there will be people like Richard and Shirley Flint to make them accessible to the public.

Chapter 22

Epilogue

The Coronado Entrada to Tierra Nueva in 1540 was a major undertaking planned, organized and financed (in large part) by Viceroy Antonio Mendoza. The main thrust of the campaign was to be a land force commanded by Captain General Francisco Vásquez de Coronado. It is well known that a second arm of the campaign consisted of two ships under the command of Captain Hernando de Alarcón who was to sail northward along the western coast of Mexico with supplies for Coronado's land force. Not quite so well known is the existence of a previous program to supply the land force. Mendoza apparently had sent men and supplies ahead to Culiacán under the leadership of Hernando Arias de Saabedra prior to Coronado's departure from Compostela to establish a depot for Coronado's Expedition. The exact nature of this effort is unknown, but it would appear that some of those supplies reached Culiacán by ship since the ship *San Gabriel* is known to have been there at the time of Coronado's arrival. The *San Gabriel* was later added to Alarcón's armada of the two ships *San Pedro* and *Santa Catarina* when he reached Culiacán, but none of the supplies carried by the armada ever reached Coronado and his ground force after they departed from Culiacán.

The Expedition began in Mexico City but did not muster and organize until Compostela, about one-quarter of the distance to Cíbola. It then marched to Culiacán (another quarter of the way) where it reorganized and rested for several weeks. This first half of the journey was a well-traveled path to the most northern of the Spanish settlements and would have been well known to the Expedition. The way station, or depot, established at Los Corazones by General Arellano was about another quarter of the distance between Mexico City and Cíbola. The route from Culiacán to Los Corazones by 1540 had a five-year Spanish history and would not have been completely unfamiliar to Coronado. Los Corazones was an Indian settlement presumably visited (and named) by Cabeza de Vaca on his epic journey in 1535. The Expedition's Advance Party included Marcos de Niza who had (if his account can be trusted on this point) previously visited Los Corazones in the company of Estevan the Moor. Estevan, himself, had been part of the Cabeza de Vaca group. It then seems highly unlikely that the name "Los Corazones" would have been misapplied to a different settlement. The Melchoir Diaz / Juan de Zaldívar group of about sixteen horsemen (and an unknown number of others) had been over this segment of the route on its way to Chichilticale and back a few weeks prior to the Expedition's passage. Since Diaz was also part of the Advance Party, it is reasonable to assume that Coronado had good knowledge of the entire first three-quarters of the route to Cíbola.

Most of the final quarter of the route would have been more of an unknown to Coronado, especially the portion north of Chichilticale. However, even this portion was not a complete unknown because some of the Indios Amigos and some of the other Indians had been over the trail with Estevan. Other Indians had been trading along the route for generations. The Expedition's use of existing Indian trade routes and local Indian guides ensured that they would follow an expedient route with minimal chance of trouble.

Marcos de Niza had been charged by the Viceroy to stay close to the coast on his 1539 entrada whereas Coronado presumably had more freedom to use the latest and best information he possessed. It is merely a supposition that the "Los Corazones" visited by Coronado was the same settlement as the "Los Corazones" visited by Marcos de Niza. It is also a supposition that "Chichilticale" was visited by Marcos de Niza. Other than these two suppositions, there is little or no evidence that the two entradas followed the same route. For that reason, information from the de Niza report has not been used in the present work.

The single most significant influence on determining the possible routes of the Coronado Expedition is the narrative of Juan Jaramillo. He alone supplied information on the majority of places visited and he alone provided distances between places. However, as he told the addressee of his work, he was not certain of that information after the intervening 20 years. Some liberties had to be taken with Jaramillo's remembered travel times in order to fit observed terrain features with several of the places in his narrative. These have been discussed in detail at the appropriate place in the text.

The method of marching employed by the Expedition is not discussed in any detail by any of the chroniclers. However, the majority of the distances between identified sites as measured on modern maps are consistent with the following supposition. It appears that the Expedition marched for a distance of one league, rested for an unknown period of time and then marched for another league. This march-rest-march-rest sequence was then repeated until six, seven or eight marches had been made in any one day. Most of the distances associated with multiple-day journeys can be closely approximated by some combination of six-, seven- or eight-league days. This supposition is also very consistent with the step-counting technique known to be employed by the Expedition for determining marching distance.

There are several instances in the available documentation of the Expedition where some additional pertinent information is given and some of that could provide clues about the route taken. The chroniclers of the Coronado Expedition mention plants and animals found at several places along the way. However, these seem to always apply equally well to both the Western Route and the Eastern Route and have proved inadequate in differentiating between the routes. On the other hand, it is known that Arellano sent a reconnaissance party under Rodrigo Maldonado from Los Corazones "downriver" to the coast in search of news of Alarcón's armada. The "Los Corazones" on the Eastern Route lies along the Rio Bavispe which flows from north to south and eventually joins the Rio Yaqui which empties into the Gulf of California just south of Guaymas. If this were the Expedition's Los Corazones, then Maldonado would have been retracing a major part of Arellano's journey from Culiacán. This seems highly unreasonable. On the other hand, the "Los Corazones" on the Western Route lies along the Rio Magdalena which flows toward the west to join the Rio de la Asunción to empty into the Gulf of California near its head. Going "downriver" along the Rio Magdalena would be a much more logical course for Maldonado to have taken. This observation would favor the Western Route over the Eastern Route.

There is another pairing of reports that may also favor the Western Route. Pedro de Castañeda implies that Coronado's Expedition followed the same route as did Marcos de Niza when he says[1]

1. F&Fdocs28, p392

> *The general and his troop crossed the land without opposition, because they found everyone to be at peace because the Indians were familiar with fray Marcos and some of those who had traveled with Captain Melchoir Diaz when he and Juan de Zaldívar went to make a reconnaissance .*

2. F&Fdocs6, p68

Marcos de Niza[2] says that somewhere along this part of the route it was "forty leagues from this settlement to the sea". He does not mention the name of this settlement and he never says that he passed through "Los Corazones." This 40 leagues (105 miles) would be correct for portions of the Western Route near the Rio Magdalena, but would be only about half the distance to anywhere along the Rio Bavispe on the Eastern Route.

The possible routes presented in this work were determined by reasonable interpretations of information given by the chroniclers of the Expedition with some freedom taken with Jaramillo's uncertain memory of distances. As such, the results cannot be considered absolutely certain. Other pathways may be possible and one, in particular, should be noted. If it were possible to find a route for which the present site of Ures, Sonora could be identified as the Expedition's "Los Corazones", then Maldonado's trip "downriver" would have been along the present Rio Sonora. This would have been a logical reconnaissance. However, such a route through Ures would still not fit into the supposition that Coronado followed Marcos de Niza's route that passed within 40 leagues of the sea. In any event, the present analysis has found no justification supporting a route through Ures and the Rio Sonora valley.

The final state of the existing knowledge regarding Coronado's route for the Expedition to Tierra Nueva in 1540 is still one of uncertainty. For the southern three-

Epilogue

quarters of the route between Culiacán and Cíbola there are two possible major branches, both of which have serious shortcomings. The Western Route depends on three unknowns

> 1. The unverified supposition that Coronado followed Marcos de Niza's route,
>
> 2. An un-accounted missing segment in the chroniclers' distances or times of travel,
>
> 3. The unverified existence of cedar trees at the Arroyo de los Cedros site, Ced3A.

The Eastern Route is dependent on

> 1. A missing 33-league segment between "Los Cedros" and the Los Corazones site Cor1,
>
> 2. The unverified existence of cedar trees at the Arroyo de los Cedros site, Ced2C,
>
> 3. The presumption that Jaramillo meant his distances along the Rio Bavispe to be measured from the end of one valley to the start of the next valley.

The northern one-quarter of the route to Cíbola is comprised of one major branch with several unresolved minor branches. Any of these could be the Expedition's path but the chroniclers have given insufficient information to discriminate between them. Archaeological evidence will be required to resolve these questions.

Coronado's Expedition of 1540 was essentially a business venture searching for portable wealth in the form of gold and silver and a more fundamental wealth in the form of encomiendas based on productive land and Indian labor to work the land. The Expedition spent two years searching for that wealth, but never found it. The only gold and silver they discovered was a few nuggets in one pot at San Juan Pueblo (Ohkay Owingeh Pueblo) in New Mexico and they could not determine its source. They did find some river valleys with good land but failed to find a native population who could be subjugated into a workforce for the desired network of encomiendas. In the Spring of 1542, Coronado realized that the purpose of the business venture would not be accomplished and led the Expedition back to Culiacán.

This Expedition was the first serious European exploration of the territory which is now the northern part of Mexico and the southwesten part of the USA. Coronado's men explored a huge part of the northern half of New Mexico, parts of Arizona and California, the panhandle of Texas, a bit of Oklahoma and a major part of Kansas. Very likely, they also crossed the southeastern part of Colorado on their return from Kansas. In doing so, they contributed a vast amount of geographical knowledge about a totally unknown portion of the North American continent.

And yet the Expedition's route remains a mystery.

Appendix A

Method of Travel

The Captain General Francisco Vásquez de Coronado organized the Expedition to Tierra Nueva in 1540 into several distinct companies, in military fashion. Each company was commanded by a Captain and was probably composed of European horsemen and footmen as well as a sizable number of servants, slaves and, perhaps some Indians who joined the Expedition along the way. There was a large number of Indian Allies (the *Indios Amigos* from southern Mexico accompanying the Expedition, but there is no indication these Indians were attached to the various companies.

The picture that emerges from the documents of the Expedition is that an individual company marched in single file, or perhaps in a narrow column, and that the companies marched one behind the other. The companies were separated from each other by some distance such that the Expedition stretched out many miles along the trail. One account says that it took an entire day for the whole Expedition to pass a given point on the trail.

1. F&Fdocs15, p201

It appears that the normal marching order consisted of a period of a one-league march (nominally 2.63 miles) followed by a rest period after which the sequence was repeated for a total of six to eight marches per day. After Coronado split off the Advance Party, it initially marched at "a fairly rapid pace" of about an average of 7.5 leagues (20 miles) per day. He probably achieved this with days of seven and eight one-league marches.

At the end of a day of marching, the Expedition would set up camp and repeat the entire procedure the next day. Every once in a while they would halt and rest for some number of days (two day and four day periods were reported). Apparently each company had its own *real*[2] (camp of tents) which they would set up for shelter. The exact form of these *reales* is unknown, but they would likely have been arrangements of individual small tents in a relatively compact area. It seems unlikely that all the companies would come together for nightly camps, but it is possible that they would assemble for the multiple-day rests that occurred periodically.

The Expedition had large herds of livestock (sheep, cattle and probably goats) being driven along the trail. Little information about how these herds were moved can be obtained from the Expedition's documents, but it might be surmised that the livestock were herded separately from any of the companies of men. It is also probable that the livestock used a different, but close-by and parallel, path than that used by the people wherever possible.

From various accounts, it seems that the Expedition routinely employed two different methods of determining the distance between designated points. One man would be assigned to count his paces and later convert the total to leagues and another man would be assigned to estimate the distance by sight from feature to feature and to keep a tally for the day's march. There are several portions of the route for which distances were stated *in leagues*, but most of the surviving distance information is expressed in a soldier's "days of travel".

2. F&Fdocs15, p396

Appendix B

Distances Between Named Places

The various places visited by the 1540 Coronado Expedition to Nueva Tierra and the distances between them are of fundamental concern in studying Coronado's trail. Fortunately, several chroniclers left a record of some of the places visited – albeit with sometimes sketchy descriptions and imprecise indications of the distances between several of those places. The two primary sources of such information are

1) the Narrative of Pedro de Castañeda de Nájera[1]
2) Juan Jaramillo's narrative[2].

1. F&Fdocs28
2. F&Fdocs30

Both of these men wrote their narratives some twenty years after the Expedition ended, so some inaccuracies might be expected. Castañeda appears to have had access to written records or, perhaps, he had a phenomenally good memory. On the other hand, Jaramillo warns his reader that his memory could be faulty after the intervening 20 years since the Expedition's journey, so his information cannot be considered as absolute.

Castañeda often supplies distances in units of leagues (almost certainly the *leguas legales* for which the conversion to miles is 2.63 miles per league) while Jaramillo almost always reports the number of *jornadas* (a day's journey) from one place to another. The obvious problem is that the Expedition did not travel at a constant rate and so a jornada probably represents different distances at different places. The type of terrain would have affected the travel rate while the choice of nightly camp sites probably determined the end of a day's march more often than not. Even so, Jaramillo's information is very often the only distance indication available for many segments of the journey.

As pointed out in Chapters 4 and 7, there are several places where an estimate of a rate of travel over certain segments of the route was able to be established.

1. Jaramillo says that the Advance Party took four days to go from San Miguel de Culiacán to Petatlán "at a fairly rapid pace" and Castañeda says that the distance is 30 leagues. The average "rapid pace" travel rate over this segment was then 7.5 leagues per day over a fairly open and flat path.

2. Castañeda states that there are 80 leagues between Chichilticale and the first pueblo of Cíbola and that it took 15 days to reach the Rio Bermejo which is 8 leagues before Cíbola. The average travel rate on this 72 league segment of the trail was then 4.8 leagues per day. Much of this segment was in mountainous terrain and involved crossing the Rio San Juan and the Rio de las Balsas. Castañeda seems to mean 15 elapsed days instead of 15 jornadas, but that is not certain.

3. Pedro López de Cárdenas, Domingo Martín and Pedro de Ledesma all indicate that the "last camp" was about 3 leagues from the first pueblo of Cíbola (and therefore about 5 leagues from the Rio Bemejo). It is highly probable that the Expedition camped at the Rio Bermejo the previous night and, if so, their rate of travel from there to the site of the last camp

would have been about 5 leagues/day. At that point in the entrada the entire Advance Party was near starvation (several people died at the small stream about 10 leagues before reaching the Rio Bermejo) so traveling at that relatively slow rate might be a bit more than should be expected.

The Estimated Distance Charts

The charts included in the Tables of this Appendix display the estimated or measured distances between any two places along the Expedition's route. They are similar to the familiar "mileage charts" found on many present-day road maps. The upper right portion of the charts of Tables B-1 and B-2 give the known information about the indicated distances while the lower left portion displays the deduced distances between the remaining pairs of locations. The black boxes indicate the diagonal of the chart where the row and column for a particular place intersect. The entry just below a black diagonal box displays the incremental distance from the place named in the black box's column to the place named in the entry's row. The numbers in bold font in these charts represent distances that were given by the chroniclers in units of leagues whereas the numbers in bold italic font (and in shaded boxes) represent distances estimated and converted from travel times.

Table B-1 (See notes at end of Appendix.)

For the purposes of the Table B-1 charts, the numbers given in leagues (bold font) are taken as fact and used as reference points for constructing the chart. This constrains the chart to the given total distance of 300 leagues from Culiacán to Cíbola and to the several other intermediate distances. The distances converted

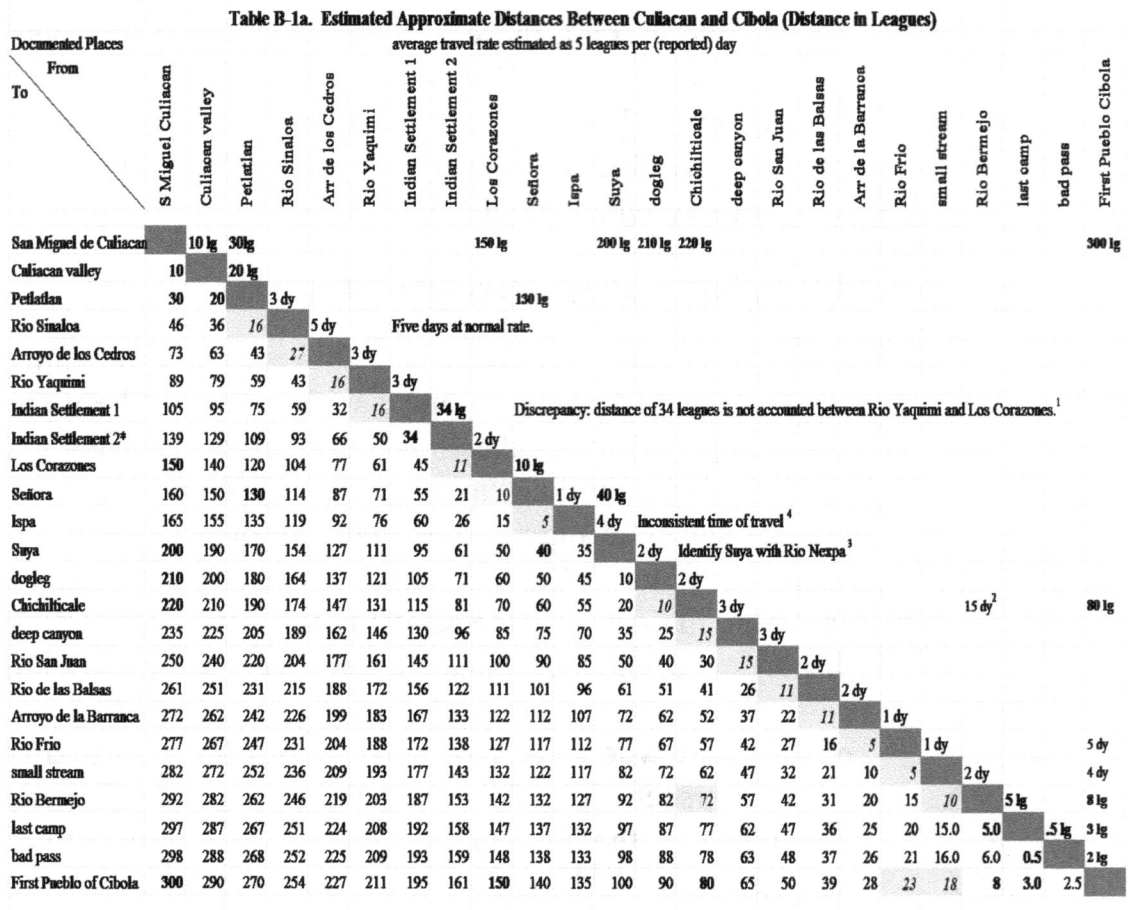

from travel times were used as estimating aids, but the actual numbers entered in the corresponding chart positions in the lower left portion just below the black, diagonal positions were adjusted somewhat arbitrarily to accommodate the reference distances. The nature of this chart is that the number in a given row and column in the lower left portion is the sum of all the incremental distances from that row to that column (inclusive). This feature -- along with the few known reference distances – provided the means of filling in the chart. But first, some

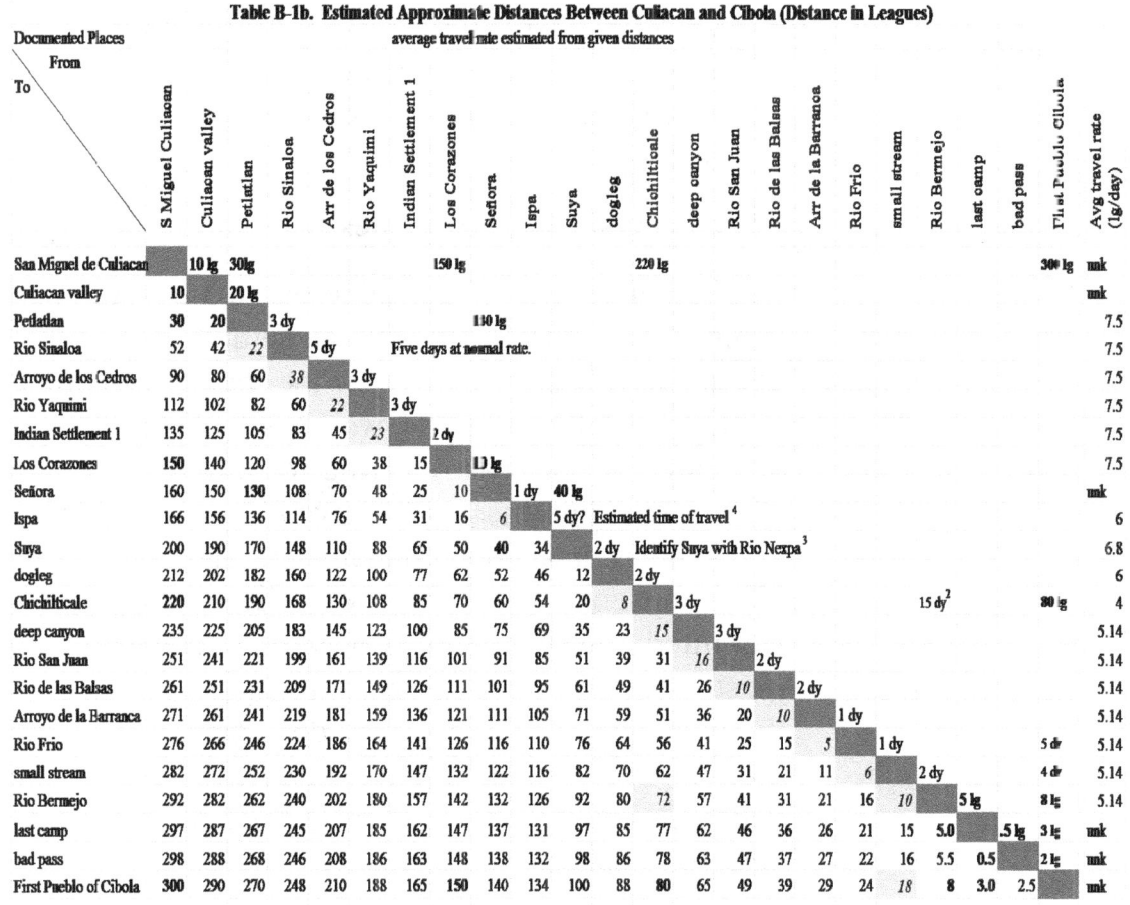

Table B-1b. Estimated Approximate Distances Between Culiacan and Cibola (Distance in Leagues)
average travel rate estimated from given distances

i. upper right of chart contains data provided by the chroniclers, lower left is derived information.
ii. distance documented in leagues denoted by **bold font**.
iii. distance converted from days to leagues denoted by ***bold italics***.

James J (Pete) Drexler Oct 2013

assumptions had to be made concerning the average daily rate of travel. These assumptions are addressed in the following two Tables.

Table B-1a

There are several occasions on various portions of the route when the chroniclers give a clear indication of a rate of travel of about five leagues per day. However, it is not clear whether that rate applies to the Advance Party or to the main body of the Expedition. It is also not clear whether the number of days refers to *elapsed days* or to *travel days (jornadas)*. Table B-1a is based on the assumption of a rate of five leagues per the number of days given, regardless of which chronicler supplied the information.

There are several difficulties with this chart.

1. Jaramillo reports that there was a 3-day journey from Rio Yaquimí to the Indian settlement and that there was a 2-day travel from the Indian settlement to Los Corazones. The way his narrative reads, it seems that he was referring to only one "Indian settlement" but this would leave a distance of about 33 leagues unaccounted between San Miquel de Culiacán and Los Corazones. Given Jaramillo's admitted faulty memory, it seems reasonable to postulate that there were actually two different Indian settlements. These are designated as "Indian Settlement 1" and "Indian Settlement 2" on the chart and have been placed 33 leagues apart to accommodate this discrepancy.

2. Jaramillo also says there was a four-day travel from Ispa to the Rio Nexpa, but that would place the Rio Nexpa about 14 leagues south of Suya where there is no other indication of a river existing. He does also state, however, that the four-day travel was through "unsettled" lands and that they found Indians at the Rio Nexpa. There is no mention of other settlements between Ispa and Suya. This argues in favor of identifying the Rio Nexpa of Jaramillo's narrative with the location of Suya and doing so is consistent with the other known reference locations on the chart.

3. The site of the snowfall and the site of the Big Boulders of the main body's experience are questionable and are not included on the chart. The segment of the route from Coronado's last camp to Cíbola then includes only information derived from the Advance Party's records.

The discrepancy of the 33 leagues is a direct result of assuming a travel rate of five leagues per day. Instead of inventing a second Indian Settlement, this discrepancy can be accomodated by adjusting the travel rate. This has been done in Table B1-b.

A second means of eliminating the 33-league discrepancy is to re-interpret Jaramillo's estimate of five days travel from Rio Sinaloa to the Arroyo de los Cedros. If he meant five days for the reconnaissance group traveling at "double pace", then about ten days travel for the Advance Party would be indicated. See Table B-4 for additional information.

Table B-1b

It is known from Jaramillo and Castañeda that the Advance Party left the Rio Sinaloa at the "fairly rapid pace" of about 7.5 leagues per day. The chart of Table B-1b is based on this rate of travel to Los Corazones. This rate and the number of days given for that segment of the route agrees with the 150 leagues recorded by the chroniclers. The other distances and travel rates tabulated in the chart were deduced in accomodation of the reference distances noted in the upper right portion of the chart. Otherwise, this chart is very similar to that of Table B-1a.

The accuracy of Table B-1 is expected to be no

Table B-2a. Estimated Approximate Distances Between Culiacan and Cibola (Distance in Leagues)
one day's travel estimated as 7.5 leagues from Culiacan to Los Corazones, 6.0 leagues north from Culiacan

From / To	S Miguel Culiacan	Culiacan valley	Petlatlan	Rio Sinaloa	Arr de los Cedros	Rio Yaquimi	Indian Settlement	Los Corazones	Señora	Ispa	Suya	dogleg	Chichilticale	deep canyon	Rio San Juan	Rio de las Balsas	Arr de la Barranca	Rio Frio	small stream	Rio Bermejo	last camp	bad pass	First Pueblo Cibola
San Miguel de Culiacan		10 lg	30 lg					150 lg					220 lg										300 lg
Culiacan valley	10		20 lg																				
Petlatlan	30	20		3 dy				130 lg															
Rio Sinaloa	52	42	22		5 dy																		
Arroyo de los Cedros	90	80	60	38		3 dy																	
Rio Yaquimi	112	102	82	60	22		3dy																
Indian Settlement	134	124	104	82	44	22		2 dy															
Los Corazones	149	139	119	97	59	37	15		10 lg														
Señora	159	150	140	124	69	47	25	10		1 dy	40 lg												
Ispa	165	156	146	130	75	53	32	16	6														
Suya/Nexpa	199	190	180	164	109	87	66	50	40	34		2 dy											
dogleg	211	202	192	176	111	99	78	62	52	46	12		2 dy										
Chichilticale	223	214	204	188	123	111	90	74	64	58	24	12		3 dy						15 dy			80 lg
deep canyon	241	232	222	206	141	129	108	92	62	46	42	30	18		3 dy								
Rio San Juan	259	250	240	224	159	147	126	110	80	64	60	48	36	18		2 dy							
Rio de las Balsas	271	262	252	236	171	159	138	122	92	76	72	60	48	30	12		2 dy						
Arroyo de la Barranca	283	274	264	248	183	171	150	134	104	88	84	72	60	42	24	12		1 dy					
Rio Frio	289	280	270	254	189	177	156	140	110	94	90	78	66	48	30	18	6		1 dy				5 dy
small stream	295	286	276	260	195	183	162	146	116	100	96	84	72	54	36	24	12	6		2 dy			4 dy
Rio Bermejo	307	298	288	272	207	195	174	158	128	112	108	96	84	66	48	36	24	18	12		5 lg		8 lg
last camp	312	303	293	277	212	200	179	163	133	117	113	101	89	71	53	41	29	23	17	5.0		0.5 lg	3 lg
bad pass	313	304	294	278	213	201	180	164	134	118	114	102	90	72	54	42	30	24	18	6	0.5		2.5 lg
First Pueblo of Cibola	315	306	296	280	215	203	182	166	136	120	116	104	92	74	56	44	32	26	20	8	3	2.5	

i. upper right of chart contains data provided by the chroniclers, lower left is derived information.
ii. distance documented in leagues denoted by **bold font**.
iii. distance converted from days to leagues denoted by ***bold italics***.

James J (Pete) Drexler   Oct 2013

better than one or two leagues and most of the uncertainty is due to the somewhat arbitrary nature of converting the "days traveled" information to actual distance in leagues. However, there are a sufficient number of reference locations to keep the errors reasonably small.

Table B-2

The previous charts were constrained to accomodate the chroniclers' statements of distances from Culiacán to Los Corazones (150 leagues), Chichilticale

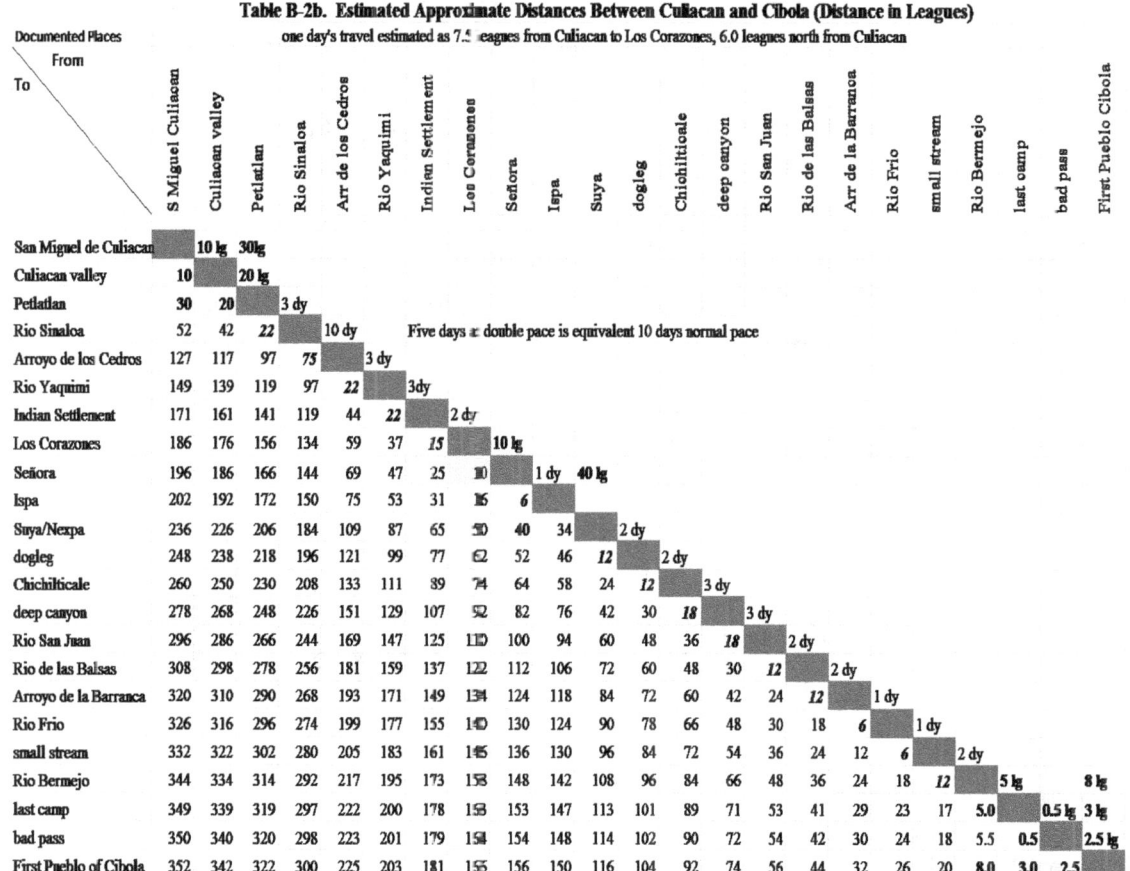

Table B-2b. Estimated Approximate Distances Between Culiacan and Cibola (Distance in Leagues)
one day's travel estimated as 7.5 leagues from Culiacan to Los Corazones, 6.0 leagues north from Culiacan

i. upper right of chart contains data provided by the chroniclers, lower left is derived information.
ii. distance documented in leagues denoted by **bold** font.
iii. distance converted from days to leagues denoted by ***bold italics***.

James J (Pete) Drexler Oct 2013

3. F&Fdocs22, p291

(220 leagues) and the First Pueblo of Cíbola (300 leagues by most reports but 350 leagues by another[3]). However, these long segment distances seem to have been broad approximations intended to convey a general concept of the geography involved in the Expedition. If those constraints were abandoned, perhaps a better estimate of the locations of the various named places would emerge. To that end, the charts of Table B-2 were constructed using a "fairly rapid" travel rate of 7.5 leagues per day from Culiacán to Los Corazones and a nominal rate of

Appendix B   277

6 leagues per day from there to Cíbola. Two charts are presented but the only difference between them is that Table B-2b applies an equivalent 10-day travel time (at normal rate) to the route segment from Culiacán to Los Corazones while Table B-2a applies a 5-day travel time. One result of lifting the forced compliance with the chroniclers' "long segment" distances in these charts is that the overall distance from Culiacán to Cíbola is now estimated at either 315 leagues or 352 leagues instead of

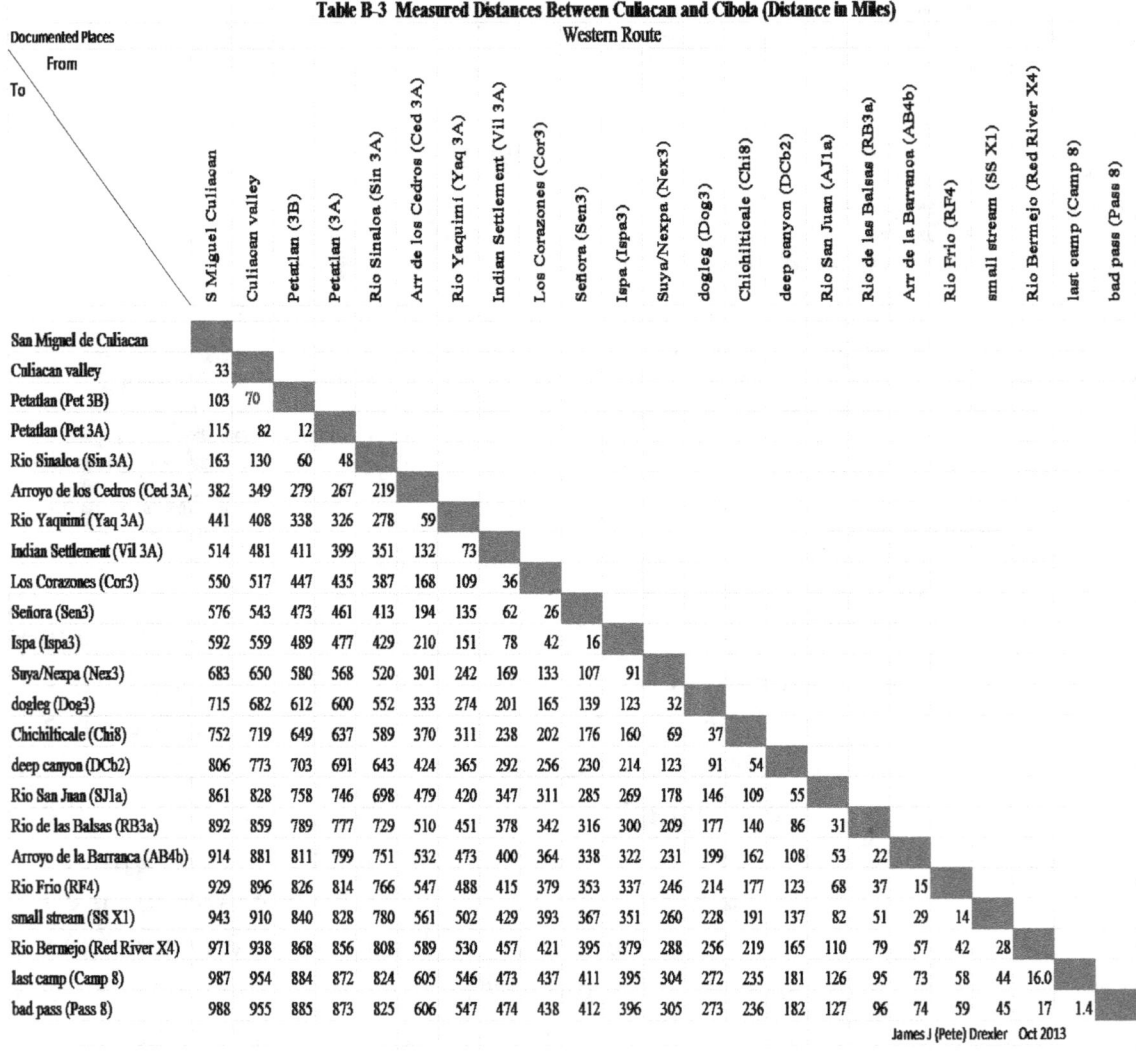

the previous 300 leagues.

The Measured Distance Charts

The charts of Table B-1 and Table B-2 presented distances estimated directly from descriptions of places as supplied by the chroniclers of the Coronado Expedition. That information formed the basis of the discovery of candidate locations of sites visited by Coronado as presented in Part 2 of this book. That investigation resulted in two viable

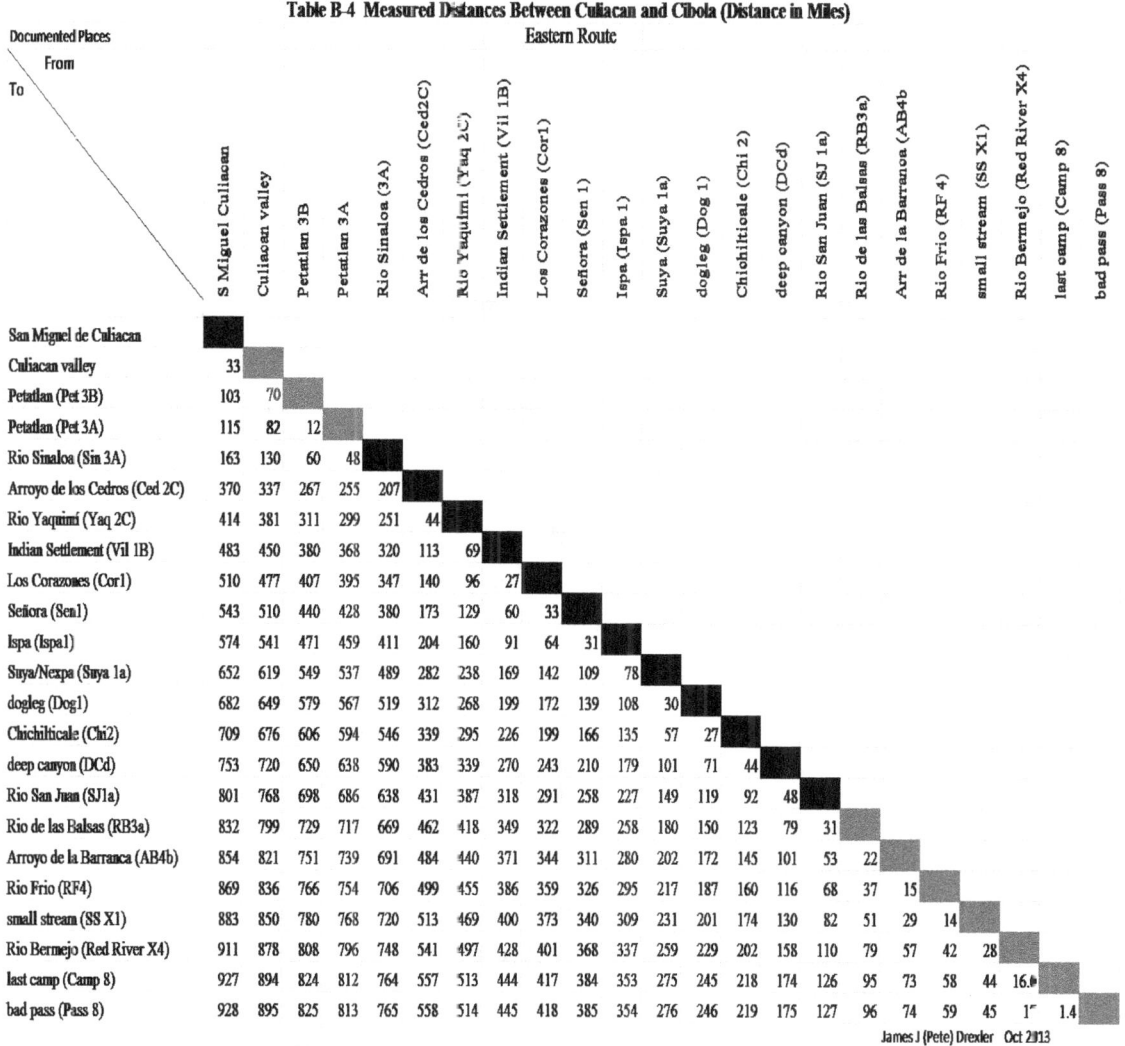

Table B-4 Measured Distances Between Culiacan and Cibola (Distance in Miles) Eastern Route

candidate routes for the Expedition to have taken in 1540. The "Western Route" stays close to the coast and follows the Rio Magdalena while the "Eastern Route" lies farther inland and follows the Rio Bavispe. Tables B-3 and B-4 present the *measured* distances between candidate sites on these two routes. These two charts list the distance in units of miles instead of leagues to emphasize that they have been measured on modern maps.

The total distance from Culiacán to Cíbola (at least as far as the "bad pass") as determined on these charts is 375 leagues (988 miles) along the Western Route and 352 leagues (928 miles) along the Eastern Route. A minor variation in these distances occurs depending upon which of the branches is chosen between the Rio San Juan and Cíbola. The longest distance stated by any chronicler is the "more than 350 leagues" by the unknown author of the *Traslado de las Nuevas*[3]. This would seem to favor the Eastern Route over the Western Route. However, the 375 leagues of the Western Route is only about 7% greater than the stated 350 leagues. This difference is within a reasonable error for the Expedition's method of distance measurement. While the Eastern Route may be slightly more likely than the Western Route, the latter cannot be eliminated as a possibility.

It might be noted that the Eastern Route distance of 352 leagues agrees with the estimated distance of Table B-2b which is based on a 10-day travel time between Rio Sinaloa and the Arroyo de los Cedros. Identification of the candidate sites along both the Western Route and the Eastern Route were also based on that travel time. The fact that no sets of candidate sites could be found for a five-day travel time between Rio Sinaloa and the Arroyo de los Cedros supports the contention that Jaramillo was referring to his own travels at double pace for that segment of the route.

Table B-1 Notes:

1. Assuming 150 leagues from San Miguel de Culiacán to Los Corazones. Arbitrarily added Indian Settlement 2 to accommodate 33-league discrepancy.

2. Average travel rate here is 4.8 leagues per day. The 80 leagues from Chichilticale to Cíbola minus the 8 leagues from Rio Bermejo to Cíbola implies 72 leagues from Chichilticale to Rio Bermejo which was covered in 15 days.

3. Suya lies at the Rio Nexpa if the distances given in leagues are correct and if the rate of travel was 5.33 leagues per day over that portion of the route.

4. If the five leagues per day is correct, Jaramillo is probably wrong on the number of days travel. If four days of travel is correct, either the Rio Nexpa would be about 14 leagues south of Suya or the travel rate would have been greater than 9 leagues per day.

Appendix C

Searching for Locations near Cíbola

The documents of Coronado's 1540 entrada into La Tierra Nueva in search of Cíbola contain descriptions of some two dozen sites and features along the route between Culiacán and Cíbola. However, none of these descriptions is sufficient to positively identify any of those sites or features with corresponding geographical locations on modern maps. The most plausible reason for this lack of adequate detail is that the Expedition was following established Indian trade routes, so the chroniclers probably did not feel the need to record a great amount of geographical information to aid later travelers in following the same path.

Present geography of the region is expected to be somewhat different from that of 1540. The climate at that time was much different from the present climate. The entire region was still in the midst of the Little Ice Age. The average temperature was lower than today's average temperature and the average rainfall (and snowfall) would have been much higher than it is today. The difference in climatic conditions would have resulted in much greater water flow in the streams and rivers and would have supported a much different distribution of flora and fauna than exists at the present time. Streams and springs probably flowed in regions which are now dry and barren. Given the same level of civilization and technology of the 1500s, the region probably would have supported a much greater and different distribution of human habitation than would be possible today.

With the above observations in mind, a search for the sites and features may begin. Because the sites mentioned in the Expedition's documents occur more frequently as Coronado nears Cíbola, that region is a logical place to begin the search.

A Synopsis of Known Places

1. **The "first pueblo" of Cíbola.** *This is the first pueblo encountered by Francisco Vásquez de Coronado and his Advance Party upon reaching the region of Cíbola.*

1. F&Fdocs22, p292

The anonymous author of *Traslado de las Nuevas*[1] says that the pueblo

> *was all surrounded by a stone wall like a city wall. The houses [were] very tall, of four and five [stories] and [some] even of six stories, each one with its flat roof and covered passageways.*

2. F&Fdocs28, p393

3. Winship, p16

Castañeda[2] describes the first pueblo of Cíbola as "spilling down a cliff" and says there are other pueblos very much larger and stronger than Cíbola. Winship[3] translates this passage as "looking as if it [had] been crumpled all up together." Castañeda also says that the Spaniards succeeded in capturing the pueblo with some significant difficulty

> *"because [the Indians] have a narrow entryway [with] twists and turns"*

while Winship's translation has

> *"since they held the narrow and crooked entrance."*

4. Davis, p155

William Watts Hart Davis[4] in his 1869 book says of the first pueblo of Cíbola

> *Instead of the large city as the friar had represented, they found it to be a village of not more than two*

> *hundred warriors, situated upon a rock, and the only means of reaching it was by a narrow and tortuous road difficult to ascend.*

Castañeda says that Cíbola was 8 leagues (21 miles) from their position on the Rio Bermejo. Jaramillo recalled a two day journey – but not two full days – so Castañeda's distance is probably close to the actual distance.

5. F&Fdocs19, p256

In his letter to Viceroy Mendoza, Coronado[5] states that a Spaniard named Espinosa, two Moors and some of the *Indios Amigos* died from hunger at a place identified by Jaramillo[5] as a "small stream". The unknown author of the *Traslado de las Nuevas*[7] states that it was four day's travel (47 to 63 miles) from the small stream to the first pueblo of Cíbola. From Chichilticale, Castañeda[2] records that it was a distance of 80 leagues (209 miles) toward the north to Cíbola. From Corazones, the author[8] of *Relacion del Suceso, 1540s* gives 150 leagues [391 miles] to Cíbola.

6. F&Fdocs30, p513

7. F&Fdocs22, p291

8. F&Fdocs29, p497

2. **The "bad pass"**. *This is the pass defended by Cárdenas the night before the Advance Party reached the first pueblo.*

9. H&R, p344

López de Cárdenas[9] reports that Coronado and the remainder of the Advance Party met up with Cárdenas and his 10 men at the bad pass the morning after the midnight battle and that they all marched on toward Cíbola on July 7, 1540. They saw four or five Indians about one league (2.63 miles) before Cíbola (or about 7 leagues (18.4 miles) from Rio Bermejo), but the Indians left without meeting with the Spaniards. Coronado's troops continued their march toward Cíbola and about a crossbow's shot (perhaps about 150 feet) just outside the pueblo they

> *found a large number of the Indians in the country outside the pueblo*[1]*. and ...they approached the*

Appendix C   285

horses' legs to shoot their arrows. ...some of them fled quickly to the pueblo, which was nearby and well fortified[10].

10. *F&Fdocs19, p257*

11. *F&Fgeo, pg599*

According to testimony[11] given at the Coronado inquiry, the Spaniards approached the first pueblo from the west.

12. *F Cruelties, p93*

Domingo Martin's testimony[12] includes the information that at the bad pass, Cárdenas "established a bivouac in a woodland" where the Spaniards were attacked after night had fallen.

13. *F Cruelties, p235*

Pedro de Ledesma[13] reports that "there were some boulders" at the dangerous pass that Cárdenas was sent ahead to guard, suggesting that the "bad pass" of the Advance group in July 1540 and the "site of big boulders" of the main body in September 1540 might refer to the same place.

3. **The site of the "last camp"**. *This is the location where the main part of the Advance Party camped while Cárdenas' group defended the bad pass.*

14. *F Cruelties, p468*

Coronado stated that Cárdenas camped that night at the bad pass which was "half a league" ahead and to the east of the Captain General's camp[14]. Many Indians attacked at midnight and Cárdenas stayed there until morning waiting for Coronado to arrive[9]. Castañeda says that the first battle (and, hence, the bad pass) was two leagues (5.26 miles) before Cíbola[2].

15. *H&R, p343*

Garcia López de Cárdenas says[9,15]

The expedition came within three or four leagues [8-12 miles] of Cíbola, without having any skirmishes with the Indians. When we reached that position, I was ahead with eight or ten horsemen and noticed

> *some Indians on a hilltop. I advanced alone to the place, making signs of peace and offering presents of things I carried to trade. With this, some of them came down and took the articles that I offered. I shook hands with them and remained at peace... and I remained there to await Francisco Vásquez and the others... At this very place, the soldiers camped for their last night before reaching Cíbola.*

Pedro de Ledesma, in his testimony[13] for the investigation into Coronado's conduct during the Tierra Neuva entrada to Cíbola and Quivira, stated that the Expedition's Advance Party was met by several Cíbolans "when they had gotten within 3 leagues of Cíbola" and that the camp was a bit beyond that meeting point, closer to Cíbola.

4. **The Rio Bermejo.** *Coronado probably camped at this river the night prior to the "last camp".*

The site of the last camp was about three leagues (8 miles) from the first pueblo of Cíbola according to Garcia López de Cárdenas[9] and Castañeda says that Cíbola was eight leagues (21miles) from their position on the Rio Bermejo[2]. Therefore the site of the "last camp" must have been about five leagues from the Rio Bermejo. There is no description of the terrain along this segment, except that there was a hill near the last camp.

Castañeda[2] gives a 15-day travel (177 to 235 miles) from Chichilticale to the Rio Bermejo and says that the river was so named because its waters

> *flowed muddy and bright red. In this river there were whiskered carp like [those] in Spain. It was here that the first Indians of that land were seen.*

The Expedition's Rio Bermejo is often associated with

Appendix C

the present Little Colorado River because it is the only river in the likely vicinity that satisfies this description in modern days.

5. The Rio del Lino.

The chroniclers give no information about this segment of the route. The Rio Bermejo and the Rio del Lino mentioned by Coronado might be the same river, but if both names are associated with the modern Little Colorado there is a problem with the distance to the first pueblo.

In his letter[5] to the Viceroy dated August 3, 1540, Coronado says of some unspecified river:

> *I saw that there was flax in very large quantities on the bank of one river, and therefore it is called Rio del Lino.*

Coronado does not specify where this river was located nor does he give any indication of its relative position in the sequence of geographical features encountered. This river has been positioned at this point in the present sequence of visited places primarily because the name "Rio de Lino" is found on General Carleton's early military map[16] of the region labeling the present Little Colorado River. There is no indication in the Expedition's documents that the Rio del Lino and the Rio Bermejo were the same river or that either lay at the location of the present Little Colorado River.

16. Carleton

6. The "small stream". *Coronado almost certainly camped at this stream which was two days' travel from the Rio Bermejo.*

Jaramillo gives two days' travel (23 to 32 miles) from the small stream to the Rio Bermejo, traveling in the "same general direction but more to the north[6]." Jarramillo's narrative implies that the direction was northeast, but Richard Flint explains[17] that it might easily have been intended to be "northwest".

17. F&Fdocs30, n67

A short portion of the southern part of this segment of the path (near the small stream) would have been through the northern edge of a pine forest, according to Jaramillo[6] and is where the Spaniard Espinosa and two others died from eating a poisonous plant. But the major portion (including the approach to the Rio Bermejo) would have been through a non-forested landscape (in 1540).

7. The Rio Frio.

Jaramillo[6] provides an uncertain one day travel time (12 to 16 miles) from the Rio Frio to the small stream going through a pine forest. On the Expedition's return trip from Tierra Nueva, Jaramillo gives the distance from Cíbola to the Rio Frio as 5 days (60 to 80 miles)[18] toward Chichilticale.

18. F&Fdocs27, p329

The Expedition named this river because its waters were cold[6] (probably in July 1540).

8. The Arroyo de la Barranca.

Jaramillo says it was a one-day travel[6] (4 to 6 leagues or 10.5 to 16 miles) between the Arroyo de la Barranca and the Rio Frio. The distance might be closer to four leagues since they were traveling through mountainous territory. He does not give any information about the terrain or the direction of travel.

Jaramillo[6] calls this a "stream" but gives no further description of this place nor of how or where the Expedition crossed it (*if* they crossed it). The name

Appendix C

could carry a number of different connotations. The word "barranca" usually applies to a cliff or to a small, steep-walled canyon. This place might be a stream flowing in such a canyon or along the base of a cliff. If the latter, could this be the cliff to which Coronado referred in his letter[5] to the Viceroy? The name could also be taken to imply that the stream flowed out of a canyon (barranca), perhaps cutting an arroyo below the mouth of the canyon. This in turn would imply that the Spaniards reached the stream below the mouth of the canyon.

9. The Rio de las Balsas.

Jaramillo says it was two "short days' travel " in a "nearly northeast" direction[6] between the Rio de las Balsas and the Arroyo de la Barranca. Here again, the uncertainty between "northeast" and "northwest" should be noted.

Jaramillo calls this a "river" and says the Expedition crossed it on rafts (balsas) because it was swollen[6]. He also says that they approached this river traveling northward.

Summary of Distances from Cíbola to the Rio Frio

The chart of Figure C-1 summarizes the above information concerning the distances between various named points along the trail near Cíbola. The bold, larger type font indicates information provided by the chroniclers and the smaller font presents additional information deduced from the information provided.

The distances converted from the number of days taken to travel between these points was done using a nominal rate of five leagues per day which seems to have been an average rate of travel in this region. However, several of the travel days were noted to be partial days and this has been reflected in the distances shown in the

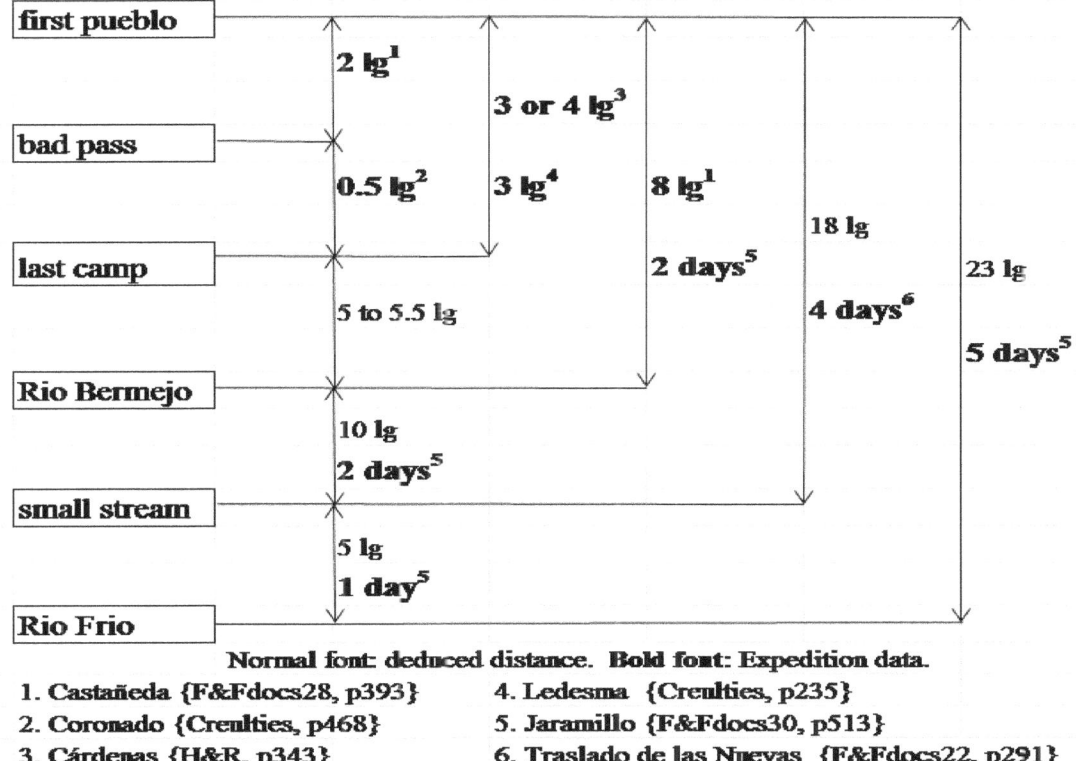

Fig. C-1. This chart displays the distance and travel time information associated with the named places visited by the Coronado Expedition as it approached Cíbola. It also includes references to the sources of that information.

chart. These distances are, of course, approximate but are consistent within the given parameters. The information in this chart served as a guide in locating possible geographical positions of the named features.

Appendix C   291

Appendix D

Tracing the Trail

It might seem odd that anyone would think it possible to determine the route of the Coronado Expedition to Tierra Nueva in 1540 almost 500 years later. The thousands of people and livestock of the Expedition would have certainly made an impression on the landscape, but 500 years of soil erosion, plant growth and subsequent use could have obliterated any trace of that activity. That would certainly be the expected result for a one-time use of any path across the desert southwestern USA and northern Mexico. However, the route taken by Coronado followed well established trails used for centuries as Indian trade routes and such use tends to form indelible traces on the terrain. Modern high resolution satellite images can reveal such traces. The primary problem with these images is that they also show the more modern trails, roads and highways as well as the scars of mining operations, urban sprawl, agriculture, pipelines and ranching operations.

This is not all bad news, however. It is well known that modern roads tend to follow old roads which tended to follow wagon roads which followed pack train trails which, in turn, followed foot trails. This old observation seems to have held true in many places until the advent of modern road building techniques. Before the early-to-mid twentieth century, roads generally followed terrain features and generally took the path of least resistance. Sometimes they took a less expedient path that represented a good trade-off between difficulty and distance to the desired destination. Older roads, then, can sometimes be an aide in finding even older trails. Especially in the desert regions, even one severe rain can drastically alter an existing arroyo perhaps forcing a re-routing of an existing trail, so it is recognized that trail routes were not static parts of the landscape. Roads and old trails cannot serve as proof of Coronado's path, but they can, and sometimes do, serve as proof of a *possibility* of a routing.

Recognition of some practical, general concerns for the routings of paths (either for the Spanish expeditions or for the Indian trade routes) also aid in searching for old trails.

1. Rivers are difficult and dangerous to cross. Cross as few rivers as possible. Cross smaller rivers if possible. It would probably be better to cross two smaller streams than to cross the one combined flow below their confluence.

2. Arroyos are difficult to cross. It would be desirable to follow the high ground upstream along (or between) arroyos and cross where the arroyo is smaller.

3. Dry arroyos often afford excellent passage and are sometimes called "highways of the desert."

4. A trail would follow in (or immediately alongside) a flowing stream only to avoid even rougher terrain farther away from the stream.

5. Water and pasture for the livestock must be found almost every day.

6. Narrow paths along steep inclines could be usable by people on foot, but may not be suitable for pack animals or livestock.

For Coronado's trail, there are eyewitness descriptions of several places along the route and approximate distances between them, both of which help locate plausible sites for those places. The chroniclers of the Expedition also supply some information about plants and animals found along the way, but most of this information is too generic to be of much help. Perhaps a biologist who is an expert in this desert region and is familiar with the fluctuations in the margins of the deserts could glean some useful information from the chroniclers' accounts.

In addition to more than a thousand Mexican Indians (the *Indios amigos*) there were several hundred European fighting men and an unknown number of additional servants with the Coronado Expedition. With all the arms, armor, equipment and supplies carried by the Expedition, it could well be expected that some artifacts are to be found along the route. Finding such artifacts and identifying them as belonging to the Expedition would be strong evidence of Coronado's route. Such artifacts, by themselves, would still not constitute proof since those items could have been collected by local Indians, subsequent inhabitants or travelers and transported from the site where they were lost to the site where they were found. However, a consistent grouping of several such artifacts would be hard to ignore.

The most straightforward means of tracing the Expedition's route seems to be locating visible traces on sattellite images. Those traces must be consistent with the known descriptions and the distances between places recorded by the Expedition's chroniclers. In addition, any suspected route segment must be a logically viable path for people and livestock.

Appendix E

Climate History of the Cibola Region

The climate of any particular region on the Earth is a determining factor in the types of flora and fauna to be found in that region. Forests expand, contract, advance or retreat up and down mountains; rivers and wetlands appear, increase, decrease or disappear; cultivated crops thrive or suffer; and populations of people move into or out of the region in response to the climate changes. The climate in northern Mexico and southwestern USA in 1540 would have had a great influence on Coronado's Expedition to Tierra Nueva, so some knowledge of the history of climate in this region is desirable. Comparison of the climatic conditions of the present with those of 1540 has led to some valuable insights into the Expedition's experience.

The climate history over a span of about six hundred years is of interest for the present purpose, but instruments for measuring climate have been in existence for only the last quarter of that period. Scientists who study this subject have found several proxy climate indicators (such as tree rings) that have allowed them to reconstruct temperature and precipitation histories. These reconstructions have a yearly resolution over a period spanning the past 1500 years or more. There are two primary limitations of these results:

1. Climate is a regional phenomenon. Knowledge of climate details of one region cannot be applied to another region.

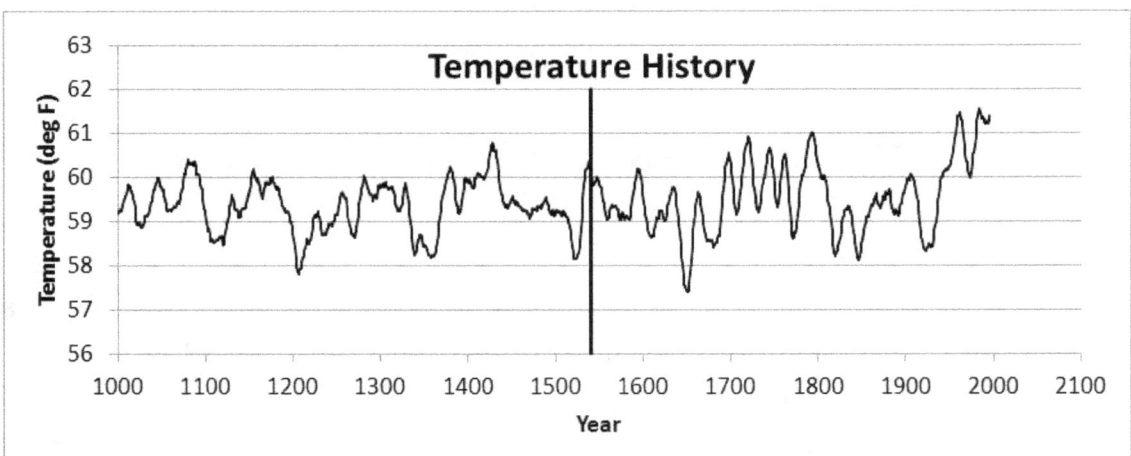

Fig E1. Reconstructed temperature record for the Colorado Plateau. Data points represent 10-year running average temperatures from 1000 to 1996. The vertical line marks the year 1540.

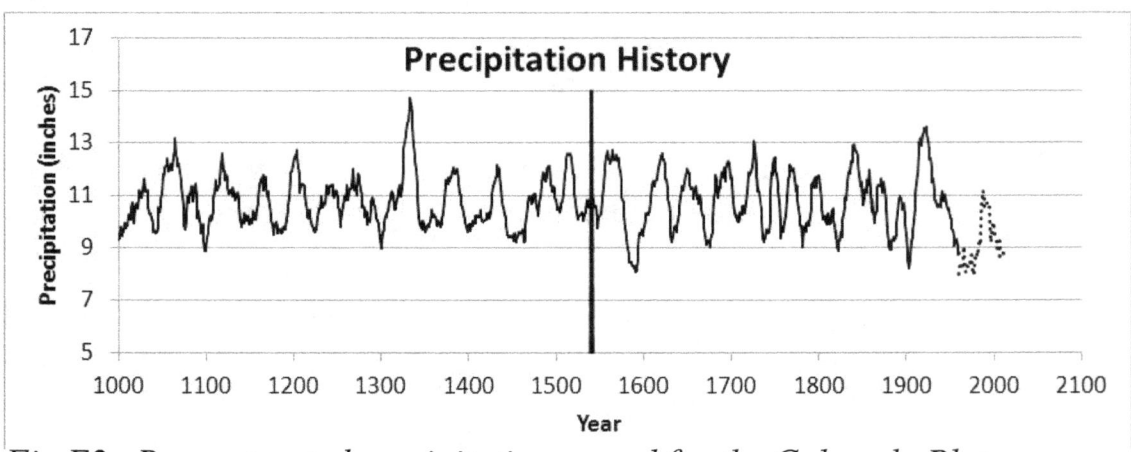

Fig E2. Reconstructed precipitation record for the Colorado Plateau. Data points represent 10-year running average precipitation. The solid line from 1000 to 1960 represents the Salzer-Kipfmueller tree ring data while the dotted line from 1960 to 2010 represents the GHCN measurements. The vertical line marks the year 1540.

2. Studies are available for only a limited number of small regions scattered around the globe.

Fortunately, the Colorado Plateau of northwestern New Mexico and northeastern Arizona is one of the regions for which such a climate reconstruction has been produced. The present Zuñi Indian Reservation, the heart of the Cíbola region, lies in the southern part of the Colorado Plateau. Those climate reconstructions are, then, pertinent to a study of Coronado's Expedition.

M.W. Salzer and K.F. Kipfmueller published an article[1] in 2005 describing the Colorado Plateau climate reconstructions of temperature and precipitation. Their data is available through the website[2] of the National Climatic Data Center (NCDC) of the National Oceanic and Atmospheric Administration (NOAA). Portions of that data have been used to produce Figures E1 and E2 which are graphs of the temperature and precipitation beginning in the year 1000. Both of these charts contain a vertical line marking the year 1540. Figure E2 includes data from the Aztec Ruins weather station in far northwestern New Mexico appended to the end of the Salzer and Kipfmueller data. The source[3] of this data is the Global Historical Climatology Network (GHCN) but is most conveniently accessed for visualization through the Weather Underground website[4].

In the documentation of the Coronado Expedition, there was found one direct reference to the climate along the route between Culiacán and Cíbola. In 1539 Fray Marcos commented that the Indians along the route (several hundred miles south of the Colorado Plateau) told him that their crops had not received rain for three years[5]. This dry condition is supported by Figure E2 where it is observed that the Expedition occurred about midway through a 20-year drought. Figure E1 shows that this dry period was also accompanied by a 20 year long warm period.

The precipitation data of Figure E2 indicates that

1. Salzer

2. NCDC, NOAA

3. GHCN

4. WUG

5. {F&Fdocs6, p67

the 10-year averaged precipitation since about 1950 has exceeded that of the 1540 drought during only one 10 year period extending from about 1985 to about 1995. Other than that short period, the present drought has been much drier than the 1540 drought period. It could be expected that in the present climate, forests would have receded from their margins in 1540 and that rivers and streams would now be flowing at much decreased volumes than in that previous period. Wetlands probably disappeared and the range of both plants and animals probably changed significantly. The ability of the land to support and sustain human populations is expected to be greatly curtailed at the present with respect to the 1540 time period.

It is clear that the present conditions of the region cannot be assumed to be the conditions encountered by the Coronado Expedition to Tierra Nueva of 1540.

Appendix F

Pack Animals

The chroniclers of Coronado's Expedition to Tierra Nueva in 1540 do not supply a wealth of information about the material goods carried by the Expedition nor about the means of transporting those goods. It is known that the fighting men of the *Indios Amigos* took their native arms and armor. They also probably carried food, repair tools, spare clothing, a cooking pot, a water jug and some sort of protection from the elements. All of this was probably carried in the familiar conical basket on their backs and in other containers slung from their backs or waist. Each of these Indian fighting men may have had a least one other person along to help carry part of the load, but that person would have also had to carry his or her own food and supplies. There is no indication that the Indios Amigos had beasts of burden.

On the other hand, the Spaniards did have pack animals and many went along with the Expedition, but the number of such animals is not discussed specifically in the documentation. However, there are two instances where sufficient information is given to allow an estimate to be made.

In chapter 2 it was noted that 600 loaded pack animals left Culiacán with the main body of the Expedition under Arellano's command. This number included an estimated 360 riding horses which were pressed into packing service. This implies that there was a estimated 240 horses and mules normally used as pack animals.

Since there were an estimated 258 Spanish fighting men in Arellano's command, it appears that normally there would be about one pack animal per fighting man.

Most of the other 360 horses and mules leaving Culiacán with Arellano were presumbly loaded with supplies to stock the supply station, San Gerónimo, that Arellano had been ordered to establish near Los Corazones.

The second instance that supports an estimate of the number of pack animals involves Castañeda's statement that there were 1000 "horses" crossing the Llano Estacado on the Expedition's route to the barrancas near Palo Duro Canyon. This number presumably includes mules, since Castañeda's statement concerned the lack of damage to the grasslands due to hoof wear. The number of horses (not including mules) at Culiacán before the Expedition split can be estimated: the 552 riding horses counted at the Compostela muster and an estimated 40 or more belonging to the Diaz/Zaldívar group. In addition to these, several more riding horses would have come with the several citizens of Culiacán who joined the Expedition. The number of these horses is estimated to be 18 so that the estimate of the total number of riding horses at Culiacán would be about 610.

An unknown number of these 610 horses were lost to starvation, hard use and Indian attacks before the Expedition reached the Llano Estacado of eastern New Mexico and the western Texas panhandle. When Castañeda made his estimate of 1000 "horses" it would, then, have included about 400 pack horses and mules. It stands to reason that some of the pack animals would have also been lost during the Expedition, so that it would be expected that more than 400 pack horses and mules were at Culiacán before Coronado left there with the Advance Party. This number is also the approximate number of European fighting men in the Expedition, so that it again appears that each European fighting man might have had one pack animal to carry his gear and supplies. There were probably several additional mules dedicated to carrying the heavy arms such as crossbows, arquebuses, and versillos as well as the bolts for the crossbows and the shot and gunpowder for the arquebuses and versillos.

If the above estimates are accurate, then the Advance Party would have had approximately 160 pack animals. This would be an average of about 1.5 pack animals per each of the 110 European fighting men in the Advance Party. It is reasonable to expect more pack animals in this group since they had to carry with them the bulk of an 80-day supply of food for the trip to Cíbola. The Advance Party anticipated finding little or no food along the route because they were traveling during the Spring of 1540 before the Indian crops had ripened.

Bibliography and Reference Key

A&R	Aiton, Arthur S. and Agapito Rey. "Coronado's Testimony in the Viceroy Mendoza Residencia." New Mexico Historical Review 12 (July 1937) 288-329.
A&P	Adorno, Rolena, and Patrick Charles Pautz, eds. and trans. *The Narrative of Cabeza de Vaca, 160.* Lincoln and London: University of Nebraska Press, 2003.
Adams&Duff	Adams, E. Charles, and Andrew I. Duff, eds. *The Protohistoric Pueblo World A.D. 1275-1600.* Tucson: The University of Arizona Press, 2004.
Carleton	"Map of the Military Department of New Mexico." David Rumsey Historical Map Collection. Series 1, Vol XLVII, map 17800998. www.davidrumsey.com. Cartography Associates, n.d. Thur. 21 Nov. 2013.
Covey	Covey, Cyclone. *Cabeza de Vaca's Adventures in the Unknown Interior of America.* Albuquerque: University of New Mexico Press, 1977.
Davis	Davis, W.W.H. The Spanish Conquest of New Mexico. 1869. Doylestown, PA. Publisher not Stated, 1869.
Epple	Epple, Anne O. A Field Guide to the Plants of Arizona. Guilford, CT: The Globe Pequot Press, 1997.
ExpTN	Flint, Richard, and Shirley Cushing Flint, eds. *The Coronado Expedition to Tierra Nueva: The 1540-1542 Route Across the Southwest.* Boulder: University Press of Colorado, 1997.
F&Fdocs	Flint, Richard, and Shirley Cushing Flint, eds., trans. and annot. *Documents of the Coronado Expedition, 1539-1542.* Dallas: Southern Methodist University Press, 2005.
F&F460	Flint, Richard. "What's Missing from This Picture? The *Alarde*, or Muster Roll, of the Coronado Expedition." In *The Coronado Expedition: From the Distance of 460 Years*, edited by Richard Flint and Shirley Cushing Flint. Albuquerque: The University of New Mexico Press, 2003.

FCruel	Flint, Richard. *Great Cruelties Have Been Reported: The 1544 Investigation of the Coronado Expedition.* Dallas: Southern Methodist University Press, 2002.
Ferguson	Ferguson, T. J. *Historic Zuni Architecture and Society: An Archaeological Application of Space Syntax.* Tucson: The University of Arizona Press, 1996.
GHCN	Global Historical Climatology Network (GHCN). http://www.ncdc.noaa.gov/temp-and-precip/ghcn-gridded-products.php. 1/18/2014.
Green	Green, Jesse. *Zuñi: Selected Writings of Frank Hamilton Cushing.* Lincoln and London: University of Nebraska Press, 1979.
H&R	Hammond, George P., and Agapito Rey. *Narratives of the Coronado Expedition, 1540-1542.* Coronado Cuarto Centennial Publications, 1540-1940, Vol. 2. Albuquerque: University of New Mexico Press, 1940.
Hodge	Smith, Watson, Richard B. Woodbury and Nathalie F. S. Woodbury. *The Excavation of Hawikuh by Fredrick Webb Hodge: Report of the Hendricks-Hodge Expedition, 1917-1923.* New York: Museum of the American Indian Heye Foundation, 1966.
Kintigh	Kintigh, Keith W. *Settlement, Subsistence and Society in Zuni Prehistory.* Tucson: The University of Arizona Press, 1985.
Krieger	Krieger, Alex D. *We Came Naked and Barefoot: The Journey of Cabeza de Vaca Across North America.* Austin: University of Texas Press, 2002.
Ladd TN	Ladd, Edmund J. "Zuni on the Day the Men in Metal Arrived." In *The Coronado Expedition to Tierra Nueva: The 1540-1542 Route Across the Southwest*, edited by Richard Flint and Shirley Cushing Flint, 187-194. Boulder: University Press of Colorado, 1997.
ModHist	"Biographic Sources On Spaniards In The New World, 16th-17th Centuries". Modern History Sourcebook. www.fordham.edu. Fordham University, NY, n.d. 15 Jan. 2013.

NCDC, NOAA	National Climatic Data Center (NCDC) of the National Oceanic and Atmospheric Administration (NOAA). http://www.ncdc.noaa.gov. 1/18/2014.
OSU	College of Earth, Ocean and Atmospheric Sciences (CEOAS), Oregon State University. http://paleomag.coas.oregonstate.edu/research/projects/arctic/arcticfig2.html. 04/07/2014.
ReffDDCC	Reff, Daniel T. *Disease, Depopulation and Culture Change in Northwestern New Spain. 1518-1764.* Salt Lake City: University of Utah Press, 1991.
Rodack TN	Rodak, Madeleine Turrell. "Cíbola, from Fray Marcos to Coronado." In *The Coronado Expedition to Tierra Nueva: The 1540-1542 Route Across the Southwest*, edited by Richard Flint and Shirley Cushing Flint. Boulder: University Press of Colorado, 1997.
Salzer	Salzer, M.W. and K.F. Kipfmueller. *Reconstructed Temperature and Precipitation on a Millennial Timescale from Tree-Rings in the Southern Colorado Plateau, U.S.A.* Climatic Change, Volume 70, Number 3, pp. 465 - 487, June 2005. Data accessed through: http://www.ncdc.noaa.gov/data-access/paleoclimatology-data/datasets/climate-reconstruction. 01/15/2014.
Winship	Winship, George Parker, ed. and trans. *The Journey of Coronado*. San Francisco: The Grabhorn Press, 1933. Reprint, New York: Dover Publications, Inc., 1990.
WUG	Weather Underground website. http://www.wunderground.com/climate/local.html?id=USC00290692&var=PRCP. 1/18/2014.

Index

Advance Party 5, 8, 11, 12, 27, 28, 29, 30, 31, 32, 33, 34, 35, 39, 46, 47, 49, 50, 51, 52, 53, 56, 62, 65, 66, 71, 74, 77, 78, 93, 94, 95, 96, 97, 98, 99, 100, 104, 115, 116, 117, 118, 121, 127, 130, 133, 138, 147, 155, 165, 177, 207, 228, 229, 232, 237, 239, 242, 243, 250, 251, 260, 267, 270, 271, 273, 275, 284, 285, 286, 287, 303
Agua Fria Creek 143, 144, 145, 151, 152, 154, 160, 161, 163, 174
Aguayaval 14
Ah:kya:ya 109
Alonso del Castillo 3
Alonso González 43
Alonso Sánchez 48
Alonzo Álvarez del Valle 47
Alonzo del Moral 42
Alonzo Manrique 47
Álvar Nuñez Cabeza de Vaca 3
Andres Dorantes 3, 5
animals 8, 26, 27, 35, 37, 38, 39, 40, 41, 51, 61, 75, 118, 250, 262, 294, 295, 300, 301, 302, 303
Antonio de Castilblanco 48
Antonio de Mendoza 3
Apache Box 188, 190, 191, 200, 202
Apache Creek 153, 154, 173, 174, 176, 180, 183, 186, 188, 190, 191
Aravaipa Creek 207, 208
Arias de Saabedra 15, 259
armor 14, 20, 21, 25, 30, 34, 295, 301
arms 14, 18, 20, 21, 28, 29, 30, 34, 36, 37, 39, 41, 46, 47, 90, 295, 301, 303
Arroyo de la Barranca 71, 72, 154, 155, 156, 157, 158, 159, 160, 161, 162, 163, 165, 166, 167, 169, 170, 171, 175, 290
Arroyo de los Cedros 64, 65, 225, 226, 227, 229, 230, 231, 232, 233, 234, 235, 237, 239, 243, 244, 246, 247, 248, 249, 264, 275, 280
artifacts 17, 99, 295
astrolabe 58

Atarque Lake 131, 132, 134, 137, 144, 145, 152, 183
bad pass 74, 95, 96, 97, 99, 118, 119, 120, 121, 122, 123, 124, 125, 126, 127, 133, 134, 135, 137, 145, 154, 280, 285, 286
Bald Knoll 189, 196
Batuco 89, 90
Bear Creek 192
Beaver Creek 167, 168, 169, 170, 175, 176, 178
Beaverhead Work Camp 181
Becker Lake 149, 156
Benny Creek 156
Bernal Diaz 14
Big Boulders 96, 275
Big Burro Mountains 186, 196
Bill Knight Gap 150, 152, 158, 159, 162, 163, 170, 171, 172, 175, 176
Binna:wa 108, 109, 112
Black Canyon 181
Black Jack Canyon 191, 202
black men 24, 36, 115
Black Ridge 139, 142
Black River 166, 167, 169, 175, 178
Blaines Lake 152, 154, 160, 161, 163, 173, 175
Blue River 178, 179, 181
bronze pieces 30
Brushy Mountain 188
Bursum Road 180, 181
Butterfield Stage 210
Campbell Blue Creek 169, 176, 178
camps 52, 75, 268
Captain General 27, 42, 45, 46, 47, 95, 155, 207, 259, 267, 286
captains 14, 28, 41, 43, 44, 45, 46, 47
Carleton 73, 288, 305
Carnero Creek 149
Carrizo Wash 143, 144, 145, 146, 152, 153, 154
Caspar de Saldana 48
cattle 8, 26, 27, 31, 37, 38, 50, 65, 118, 268
Ceadro Spring 130
chain mail 21

Chalo:wa 109, 117, 135
Chiametla 10, 22, 23, 43, 45
Chiricahua Mountains 210
Christianity 4, 17
Cíbola 3, 4, 5, 6, 7, 8, 9, 10, 11, 13, 14, 15, 17, 22, 26, 27, 28, 31, 32, 33, 36, 41, 46, 47, 49, 50, 53, 55, 56, 58, 61, 62, 63, 65, 68, 69, 70, 71, 72, 73, 74, 76, 77, 78, 79, 80, 82, 83, 84, 85, 87, 88, 91, 93, 94, 95, 96, 97, 98, 99, 100, 103, 104, 105, 106, 107, 108, 109, 111, 113, 114, 115, 116, 117, 118, 119, 121, 122, 123, 124, 125, 127, 128, 133, 134, 135, 138, 140, 141, 142, 147, 149, 151, 154, 176, 183, 184, 225, 228, 249, 251, 252, 256, 259, 260, 264, 270, 271, 275, 277, 278, 280, 281, 283, 284, 285, 287, 289, 291, 299, 303, 306
Climate 61, 297
Colima 14
Colorado River 15, 27, 37, 49, 53, 55, 73, 79, 80, 82, 103, 140, 141, 142, 145, 148, 156, 157, 288, 289
Compostela 10, 18, 19, 20, 21, 22, 23, 24, 26, 27, 30, 35, 36, 37, 41, 44, 45, 82, 83, 84, 239, 259, 302
Concho Creek 139, 140, 142, 144, 145, 148, 152
Concho Lake 148, 156
Corn Mountain 7, 108, 113
Coronado 3, 4, 5, 6, 7, 8, 9, 10, 11, 12, 13, 14, 15, 16, 17, 18, 19, 20, 22, 23, 24, 25, 26, 27, 28, 29, 30, 31, 32, 33, 35, 36, 37, 41, 42, 43, 44, 45, 46, 47, 48, 50, 52, 55, 56, 58, 59, 60, 61, 62, 63, 64, 65, 68, 69, 71, 72, 73, 74, 75, 77, 78, 79, 80, 81, 82, 83, 84, 85, 87, 90, 93, 94, 95, 97, 99, 100, 103, 104, 105, 106, 107, 108, 111, 114, 115, 116, 117, 118, 119, 120, 121, 122, 123, 124, 125, 127, 130, 132, 133, 134, 135, 137, 138, 139, 140, 141, 142, 144, 145, 146, 147, 150, 154, 155, 162, 167, 169, 176, 177, 181, 184, 185, 186, 195, 200, 204, 205, 207, 213, 215, 220, 224, 225, 226, 227, 228, 229, 231, 237, 239, 240, 242, 243, 244, 246, 247, 248, 250, 251, 253, 258, 259, 260, 261, 262, 263, 264, 265, 267, 269, 275, 279, 283, 284, 285, 286, 287, 288, 289, 290, 291, 293, 294, 295, 297, 299, 300, 301, 303, 305, 306, 307
Coronado Expedition 5, 10, 13, 16, 18, 19, 23, 25, 26, 31, 35, 36, 41, 43, 47, 55, 56, 59, 60, 62, 64, 75, 77, 82, 83, 93, 95, 103, 107, 108, 114, 118, 119, 120, 123, 127, 134, 135, 137, 139, 144, 146, 154, 162, 167, 169, 177, 181, 184, 185, 186, 195, 200, 207, 213, 215, 220, 224, 231, 237, 246, 248, 250, 251, 253, 258, 261, 262, 269, 279, 291, 293, 295, 299, 300, 305, 306
Cortes 3, 4
Cottonwood Canyon 180, 182
Cottonwood Wash 220
couriers 13, 82, 85, 91
Cow Springs Draw 150, 159, 160, 163, 172
Coyote Creek 150, 158
Crescent Lake 150, 166, 168
criados 24, 36, 38
Cristóbal de Escobar 78
Cristóbal de Oñate 19
crossbow 30, 47, 97, 285
Culiacán 3, 4, 5, 6, 7, 9, 10, 11, 12, 13, 14, 15, 16, 17, 18, 20, 21, 22, 23, 24, 25, 27, 28, 29, 30, 31, 32, 33, 34, 35, 36, 38, 43, 44, 45, 46, 47, 55, 56, 58, 60, 61, 62, 63, 64, 66, 67, 68, 69, 74, 76, 77, 81, 82, 83, 84, 85, 87, 90, 91, 239, 240, 241, 242, 243, 244, 245, 246, 247, 248, 249, 250, 259, 260, 262, 264, 265, 270, 271, 274, 276, 277, 278, 280, 281, 283, 299, 301, 302, 303

daggers 21
daily travel 236
Daniel 306, 48
Deep Canyon 69, 184, 185, 186, 187, 188, 189, 191, 192, 193, 194, 195, 197, 198, 200, 201, 202, 203, 204, 205, 211
Deep Creek 178
despoblado 70, 73
Diego de Alcaraz 79, 81
Diego de Guevara 42, 44, 45
Diego de Guzman 63
Diego Gutiérrez de la Caballería 42, 45
Diego Hernández 42
Diego López 42, 45
diseases 114
Distance Charts 271, 279
Dogleg 68, 207, 208, 209
dogs 26, 41
Domingo Martín 47, 94, 96, 270
Doubtful Canyon 198, 209
Dowa Yalanne 7, 108, 113, 116, 117

dry arroyo 65, 225, 230, 231, 232, 234, 235 236, 237
Eagle Creek 178
Eastern Route 262, 263, 264, 280,
East Fork of the Black River 166
El Fuerte River 245
encomiendas 4, 264, 265
España 14, 18, 19, 38, 79, 80
Espinosa 72, 73, 138, 147, 285, 289
estate of Juan Jiménez 87
Esteban 3, 6, 7, 8, 9, 69, 99
Esteban de Dorantes 3, 6
European 24, 25, 28, 29, 34, 265, 267, 295, 303
exploratory groups 4
fame 4, 16, 17
first battle 95, 286
first pueblo of Cíbola 7, 11, 28, 32, 74, 84, 93, 94, 96, 97, 98, 99, 100, 105, 106, 115, 116, 117, 119, 133, 135, 138, 256, 270, 284, 285, 287
foot soldiers 10
Francisca de Hozes 48, 49, 50
Francisco de Barrionuevo 44
Francisco de Ovando 43, 44, 84
Francisco Torres 48
Francisco Vázquez de Coronado 3, 6, 44, 45, 46, 47
Frank Cushing 7, 99
fray Marcos 263
fray Onorato 6
Galestina Canyon 113, 115, 121, 122, 125, 126, 131
Galiuro Mountains 208
Game Department Road 196
Garcia Lopez de Cárdenas 29
geographical features 114, 123, 215, 288
geography 5, 16, 228, 277, 283
Gila River 15, 49, 188, 189, 190, 191, 192, 196, 198, 199, 200, 202, 203, 204, 250
goats 268
Gomez Suarez 48
Granada 44, 105, 106
Grand Canyon 55, 82, 103
Greer Lakes 156
Halona:wa 108, 109, 112, 114, 116, 123
Hannagan Meadow 150, 168
Hardcastle Gap 173
Hardscrabble Wash 128, 129, 131, 134, 137, 139, 140, 141, 142, 145
harquebuses 10
Harris Canyon 154, 174

Hawikuh 8, 99, 100, 106, 108, 110, 112, 115, 116, 117, 121, 122, 124, 127, 135, 256, 258, 307
H Bar Y 189
headgear 21
Hemlock 115
Hernando Arias de Saabedra 15, 259
Hernando de Alarcón 14, 52, 78, 79, 259
Hernando de Alvarado 42, 44, 45, 47
Hernando Martín Bermejo 47
Hopi 52, 55, 78, 82, 84
Hornbrook Mountain 196, 203
horsemen 9, 10, 11, 20, 21, 24, 26, 29, 30, 31, 34, 35, 39, 42, 43, 44, 45, 64, 65, 79, 93, 94, 95, 226, 239, 260, 267, 287
horses 8, 11, 12, 20, 24, 25, 26, 27, 31, 35, 37, 39, 41, 51, 52, 75, 97, 118, 185, 190, 201, 226, 227, 285, 301, 302
Huásabas 221, 233
Hulsey Lake 170
Indians 6, 7, 8, 12, 13, 15, 18, 24, 25, 27, 46, 49, 50, 51, 53, 60, 66, 67, 68, 69, 72, 81, 89, 94, 95, 97, 98, 105, 116, 124, 138, 140, 191, 210, 213, 225, 260, 263, 267, 274, 284, 285, 286, 287, 288, 295, 299
Indian Village 210
Indios Amigos 260, 267, 285, 301
Ispa 67, 68, 213, 214, 215, 216, 217, 218, 221, 222, 224, 274
Jaralosa Draw 121, 130, 132, 133, 134, 137, 144, 145
Jeff Lake Draw 148, 156
Jenkins Creek 171
jornada 57, 75, 269
Juan Bermejo 26, 47
Juan de Contreras 47, 88
Juan de Cuevas 20, 21, 26, 42
Juan de Padilla 48
Juan de Villareal 42
Juan de Villegas 48
Juan de Zagala 48
Juan de Zaldívar 4, 9, 20, 22, 43, 44, 45, 201, 260, 263
Juan Galeasso 38
Juan Gallego 44, 47, 68, 79, 82, 83, 88
Juan Jaramillo 29, 47, 55, 63, 105, 107, 120, 137 147, 155, 165, 177, 185, 189, 200, 202, 213, 225, 239, 252, 261, 269
Juan Jiménez 87, 88

Juan Navarro 42
Juan Torquemada 42
Juan Troyano 26, 48
Julian calendar 79, 140, 165, 177, 239
Kechiba:wa 100, 108, 110, 117, 121, 122, 124, 127, 135, 256
Kiakima 7, 8, 9, 99, 100, 115, 117, 256, 258
Knight Peak 196, 203
KP Creek 179
Kwa'kin'a 108, 110, 116
Kwakina 116
Kyaki:ma 108, 109, 113, 115, 122, 125, 126, 127, 135, 256
lances 21, 30, 34, 35, 39
land 3, 4, 15, 17, 19, 57, 63, 68, 69, 70, 71, 72, 107, 108, 177, 190, 191, 213, 222, 259, 263, 264, 265, 288, 300
Largo Creek 153, 161, 172
Lark Creek 162
Last Camp vii
Latitude 58, 59, 258
Lazy B 199
league 12, 22, 51, 57, 62, 65, 66, 71, 95, 97, 107, 120, 124, 126, 132, 133, 137, 225, 226, 229, 246, 249, 261, 262, 264, 267, 269, 270, 275, 281, 285, 286
legua comun 57, 120
legua legal 57, 62, 120, 121
letter 7, 11, 12, 28, 31, 32, 73, 78, 79, 81, 83, 226, 227, 228, 285
Little Colorado River 73, 140, 141, 142, 145, 148, 156, 157, 288, 289
little ice age 61
Little Ortega Lake 148, 152
livestock 11, 12, 14, 15, 26, 27, 31, 35, 36, 37, 38, 39, 41, 51, 61, 65, 78, 148, 190, 226, 268, 293, 294, 295
Llano Estacado 63, 302
Lope de Gurrea 42
Lope de Samaniego 22, 42, 45
Lorenzo de Tejada 44, 48
Los Corazones 12, 15, 31, 32, 33, 65, 66, 74, 77, 82, 89, 90, 91, 213, 214, 215, 216, 217, 218, 220, 221, 222, 223, 224, 225, 226, 227, 228, 229, 230, 233, 234, 235, 237, 241, 248, 249, 250, 260, 261, 262, 263, 264, 274, 275, 276, 277, 278, 281, 302

Luis de Figueredo 47, 83
Luis de Úbeda de Escalona 48
Lyman Lake 142, 143, 144, 145, 149
magnetic pole 59
main body 5, 12, 13, 28, 30, 33, 34, 46, 49, 50, 52, 53, 55, 63, 65, 66, 77, 78, 79, 95, 96, 98, 239, 242, 273, 275, 286, 301
Mangas Trench 181, 186, 188
marches 51, 57, 63, 229, 261, 267
Marcos de Niza 4, 5, 6, 7, 8, 9, 11, 18, 20, 32, 43, 48, 69, 74, 79, 99, 115, 226, 228, 250, 260, 261, 262, 263, 264
Mar del Sur 37, 84
Mats'a:kya 104, 106, 108, 112, 116, 118, 123
Matsima 116, 118
Mazaque 104, 106, 107, 118
McCauley Road 189, 196
Melchior Diaz 4, 9, 11, 20, 22, 31, 44, 64, 79
Melchoir Pérez 27, 36, 47
Melchoir Pérez de la Torre 47
melons 67
members 18, 19, 23, 24, 27, 53, 56, 75, 82, 106, 120, 251, 258
Mendoza 3, 4, 5, 6, 7, 9, 11, 13, 15, 18, 19, 20, 22, 24, 25, 31, 38, 43, 71, 73, 74, 79, 82, 83, 104, 226, 228, 259, 285, 305
mesquite beans 67
Mexico City 4, 6, 7, 13, 14, 18, 19, 20, 22, 79, 81, 82, 83, 85, 87, 91, 259, 260
Mimbres River 181
Moors 73, 138, 147, 285
Mount Graham 199, 200
Mule Creek 186, 187, 191
mules 11, 25, 26, 31, 35, 37, 39, 41, 51, 301, 302, 303
Mullen Canyon 113, 115, 122
muster 19, 20, 24, 25, 26, 27, 30, 35, 36, 37, 41, 42, 43, 44, 83, 84, 259, 302
Muster Role 19, 20
Narváez 3, 5
navios 14
non-Indian people 24
Nueva Galicia 4, 6, 10, 17, 19, 77, 90
number of Indians 6, 25
number of people 25, 34, 36, 37
Nutrioso Creek 158, 159
Orange Butte 197

312   Coronado's Journey

oxen 11
Pablo de Melgosa 42, 45, 47
Palo Duro Canyon 56, 302
Panfilo de Narváez 3
Park Lake 198
Pecos Pueblo 55
Pedro de Ávilar 81
Pedro de Castañeda de Nájera 55
Pedro de Ledesma 47, 94, 270, 287
Pedro de Tovar 42, 45, 52, 78, 81, 84
Pedro Méndez de Sotomayor 5
Peloncillo Mountains 197, 198, 199
Petlatlán 62, 63, 64, 90
pigs 26, 27, 31, 38, 41
Pine Spring Wash 130, 131, 134, 137, 142, 143, 144
Pinitos Draw 131, 132, 134, 144, 145
pitahayas 63, 67, 68
Pizarro 4
Plumasano Wash 110
poisonous plants 138, 147
polar north 59
Presa La Angostura 218
prickly pear cactus 67
province of Cíbola 99, 106, 108
Pueblo of Cíbola 73, 99, 277
pueblo of Kiakima 7, 99, 115
Pueblo of Zuñi 3
pueblos of Cíbola 87, 103, 104, 107, 141, 251, 252
purposes 271, 17
Quemado Lake 160, 162, 163, 174
Quivira 287, 5, 17, 23, 37, 48, 56, 61, 81, 82, 84, 85, 87, 94
rafts 291, 71, 141, 169, 204
rams 27, 37, 38, 70
rate of travel 10, 11, 23, 31, 32, 33, 35, 75, 76, 94, 138, 139, 229, 237, 250, 252, 270, 273, 275, 281, 292
reales 52, 53, 268
recruitment 18
religious men 20
Rio Bavispe 218, 219, 220, 224, 232, 235, 262, 263, 264, 280
Rio Bermejo 32, 72, 73, 74, 94, 95, 96, 97, 119, 120, 128, 129, 130, 131, 132, 133, 134, 137, 138, 139, 140, 141, 142, 143, 144, 145, 146, 151, 152, 204, 270, 271, 281, 285, 287, 288, 289
Rio Chico 248
Rio Culiacán 63, 241, 242, 243, 244

Rio de Aros 232, 235
Rio de Guisamopa 235
Rio de las Balsas 71, 72, 141, 155, 158, 163, 165, 166, 167, 169, 170, 171, 172, 173, 174, 175, 177, 178, 179, 180, 181, 182, 183, 191, 204, 270, 290, 291
Rio del Lino 72, 73, 288, 289
Rio El Fuerte 245, 246
Rio Frio 72, 87, 88, 120, 138, 146, 147, 148, 149, 151, 152, 153, 154, 155, 156, 157, 160, 162, 289, 290, 291
Rio Fuerte 245
Rio Gila 200
Rio los Cedros 247
Rio Magdalena 222, 223, 224, 235, 262, 263, 280
Rio Nexpa 68, 82, 204, 205, 207, 208, 209, 210, 211, 213, 214, 215, 216, 217, 218, 221, 222, 224, 274, 281
Rio San Bernadino 218
Rio San Francisco 182
Rio San Juan 71, 173, 176, 177, 179, 180, 181, 182, 183, 184, 185, 186, 189, 192, 194, 204, 270, 280
Rio San Lorenzo 22, 62, 240, 241
Rio San Pedro 207, 208, 210, 211, 222, 224
Rio San Simon 207, 210
Rio Sinaloa 63, 64, 65, 240, 243, 244, 245, 246, 247, 248, 249, 275, 280
Rio Tizon 53, 79, 80, 81, 85
Rio Yaqui 208, 218, 248, 262
Rio Yaquimí 11, 31, 65, 78, 225, 226, 227, 230, 231, 232, 233, 234, 235, 236, 237, 248, 274
Rodrígo de Frias 47
Rodrigo Maldonado 42, 45, 78, 262
Rodrigo Trujillo 87
Rodrígo Ximon 48
Rosey Creek 156
sacred lake 140
saguaro cactus fruits 67
Saliz Canyon 180, 183
San Augustine Plains 181
San Francisco River 170, 172, 176, 178, 179, 183
San Gerónimo 13, 37, 46, 48, 60, 66, 67, 77, 78, 79, 80, 81, 82, 83, 84, 85, 302
San Miguel de Culiacán 21, 22, 28, 62, 64, 90, 239, 242, 243, 244, 270, 281
San Pedro River 208, 223
Santa Cruz de Terrenate 211

satellite imagery 121, 125, 133, 134, 139, 144, 147, 155, 165, 177, 186, 195, 200, 207, 243, 251
sea coast 6
Señora 13, 46, 64, 66, 67, 78, 79, 80, 81, 82, 83, 84, 88, 89, 91, 213, 214, 215, 216, 217, 218, 219, 220, 221, 222, 224
Separ Road 196
Sepulveda Creek 152, 160
servants 10, 13, 20, 24, 27, 29, 34, 36, 37, 46, 51, 87, 267, 295
Seven Cities of Gold 3, 16
sheep 11, 26, 27, 31, 38, 39, 41, 50, 65, 118, 268
ships 14, 15, 79, 80, 259
Sierra San Diego 218
Skunk Flat Tank 159, 162, 171
slave hunters 3
small pass 66, 213, 216, 219, 221
Small Stream 72, 137, 139, 141, 143, 145
snowfall 95, 96, 275, 283
snow storm 13, 96, 123
Socorro 55, 56, 80
Soldiers Farewell 196
Sononan Desert 203
Sonora River 236
souls 4, 17
southbound routes 88
South Fork of the Little Colorado River 157
squash 65, 225
starvation 12, 33, 271, 302
Stone Creek 159, 171
Strayhorse Canyon 179
Sulphur Springs Valley 199, 200, 210
Summit Hills 196
supply depot 13, 33, 36, 37
Suya 48, 50, 67, 80, 81, 82, 85, 88, 89, 90, 91, 213, 214, 215, 216, 217, 218, 221, 222, 224, 274, 281
swine 11
swords 21, 30, 34, 39
Sycamore Canyon 193
tents 52, 53, 268
the San Gabriel 14, 15
the San Pedro 14, 210, 223
the Santa Catarina 14
Thompson Canyon 196
Thunder Mountain 7
Tierra Nueva 4, 5, 17, 18, 36, 41, 43, 48, 61, 77, 83, 85, 91, 134, 155, 253, 258, 259, 263, 267, 283, 289, 293, 297, 300, 301, 305, 306
Tiguex 48, 56, 80, 81, 82, 106
topographic maps 139, 144, 147, 155, 165, 177, 186, 195, 200, 207, 243
Trade Goods 40
trade routes 260, 283, 293, 294
trading 40, 49, 103, 118, 134, 260
trails 8, 150, 166, 184, 188, 190, 205, 210, 293, 294
Trapped Rock Canyon 122
travel rates 246, 275
Tristán de Arellano 12, 45, 46, 80, 89, 239
Tularosa River 174, 190
Tutahaco 80
un-named Indian village 90, 211, 224
valley of Culiacán 34, 62, 90, 239, 240, 241, 242, 244, 245
Velasco de Barrionuevo 33
Venadito Draw 121, 122, 124
versillos 26, 35, 39, 303
Viceroy Mendoza 4, 5, 6, 7, 9, 11, 15, 18, 24, 31, 43, 71, 73, 74, 79, 82, 83, 104, 226, 228, 285, 305
Villa Hidalgo valley 233
villa of Culiacán 62, 63, 240, 241, 242, 244
villa of San Miguel de Culiacán 62, 90, 239, 243
wealth 4, 7, 9, 16, 17, 41, 82, 264, 265, 301
western route 250
West Fork of the Black River 166, 175, 178
West Fork of the Little Colorado River 156
Whitlock Mountains 198, 200
Wilcox Playa 207, 208
Zuñi River 109, 110, 112, 113, 117, 122, 124, 130, 131, 140, 141
Zuñi Salt Lake 144, 146, 154